ANCIENT TEXTS ALIVE TODAY:
THE STORY OF THE ENGLISH BIBLE

ANCIENT TEXTS ALIVE TODAY:
THE STORY OF THE ENGLISH BIBLE

by John Stevens Kerr

Edited by Charles Houser

AMERICAN BIBLE SOCIETY
NEW YORK

Copyright © 1999, American Bible Society

Printed in the United States of America
Ancient Texts Alive Today-105053
ABS-1/05-500-2500–SMG-1(2)

PREFACE

I had perceaved by experyence, how that it was impossible to stablysh the laye people in any truth, excepte the scripture were playnly layde before their eyes in their mother tonge...

William Tyndale

The story of the English Bible spans more than 13 centuries of fascinating history. In that period, the English language formed and developed. As the language spoken by the people changed, so did the language of the English Bible. For much of that time, religion and politics were intertwined to the extent that the coming of a new British monarch affected the fortunes of English Scripture. Religion also affected language, as the debate over Latin roots and Anglo-Saxon roots reflected the conflict between Roman Catholics and Protestants. The passions of the Reformation era, the struggles between Protestants and Roman Catholics, as well as the conflicts among Puritans and the established church in England, have all contributed to the shape and style of our English Bibles.

For English-speaking Protestants, the beloved *King James Version* long claimed priority, and that version substantially shaped how people throughout the English-speaking world spoke and wrote. But the English language continued to grow. This, along with new discoveries in biblical studies, challenged the preeminence of the *KJV*. A number of modern language translations came from the pens of several biblical scholars in the first decades of the 20th century. Their efforts set a new standard that has been followed by subsequent translations.

Today there is a wider variety of English translations than ever before. Some of these continue the *King James* tradition, while others take a different approach. Protestants, Romans Catholic and Jewish translators are all active, and they are working together in a cooperative spirit that would have amazed their forebears.

To tell the story of the efforts to render God's Word into the language of the people—the dream of the great William Tyndale—is the purpose of this book. The story requires attention to cultural, political, historical, and linguistic issues, for all of these matters have affected English Bibles. It also demands a look at the experiences and struggles of key personalities who have left their imprint on the English Bible.

v

"Ancient Texts Alive Today" expands on the earlier pamphlet produced by the American Bible Society and last revised in 1983, *A Concise History of the English Bible*. That work first appeared in 1935, under the title "A Ready Reference History of the English Bible," to commemorate the 400th anniversary of the printed English Bible. It was prepared by the late Miss Margaret T. Hills, M.A., librarian of the American Bible Society. She revised it in 1962, and several further revisions were made by the ABS library staff under her successor, Miss Elizabeth J. Eisenhart, and others.

The present volume includes much new material, as well as a different arrangement of the contents and the addition of illustrations. Interesting sidelights and brief biographies appear in boxes for easy reference. The author and editor of this revised edition wish to thank Dr. David G. Burke and Dr. Erroll F. Rhodes for their careful review of the manuscript and many helpful suggestions. While directed to the general reader, it does include basic information about various editions of the English Bible. However, the specialist and collector will find complete bibliographic information in *Historical Catalogue of Printed Editions of the English Bible*, 1525-1961, by A.S. Herbert, published jointly by The British and Foreign Bible Society, London, and the American Bible Society, New York, in 1968 (now out of print, but in the collections of many seminary libraries).

If this book deepens your appreciation for the heritage of the English Bible, helps you understand where your favorite English version fits into the broad picture of English Bibles, and encourages you to explore God's Word in other translations and renderings, it will have fulfilled its purpose.

TABLE OF CONTENTS

PART I

THE
ENGLISH BIBLE
BEFORE PRINTING

1 THE BEGINNINGS

The English Bible holds our interest at many levels. English-speaking Christians are concerned primarily because the English Bible brings God's Word into the language they understand. Though good texts are available in biblical Hebrew for what Christians call the Old Testament and in Greek for the New Testament, only a very few people possess sufficient command of Hebrew and Greek to read the Bible in its original tongues.

How did the English translation we now read come down to us? How does it relate to the scores of other versions that have been prepared over the years? The search for answers to these questions covers fascinating ground.

Those with less fervent commitments to the Christian faith also find fascination in the history of the English Bible because of its longevity. The various English versions done over the centuries embody the changes in our language as it evolved. Versions of the Bible reveal their times in other ways, too. Reflected in their pages we catch glimmers of ecclesiastical trends and conflicts, secular struggles, economic and social trends, and intellectual developments–the stuff from which English-speaking civilization is formed.

We cannot appreciate the history of the English Bible in a vacuum. It belongs to the wider sweep of history. Our journey begins at the time Christianity came to Britain, when the people spoke Celtic languages, long before the first, crude sounds of what would become English were uttered.

The Coming of the Faith

The islands of Britain, where our story begins, sit off the European continent, separated from the larger land mass by the North Sea and the turbulent English Channel. In ancient times, when ships were small and frail and seafarers limited in their skills, people feared embarking on the terrifying sea. Yet some, urged on by the profits of trade, the desire for new homes, or the sheer adventure of it all, did venture across the sea. Visitors arrived regularly on British shores and returned to the Continent to tell about the island. Alexander the Great (*d.* 323 B.C.) knew of the island and traders dealt in the metals from British mines.

At the time of Christ, Rome dominated the Mediterranean and was extending its power northward across the towering Alps into Gaul (modern France). In A.D. 43, Britain fell into the embrace of the power and glory of the Roman Empire, when Emperor Claudius invaded the island and planted the Roman eagle. A century earlier, Julius Caesar had made forays into Britain during his campaign to conquer Gaul, perhaps to stop the Britons from coming into Gaul. While Caesar did not build settlements, Claudius intended from the start to establish Britain as a permanent, garrisoned Roman province.

Christianity came to the island in the wake of Claudius' legionnaires, yet exactly how the faith first obtained a foothold among the Britons we cannot say. The details are obscured in the mists of time.

We do know that in A.D. 314 , three British bishops attended a church council in Arles, in southern Gaul, and British church leaders were represented at the Council of Rimini in 359. In the fifth century, a British congregation welcomed a Gallican bishop. In one of his writings, the Church father Quintus Septimius Florens Tertullianus (c. 160–c. 225, known as Tertullian), who worked in Carthage (modern Tunis) in North Africa, mentions "Places of the Britons, unreached by the Romans, but subject to Christ."

Another Church father, Origen (c. 185–254), makes at least three references to British Christianity between A.D. 238 and 240. One appears in his commentary on Ezekiel:

CAESAR AND CLAUDIUS

Caius Julius Caesar (c.102–44 B.C.) came from a notable Roman clan, the Julians. He was a popular leader, but the aristocratic Senate distrusted him. His illustrious career was capped by his notable campaigns in Gaul, from 58 to 49 B.C., when he brought Gaul under Roman authority. He wrote of his experiences in De Bello Gallico, or "The Gallic Wars."

Tiberius Claudius Drusus Nero Germanicus (10 B.C.–A.D. 54) was Emperor from A.D. 41-54. The nephew of Tiberius (see Luke 3.1), he had a speech impediment and other disabilities and preferred a literary life, but the elite Praetorian Guard hailed him as Emperor.

Roman legions carried standards topped with the image of an eagle. Below the eagle were the letters "S.P.Q.R.," the Latin abbreviation for "The Senate and People of Rome" in whose name the legions marched. The army included troops from everywhere in the Empire.

> When, until the coming of Christ, did the land of the Britons accept belief in one god?...But now there are churches on the frontiers of the world, and all the earth shouts for joy to the God of Israel.

These few notices suggest that Christianity was reaching the British by perhaps A.D. 200. But how the faith first came to the islands remains a mystery.

We can imagine that among the Roman soldiers serving in the occupation forces there were Christians who with their families settled in the towns and garrisons the Romans established. Through their witness, Christian communities may have gathered. Christians, though, would represent a tiny fraction of the first waves of Roman occupiers. The Roman legions did not turn to Christianity early on.

As the Romans settled into towns, garrisons, and villages, they interacted with the Britons in the daily course of life. Some Britons, impressed by Roman culture, became "Romanized," adopting the manners of Roman civilization and Latin culture. This social intercourse may have helped to plant the Christian faith in British hearts, especially as Christianity spread more and more among the Romans. Christians, in any case, tended to concentrate in towns. The countryside remained largely pagan. Yet this small church established a heritage of Celtic Christianity.

The major missionary thrust into Britain began at the end of the sixth century, long after the Empire's armies had taken their eagles back to Rome. The new missionaries came to a people quite different from those Claudius encountered. But that story comes later.

The Early Britons

The English have been called the most mongrel of all races. Daniel Defoe (*c.* 1660-1731), author of *Robinson Crusoe*, wrote that the "true-born Englishman" is

> A metaphor intended to express
> A man that's kin to all the universe.

The mixing of peoples began centuries before Claudius arrived, and invaders and settlers continued to mold and mingle the British population as late as the 11th century. This amalgam of peoples and their various tongues eventually evolved into the English language as we recognize it today, but the process took a long time.

The islands had been connected to the continent by a land bridge over which migrating tribes could travel. About 7,000 years ago, the land bridge subsided, and the ocean flowed in to slice Britain from the Continent with the North Sea as a water barrier. Now immigrants could arrive only by boat, and prehistoric ships were very small. Massive invasions by sweeping hordes were out of the question. New settlers were forced to arrive in small groups, which led to a pattern of peaceful assimilation as new, small groups of people blended over time into the native population.

The earliest Britons were hunters and gatherers. The first soil cultivators arrived about 2500 B.C. from the Mediterranean by way of Spain. Early Britons mined gold and tin, did weaving, and engaged in trade, as well as pursuing settled agriculture. When they discovered how to blend Cornish tin with Irish copper, they entered the Bronze Age.

These prehistoric peoples have left monuments we can still visit—the long barrows and cairns, originally communal graves, that dot the Scottish Highlands, Wales, and southwest England. And the famous Stonehenge, a circular arrangement of massive stones carefully constructed for a purpose we can only guess at today.

Beginning in 1900 B.C., another wave of immigration flowed from the east off the Continent. These were the "Beaker Folk," so-called after their distinctive pottery. They were more warlike than the native Britons, given to pasturing flocks more than tilling the soil, and more ready than the natives to adopt bronze for tools and weapons.

ABOUT THE CELTS

Muireadach's Cross, Monasterboice, Ireland, shows the classic form of a Celtic Cross.

Celts, or Kelts, emerged in the second millennium B.C. in southwest Germany and eastern France. They introduced the new technology of iron and adopted the chariot from the Greeks. Their art was richly ornamented. Celts organized their life on a tribal pattern and lived in semi-fortified villages. They had a complex, nature-oriented religion. Their priests, called Druids, also exercised political power.

Celts swept over most of Europe, including Britain. Gaelic, still spoken in Scotland and Ireland, is a Celtic language, as is Welsh.

Celts favored circular houses. They dwelt in communities large enough for Caesar to call them *urbes,* or towns. These towns were situated on hills and enclosed by fortifications, usually a sheer wall of timber. One town, at Stanwick in North Yorkshire, enclosed 850 acres with six miles of ramparts and ditches. Another, in Scotland, embraced 300 dwellings within its 40 acres. Many towns covered more than 15 acres.

Then waves of Celtic people from the region of Gaul crossed the waters in large numbers in the fifth century B.C. to claim land on the island. The Celts brought their Iron Age culture against which the simpler Bronze Age culture of the native Britons could not compete. The Celts pressed the Britons westward and dominated the eastern portion of the island.

The Romans Arrive

The last wave of new settlers, before the Roman invasion, were the Belgae, a Celtic people who arrived from the densely wooded forests of northern Europe about 75 B.C. They brought with them iron plows of superior design to anything on the island. With these plows, the Belgae could cultivate the clay soil of the river valleys in southern Britain.

The arrival of the Belgae shifted the pattern of settlement from the hilltop villages, favored by the Celtic tribes for reasons of protection, to towns on the plains. Winchester and Chichester became tribal centers. The Belgic warrior princes established Verulam (St. Albans) and Camulodunum (Colcester). From Colcester, the Belgic ruler, Cymbeline, established ascendancy in southern Britain and carried on a brisk trade with Gaul in wheat, slaves, and hunting dogs.

Roman traders took part in the commerce, of course, and Claudius may have sought to conquer Britain in order to fatten the Empire's granaries with the abundant crops of the island. In any case, Claudius landed in the territory of the Cymbeline kingdom. Before long, the Romans gained enough control to create the Roman province of Britannia.

Roman advances did meet resistance, though. Twenty years after Claudius began the Roman conquest, Boadicea, queen of the Iceni (who lived near modern Norfolk), led a revolt that sacked several Roman settlements. The Roman governor Paulinus quelled the rebellion after a great loss of life, and Boadicea took poison.

The Romans continued to build military roads and moved ahead with their subjection of the island. However, the Romans could not push their authority beyond the Welsh highlands. Hadrian's Wall, built about A.D. 128, marks the northern limits of their control. Like the Great Wall of China, it was constructed to keep out the barbarians, in this case the Picts, who roamed what is today called Scotland.

Boadicea, queen of the Iceni, who led a revolt against the Roman invaders in the first century A.D.

Culture and Mission

Roman culture soon infused the island, even though the Romans never made up more than 10 per cent of the island's population. They built the city of Londinium (London) as a supply depot. They established *coloniae*, official colonies settled by ex-legionnaires and their families. Towns and cities sprouted the amenities of Roman life: aqueducts, hot and cold running water, gymnasiums, and homes with atriums and mosaic tile work. A spacious villa nestled in splendid isolation amid the cultivated fields of its estate, a common sight in Italy, soon appeared in Britannia.

THE PICTS

The Picts, ancient inhabitants of central and northern Scotland, were probably descendants of late Bronze Age and early Iron Age invaders of Britain. The Romans never conquered them. They may have spoken a language that blended Celtic with an earlier, non-Indo-European language of their own.

As everywhere they went, the Romans built good military roads, radiating from southeast into all parts of the island. These roads provided the transportation network for medieval and later England. One, called Watling Street in modern times, ran from London north and west to Shrewsbury, a distance of 100 miles. Parts of this road are still used today.

In addition to roads, the Romans left another legacy of surpassing worth—the Latin language. That language would endure for centuries as the universal language of European civilization and through it the culture of the Roman Empire would pass to the barbarian hordes who defeated Rome. It was the language of the Roman Church and its missionaries. Christians in this period of British history would have read Scripture in Latin. In fact, the Latin Bible was the mainstay translation for centuries.

Was the Bible translated into the Celtic tongues? If so, no copies have survived. Tertullian's comment that the Gospel in Britain had extended beyond the reach of Roman arms suggests that there were pioneering missionary efforts, especially from the third century to the time when the Roman armies abandoned Britain. One of these missionaries was St. Ninian, who reached beyond the limits of Roman authority to convert the Picts in Scotland. St. Ninian (c. 360–c. 432), missionary to Scotland, left his home as a youth and went to Rome. Consecrated bishop in 394, he returned to Scotland with some monks to preach to the Britons and Picts, founding a church known as "Candida Casa" (White House), probably named after the whitewash he applied to the gray stone, which would seem very unusual to the Britons.

On the Continent, Ulfilas, missionary to the Goths, had translated the Gospels into the Gothic language, developing for their use an alphabet based mostly on Greek letters. Other missionaries, now lost to history, may have done the same kind of translating for Celtic-speaking Britons. Certainly any missionary would have to tell the Gospel story in the language of the people, but probably they would have relied on verbal, paraphrased translations which they made up as they spoke.

Still, the Christians concentrated in towns, and were identified with Latin culture. From the late third century onward, the Latin world became increasingly Christianized and that movement spread the faith in Britain. As for the Celtic-speaking Britons away from the occupied towns, few could read and few needed to. Celts knew how to write but they preferred to rely on oral transmission of their customs and heritage. The many tribes spoke a welter of dialects and this would pose barriers to written translations.

Besides, a rich, written language already existed which those who so desired could learn—Latin. Romans and Britons, at least in the major garrison towns and *coloniae*, knew each other, traded together, and had many social interactions. Britons would learn Latin, even as the Romans would acquire the local Celtic language. Some Britons in fact became very "Romanized" and adopted the Roman style of dress. We call this the Romano-British period, meaning a blend of cultures in settled, urban areas. A parallel might be drawn with the more modern Anglo-Indian culture, where long British occupation gave many Indians a passion for the English language and English culture, including polo and cricket.

We can summarize the little we know in this way: Christian communities probably appeared in Britain around the second century. They concentrated in towns and, at least to some extent, received the faith through Roman settlers who were Christians, in addition to work by missionaries from Rome and Gaul. On more certain ground, we can say that by the time the Roman armies departed, Christianity was common among those Britons identified with Latin culture. (The great persecution of A.D. 303 seems to have reached into Britain, indicating the presence of a significant Christian community.) In the countryside, paganism and the old nature religions prevailed, but not everywhere.

The Roman Eagle Departs

From A.D. 275 onward, Saxon pirates threatened the southeastern coast of the island. A joint Roman and British fleet was organized for their defense. In the middle of the fourth century, the barbarians—Scots of Northern Ireland and the Picts in Scotland—breached Hadrian's Wall by raiding Britannia from the

THE BIBLE IN LATIN (THE VULGATE)

When the early Christian missionaries taught, they quoted from versions of the Septuagint (so-called because some 70 scholars, according to tradition, worked on this translation of the Hebrew Scriptures into Greek). It was done in the mid-third century B.C. by scholars in Alexandria, Egypt. The translation was to serve the needs of Jews outside of Palestine who could no longer read or understand Hebrew, but could speak Greek, either as a first language or as a strong second language.

The early Christians wrote in Greek (the language of the New Testament) and worshipped in the same tongue. As time passed, however, Roman Christians adopted Latin. This led to a need for Latin translations, which were prepared as early as 175 to satisfy the needs of Latin-speaking North African Christians. By the third century A.D., a number of Latin versions circulated in Italy, Gaul, and Spain—and perhaps Britain.

These Old Latin versions were not always well done. Variant readings and other inconsistencies abound. The situation reached a point where Augustine of Hippo (354–430) complained that "in the early days of the faith, every man who happened to gain possession of a Greek manuscript and who imagined that he had any facility in both languages (however slight that may be) dared to make a translation" (*On Christian Doctrine*, II, 13).

Under the urging of Augustine and many others, Pope Damasus, in 382, commissioned the best biblical scholar of the time, Eusebius Hieronymus–known today as Jerome–to prepare an official Latin translation. Jerome compared several Old Latin versions with the Septuagint in various forms and consulted the Hebrew text, always seeking the best reading. Jerome completed his first version of the Gospels in about two years, but continued to improve his translation for several years. He even lived in Palestine for 20 years in order to consult with rabbis on the fine points of the Hebrew text of the Old Testament and to gain access to the best Greek jmanuscripts.

Jerome made so many changes from the crude Latin translations people were accustomed to that he was accused of rewriting, rather than translating. Yet as time passed, the high quality of his work became recognized. Jerome's version, now known as the "Vulgate," became the authoritative Bible version for western Christianity.

Jerome (c.340-420) translating the Bible, a copper engraving by Albrecht Dürer, 1514. Dürer pictures Jerome as working in a 16th-century house. The artist surrounds Jerome with allegorical symbols. For instance, the skull represents mortality. The fox and lion sleeping peacefully together recalls the vision of the peaceable kingdom in Isaiah 11.6-9.

northwest. Using the excellent roads the Romans had conveniently built, the invaders reached as far south as Kent. General Theodosius, who later became Emperor, valiantly tried to stop the incursions using the full garrison of 50,000 Roman regulars and auxiliaries.

Later commanders in Britain lost interest in defending the island. Their attention turned to the Continent, and to Rome itself, which was continually threatened by Germanic tribes. Generals who aspired to become

ROMANO-BRITISH CHRISTIANS

A mosaic from a villa in Lullingstone, Kent, shows a Romano-British Christian with his hands raised in prayer.

Emperor knew they had to be in the center of the political maelstrom. A "front porch" campaign from headquarters in Britain would not do. The chaos wrought by barbarian invasions almost completely severed the western part of the Roman Empire from the eastern half, where the wealth and splendor of the Second Rome, Constantinople, continued to glitter. But in the west, the Dark Ages were beginning.

The last of the commanding generals, Constantine III, abandoned the island with all his troops in 407. Later pleas for help from the Britons fell on deaf ears. Rome simply did not have the resources to be everywhere when the city of Rome itself was under siege. (In 410, Alaric, the Goth, sacked Rome.) Britain was never re-garrisoned. They now had to provide for their own defenses against invaders.

For nearly 400 years—about the span that separates us from Shakespeare—the British lived under Roman rule. When the Roman armies left, Britain's Christian community had to face the future alone.

2 THE EARLIEST ENGLISH BIBLES

The departure of the Romans left the Celtic church to its own devices in a society beset by struggle. Invaders flowed from Europe, and the Britons, valiantly trying to resist them, could not get help from the Romans. Internally, the country fell into an economic depression because farmers and merchants lost tens of thousands of customers when the Romans departed. Exports to Rome fell because Rome had its own crises to deal with. British towns disbanded; the Celtic Christians struggled to survive.

The Invaders

The Saxon raid that the Romans fought off with British aid in A.D. 275 was only the first of many such expeditions. Without the protection of Roman legions, the British made vulnerable prey for land-hungry Germanic tribes. Their incursions into Britain form part of the same mass movement of people as was pressing upon Rome. The northern tribes were on the march and their might was formidable indeed.

Three peoples took part in this new invasion: the Saxons, from what we now call Schleswig, on the southern end of Denmark; the Angles, a neighboring tribe; and the lesser-known Jutes, probably from the area of the mouth of the Rhine.

The serious invasions began in 450 with an act of treachery. Some British chiefs or princes had invited Jutish warriors to help them in the defense of southeast Britain. The Jute mercenaries turned against their employers and opened the way for their people to conquer Kent.

The Angles and Saxons followed. The Angles moved into the eastern, central, and northern parts of the island. They established the later kingdoms of East Anglia, Northumbria, and Mercia. These kingdoms held so much power that the nation got the name England. The Saxons settlements later became the kingdoms of Sussex, Wessex, and Essex.

The Anglo-Saxons referred to the native Britons as "Welsh." Under the pressure of the invaders, the Britons, or Welsh, were pushed westward into modern Wales. Some returned to the continent, to the area of France now called Brittany.

The Britons fought valiantly to keep their land, but their decentralized tribal society could not cope with such a massive invasion. Still, they had some successes. At one stage, for about a generation, the influx stopped, the Britons regained some ground, some Angles and Saxons went home, and military engagements largely ceased.

It is this period that gave rise to the legend of King Arthur. One cannot think that the title King at this time referred to a ruler of the whole land. The word derives from

ANGLO-SAXON

The term "Anglo-Saxon" was first used in Continental Latin sources to distinguish the Saxons in Britain from their Continental counterparts. Eventually it came to mean "English," to describe the new population of Britain. With the Anglo-Saxon conquest, we begin to speak of England (from Angle-land) rather than Britain. The more precise use, to refer to non-Celtic inhabitants of England, stems from the sixteenth century.

the Anglo-Saxon word for "chief." We can think of these kings more as tribal chiefs. (The most powerful king at a given moment—who could command other kingdoms as well as his own—was called the *bretwealda*. This Old English word combines two words meaning "ruler of Britain.")

Many of the Britons were Christians. They were fighting pagan hordes. Arthur would have been a chief of one of these British tribes. The Arthurian legend is just that—a legend—but one that scholars believe has some factual basis. A Romano-British general named either Arthur or Ambrosius led the Britons in twelve successful battles sometime around A.D. 500.

When the stormy Anglo-Saxon conquest came to its successful end, the Scots in Ireland and the Picts in Scotland remained unconquered. The Welsh (Celtic Britons) were pushed into Wales, Devon, and Cornwall. These Celts hated the Anglo-Saxons. Fighting continued along the Welsh-English border for centuries.

Celtic Christianity

The pagan Anglo-Saxons had little use for Rome and its ways. They swept aside Roman place names and settlements, destroying every vestige of Romano-British culture. Since that culture was, by this time, well Christianized, the Anglo-Saxon conquest shook the church to its roots. Missionary activity continued, however, in the unvanquished north, led by Celtic missionaries. Their names are legendary in English church history, and to them we owe a great deal for preparing the way for an English Bible.

One was St. Patrick (c. 390–c. 460), known as the patron saint of Ireland. Actually, he was British, a third-generation Christian and son of a deacon and a town councilor under the Romans. Captured by Irish pirates as a youth, Patrick tended flocks for six years as a slave in County Mayo. He escaped and after some years was able to fulfill his vision as a missionary to Ireland. Patrick's mission created a vital Celtic church. From the Emerald Isle, Celtic missionaries brought the Gospel to Pictland (modern Scotland) and northern England.

Patrick gives us a glimpse into the importance of the Bible in the Celtic mission. Most monks knew the Psalter by heart, but Patrick lived freely with the whole of Scripture. We have two writings that very likely come from his hand: *The Confession*, his life story, and *The Letter to Coroticus*, in which he rebukes a British king for taking captive Irish Christians. The two works, in one edition, amount to 756 lines. They include 189 Bible quotations, or one every fourth line. Patrick must have memorized vast quantities of Latin Scriptures. Undoubtedly, he would quote Scripture as he preached, translating or paraphrasing into Celtic.

Another missionary was Columba (*c.* 521–597), an Irishman of noble birth. In 563, he established a monastery at Iona, an island on the rugged west coast of Scotland. He chose only twelve companions to symbolize a mission based on that of the original Apostles. From this base, Columba evangelized the northern Picts of Scotland and reached into the Anglo-Saxon territory of Northumbria.

Columba worked with individuals, rather than converting an entire tribe through the agency of the chieftain adopting the Christian faith. He needed an interpreter to preach to the Picts and the Anglo-Saxons in their tongue. This incident is described in *Life of St. Columba*, written a century after his death by Adamnan, then Abbot of Iona:

> When the Saint [Columba] was staying for some days in Skye...a boat arrived with an aged Pict, chieftain of his tribe, in its bows, and two youths who lifted him out...And he received the word through an interpreter, and believed and was baptized *(1,33; also III, 14)*.

The "word through an interpreter" doubtless included oral translations of Scripture passages.

Columba was a good copyist. That is, he copied manuscripts and books by hand, the only means of publishing before the introduction of printing. The Scriptures he copied, as far as we know, were in Latin.

Iona became a vital center of Christian mission and, through the energy of its fervent faith, evangelized much of England. Oswald (*c.* 605–642), later king of Northumbria, was converted to the Christian faith while spending an exile under the protection of the Ionian monks. Regaining his throne in 634, he

MAKING BIBLES BEFORE PRINTING

The *Book of Kells*, one of the most beautiful illuminated manuscripts, is an eighth-century rendition of the Latin Gospels, with notes about local history added to it. It was done in the monastery at Kells (or Ceanannus Mor), in Ireland, founded by Columba in the sixth century.

Before printing, all books were copied by hand, with monks doing the work because they were the largest body of literate people. Most monasteries had scriptoria or writing rooms. Monks used parchment, a writing material made from the skins of goats, sheep, or calves, because it was readily available. Papyrus had to come from Egypt and paper, from Asia, was not readily available in Europe until the twelfth century.

Monks took four sheets of parchment folded together to make an eight-leaf, sixteen-page copybook called a quaternion. Up to twenty of the copybooks would be assembled in one binding to make a book.

The copyists sat, up to twenty in a room, on benches with footstools and bent over in such a way that they wrote on their knees. Monks wrote on a desk, with a side table for their quills, ink, knife, eraser, compasses, and rulers.

The scribes worked in silence. Each would copy from another manuscript. In the mass production mode, several monks would transcribe what a senior monk dictated. They worked in silence, but some expressed their thoughts in marginal graffiti: "Christ, favor my work," "This work is slow and difficult," "Only three fingers are writing; the whole body is in agony."

The work of copying was necessarily slow, though some copyists, like Columba, developed great speed and accuracy. Tradition has it that Columba could write twenty or thirty pages a day with barely an error. Normally, an entire scriptorium would need to work a full year in order to produce one top-quality Bible. It would appear as two or three large volumes. Such slow production made books rare and expensive. In the eighth century, a library with 100 volumes was remarkable.

For many modern people, the greatest delight of these medieval manuscripts lies in their illuminations, the miniature paintings and designs used to ornament initial letters in particularly special and elegant copies. The artist would draw the outline, perhaps following a copybook with a selection of basic images he could incorporate into his design. Then the artist would add gold paint, followed by the other colors of paint. Finally, he would redo the outline. Monks generally added the illuminations, but in some cases monasteries hired lay artists for this work.

English monasteries that had active scriptoria include Canterbury, Ripon, Wearmouth, Jarrow, York, and Lindisfarne. In Ireland, Bangor, Burrows, and Kells were notable.

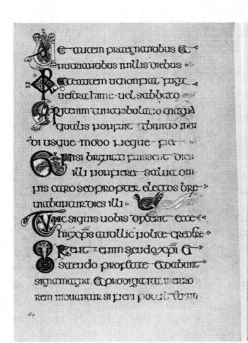

Two pages of the Gospel of Matthew, from the beautiful Book of Kells, *dating from about A.D. 800. The right-hand page is a hand-done illumination of St. Matthew. The halo, or nimbus, about his head was a standard way to depict a saint. The use of angel-like wings, however, is unusual. The left-hand page shows part of Matthew's Gospel, written in Latin. Note the beautiful illuminated letters. A black-and-white reproduction cannot capture the beauty of the colors in the original. This manuscript contains the Latin Gospels, with additional notes on local history. It is generally considered to be the finest example of Celtic illumination. The* Book of Kells *is named after the town near which St. Columba founded a monastery in the sixth century A.D.*

asked the monks of Iona to help in the conversion of his kingdom. The Abbot of Iona sent a rather austere monk who met with little success. The frustrated monk returned to Iona and gave his report:

> I have achieved nothing in teaching the people to whom I was sent. They are uncivilized men, of a hard and barbarous disposition.

Aidan, a monk at Iona, told the unsuccessful missioner that he took the wrong approach. Aidan said:

> It seems to me, Brother, that you were too harsh with your ignorant hearers, and forgot the Apostle's instruction to give

them first the milk of simpler doctrine, till little by little, nourished by God's word, they should be able to receive that which
is more excellent, and to fulfil God's loftier commands.

The senior monks promptly dispatched Aidan to continue the mission.

They made an excellent decision. Aidan based his mission in Lindisfarne, a monastery on an island off the east coast of Scotland. Until he learned the language, Aidan would preach through an interpreter who was often King Oswald himself "interpreting the word of God to thanes [retainers] and ministers [king's councilors]" and the people "gladly came flocking to hear the word." Oswald had learned the Scots language while staying at Iona.

Irish or Celtic Christianity, and its outposts in Iona and Lindisfarne, shone brightly in the Christian firmament. Its spiritual influence extended into Gaul on the Continent. Celtic monks, though, were less disciplined than Rome would like. They cared little for episcopal authority. Basically, they were pilgrims and wandering preachers, given to austere styles of life and frequently withdrawing into a monastic cell or a cave for isolated meditation. If we think of the Roman church as the "Establishment," then the Celtic church and its monks would represent the "counterculture."

Roman Christianity

Gregory I (c. 540–604) occupied the Papal throne from 590 until his death and also headed the secular government of Rome. Born of patrician parents, he gave away his immense wealth to the poor. He established seven monasteries and entered one of them himself. His interest was awakened to England by a famous incident in a Roman marketplace where fair-headed Britons, captured and enslaved by Anglo-Saxons, were for sale. Tradition has it that when he saw these lads he exclaimed, in a manner that showed his love for plays on words:

> Of what nation? Angles! They have the faces of angels. Of what province? Deira [Yorkshire]! They shall be saved *de ira* [from wrath]!

> And their king? Aellia [king of Deira]! Then must Alleluia be sung in that land.

But it was not the Pope but a missionary sent by him who arrived in England: Augustine (of Canterbury; not to be confused with the earlier, North African Church Father, Augustine of Hippo).

Augustine (died *c.* 607) arrived in Kent on the Isle of Thanet in 597 accompanied by 40 Frankish monks (the tribe which dominated the former Roman province of Gaul) to serve as interpreters. A rather unimaginative person,

Augustine did not learn Anglo-Saxon in preparation for his mission. However, he did realize the value of visual aids. When King Ethelbert of Kent received the band of missionaries,

> They came with a silver cross as their standard, and on a board a picture of our Lord and Saviour.

Pope Gregory may have suggested the idea of visualizing the Gospel, for he had once written, "Pictures are to the illiterate what books are to educated men."

Queen Bertha, Ethelbert's wife and a Frankish Christian, helped to smooth the way, perhaps with Gregory's encouragement, for her husband to receive baptism. A number of the king's thanes followed his example. Augustine conducted his mission with a careful strategy, unlike the efforts of the more mercurial Celtic monks. Augustine stressed group or tribal conversions, in contrast to the individualistic approach of the Celts, with the king or chieftain first receiving the faith and his people following his example. Instead of demolishing pagan shrines, he "baptized" them as churches and worked pagan festivals into the Christian calendar. Augustine also established sees, or episcopal jurisdictions, to develop an organized ecclesiastical structure.

In 625, the pagan King Edwin of Northumbria asked to marry Ethelburga of Kent, the Christian daughter of Ethelbert and Bertha. (Edwin was the son of Aellia, King of Deria, whose subjects Gregory had seen in the Roman slave market.) As Ethelburga traveled to her new husband, she was accompanied by Paulinus, who was also sent to England by Gregory.

Edwin was open to the new faith. He gathered his Witan (wise men or tribal council) to hear a debate between Paulinus and the pagan high-priest Coifi. Bede (c. 673–735), a monk at Jarrow and the earliest writer of English history, relates the story in his great work, *The Ecclesiastical History of the English People*. He records that the high-priest ended the debate convinced for the new faith, saying:

> I have long concluded that there is nothing in what we [the pagans] worship, for the more zealously I sought the truth in our religion, the less I found...So I say, O King, let the temples and altars which we vainly have held as sacred, be forthwith accursed and put to the flames.

Edwin and his nobles were baptized on Easter, 627. Edwin was later killed by Penda, pagan king of Mercia. His successor, Oswald, re-Christianized Northumbria through the work of Aidan, as mentioned above. And so in England two Christian traditions competed: the Roman heritage of Paulinus and Augustine, and the Celtic tradition represented by Aidan. Penda, a powerful bretwealda, remained a pagan to his death, but his sons were baptized. The march of England toward the Christian faith gained momentum.

One Country, One Faith

The Celtic and Roman factions in the church tried to reconcile their differences, including the date of Easter, at the Synod of Whitby in 664. (A synod is a gathering of ecclesiastical leaders.) King Oswey of Northumbria, the successor to Oswald, played a key role in the synod. He led the group to cast their votes in favor of Roman practice. The Celtic monks objected. They were a long time in accepting the Roman tradition. Many simply retired to the wilderness to live alone. The future for Christianity in England lay with the Roman way of celebrating the faith, but the fire and commitment—along with the ascetic strain—of the Celtic tradition continued to infuse the English church.

Into a rapidly Christianizing England came two new peoples: the Danes and the Normans.

The first were the Danes, or Vikings, in the ninth century. These wanderers from Scandinavia presented two faces to the English. Some were coastal raiders and plunderers, the sort of destructive and fearsome pirates we associate with the popular image of Vikings. They pillaged monasteries such as Iona and, over the years, pretty much quenched the bright flame of Irish Christianity.

Most Danes, though, were better called settlers. They came for land and brought their families. These newcomers put down roots in the less inhabited areas of eastern and northern England (settling in modern Lincoln, Leicester, Derby, and Nottingham), from whence they made raids on the rest of England. Some would stay in England during the growing season and return home after harvest.

The advent of the Danes helped the warring factions among the English to reach a kind of unity. The first reasonable claimant to the title of King of all the English emerged in Wessex (meaning, West Saxons). His name was Alfred, called The Great (849–899). After many battles, Alfred and the Danes agreed to divide England into their respective spheres of influence. That of the Danes, in the eastern and northern sections of England, was called the Danelaw and Alfred reached this settlement after paying a large tribute, called a Danegeld. Alfred also managed to get Guthrum, the Danish leader, to accept Christian baptism. With the Danes cordoned off in the Danelaw, the south and west of England fell under the overlordship of Alfred.

Alfred had stayed in Rome as a youth. He was a Christian, a scholar, and a great admirer of Latin culture. Fearing that the Danish invasions imperiled all civilized culture, he instituted a great revival of learning. He codified English law for the first time, and added to the law an Anglo-Saxon translation of the Decalogue (Ten Commandments). He personally translated several important Latin works into English and inspired an English translation of Bede's great history. His influence generated the famous *Anglo-Saxon Chronicles*, a running history of England written in English by monks and drawing upon Bede's earlier work in Latin. The *Anglo-Saxon Chronicles* still survive pretty much intact.

The next invasion, that of the Normans, established a long-lived Norman line on the English throne. The Normans and the Danes were ethnically related. Normandy was named after the Norsemen (Vikings or Danes), who had conquered this territory in the tenth century, more or less parallel to the Danish invasions of England. They soon gave up piracy and settled down, adopting both Christianity and the emerging French language which was replacing Latin.

The English King, Edward the Confessor, having no heirs, decided to give his throne to his Norman kinsman, William. As a token of good faith, Edward appointed a Norman as Archbishop of Canterbury. These actions provoked an anti-Norman uprising and William had to claim his throne by force, a struggle that led to five years of intense war. "Modern" English history begins with the Normans, who under William, duke of Normandy (called the "Conqueror"), defeated an English army at the Battle of Hastings in 1066.

Now enthroned as William I, he conducted a thorough general census of England (1085-86) for the purpose of imposing taxes. This valuable historical source has come down to us today. It is called, understandably enough, *The Domesday* [or Doomsday] *Book*.

This illustration from an old manuscript shows Aldhelm (c.639–709), Abbot of Malmesbury and one of the great scholars of his time, reading one of his books to a group of nuns. Oral reading to groups often replaced private reading when books were handmade and very expensive.

The Growing English Language

The Normans spoke Anglo-Norman, a variation of French which, like other Romance languages, continues Latin in another guise. As the Norman nobility established itself throughout England, Anglo-Norman became the language of the elite, much as Latin had been in the Roman period. The masses of farmers and yeomen, though, continued to speak Anglo-Saxon. The ordinary Englishman would hear Latin in church, Anglo-Norman in the law courts of the shire (county) and hundreds (county subdivision), and Anglo-Saxon on the streets.

Scholars divide the history of the English language into three periods:

1. Old English—from about 450 to about 1200

2. Middle English—from 1200 to about 1500, subdivided into three periods:
   Early—1200 to 1300
   Late—1300 to 1400
   Transitional (to Modern English)—1400 to 1500

3. Modern English—from 1500 to the present.

Anglo-Saxon, strictly speaking, was the form of Old English spoken in Wessex, the realm of Alfred the Great south of the Thames. Between the Thames and Humber rivers, the Mercian dialect prevailed. In Northumbria ("north of the Humber"), Bede's old territory, they spoke the Northumbrian or Anglian dialect. At the time when Modern English emerged, the Midland (Mercian) dialect prevailed, the language of Chaucer and Wyclif.

Old English used some letters we no longer need, such as Þ, called the *thorn*, and ð, called an *edh*. Another was the *wyn* ƿ, later replaced by *w*, and the *yogh* ȝ, replaced by *g* or *y*. The thorn and edh represented *th* sounds. (Much later, printers would take the idea of a thorn to abbreviate *th* by using a *y*. Thus, "Ye Olde Tea Shoppe.") Old English was also a highly inflected language, using word endings and changes in the body of a word to indicate the relationships for which we now use prepositions and pronouns.

As time went on, endings changed to a final *e* (which they pronounced) which eventually fell into disuse:

Old	*Middle*	*Modern*
(450–1200)	(1200–1500)	(1500–present)
leornian	lernen	learn
mona	monee	moon
stanas	stones	stones
sunne	sunne	sun
sunu	sune	son

That language changes so much ought not surprise us. Today some 3,000 new words and usages appear between editions of a major dictionary. Look, for instance, at a reproduction of the Declaration of Independence, which was written in 1776. The spelling, the script, and the style of expression all differ from what we read in contemporary books. We can read it, but only with difficulty.

Old English Versions of the Bible

Of all the Old English literature, not much has survived. The poetry we have bulks about as large as a modern paperback, and the prose taken together would fit into four or five thick paperbacks. Poetry came before prose as in most languages. Most of the prose—excluding the historical work by Bede—stems from the time of Alfred the Great.

So, we are not surprised that few Old English versions of the Bible have come down to us, and many of those only in fragments. Some, such as Caedmon's poems, were paraphrases of Scripture.

Bede tells the charming story of Caedmon (*fl.* 670). He tended cows and was ashamed of his wretched singing voice. When they passed the harp around during a feast, signalling time for song, Caedmon would excuse himself.

One night, when he had slipped into the barn to hide from the songfest, he fell asleep and in a dream an angel told him to sing of the Creator. Caedmon awoke and remembered the hymn he dreamed and sang it. He later became a monk and devoted his life to composing English Christian verse.

This is the hymn he dreamed, the one work surely from Caedmon's hand. He wrote in Northumbrian dialect and used the form of Old English verse: each line contains four accented syllables, divided into two half-lines with a break or pause between. People would have sung it to the accompaniment of a harp. A literal translation in modern English appears below each line; the space in each line indicates the break or pause.

Nu sculon herigean   heofonrices Weard
Now we must praise   *heaven-kingdom's Guardian*

Meotodes meahte   and his modge-ane
the Creator's might   *and his mind-plans*

weore Wuldor-Fder   swa he wundra gehwæs
the work of the Glory-Father   *when he of wonders of every one,*

ece Drihten   or onstealde
eternal Lord,   *the beginning established*

He ærest sceop   ielda bearnum
He first created   *for men's sons*

heofon to hrofe *heaven as a roof,*	halif Scyppend *holy Creator;*
-a middangeard *then middle-earth*	moncynnes Weard *mankind's Guardian*
ece Drihten *eternal Lord,*	æfter teode *afterwards made-*
firum foldan *for men earth,*	Frea aelmihtig *Master almighty.[1]*

"The Dream of the Rood [Cross]," a delightful poem from the seventh century and sometimes attributed to a poet named Cynewulf, contains many deeply spiritual lines, one of which in a modern rendering reads: "For through the Cross shall every soul who thinks to dwell with the Lord seek his [the Lord's] kingdom in his earthly journey."

The monks usually translated portions of the Bible—favorite sections such as Psalms, the Lord's Prayer, and other Gospel portions—for the edification of the clergy or one of the rare laypeople who could read. These translations often take the form of glosses, or a literal Old English translation written between the line of a Latin manuscript. Try reading aloud the Modern English interlinear on Caedmon's "Hymn," above. It sounds stiff and disjointed because it is literal. The Old English glosses would seem equally awkward, compared with the Latin.

This list summarizes the major Old English translations:

Bede and Others—In the seventh and eighth centuries, we have Caedmon's poetic paraphrases, and those of Aldhelm, abbot of Malmesbury. A number of Psalm translations appeared, along with small sections of Scripture such as the Lord's Prayer and the Decalogue. Bede, it has been said, completed his translation of John's Gospel the moment he died in 735. Aldhelm, bishop of

An early ninth-century depiction of the Venerable Bede (d. 735) by an anonymous artist, from a manuscript in the British Museum. The page is poorly trimmed on the right, but the four figures in the corners are the symbols of the four Evangelists (Gospel writers). Clockwise from upper left, Matthew (a man), John (an eagle), Luke (an ox), and Mark (a lion). These symbols derived from Revelation 4.7. The artist used the symbols to remind viewers of Bede's work in translating the Bible.

Sherborne who died in 709, translated the Psalms into Anglo-Saxon, and at his request Egbert, bishop of Holy Island [Lindisfarne], translated the Gospels.

In the tenth century, Alfred the Great took great interest in Bible translations. He initiated a translation of the Psalms and the Decalogue. Other parts of the Pentateuch appear in translation in his law codes. Alfred may have translated some of the Psalms himself, and they might be Psalms 1–50 in the *Paris Psalter*, a rendering in Old English with interpretative comments. With the exception of some works by Caedmon and some by Alfred the Great, no copies of these translations have survived.

Vespasian Psalter—The earliest surviving gloss in English on any part of the Bible, this psalter dates from the ninth century. Its Old English reads like a foreign language and uses unfamiliar characters. This is how Psalm 23.1-4 looks in this psalter:

> dry[h] receő Ĵ noþiht me þonu biő in sto[th]e lesþe őer mec
> gesteaőelade ofer þeter gereodnisse aledde mec saþle mine
> gecerde gelaedde me ofer stige rehtþisnisse fore noman his
> þeotudlice Ĵ őaeh őe ic gonge in midle scuan deaőes ne
> ondredu ic yfel for őon őu mid me er gerd őin Ĵ cryc őin hie
> me froefrende þerun.

Lindisfarne Gospels—These Gospels consist of a Latin version, copied by Bishop Eadfrith of Lindisfarne around 700, with a very literal Northumbrian interlinear translation added by Aldred at Durham, in about 950. This beautiful manuscript features illuminations that display fine Celtic designs. The magnificent opening letter on folio 149r is surrounded by 10,600 dots; a perfect jewel. This manuscript now resides in the British Library.

Luke's version of the Lord's Prayer looks like this in the Lindisfarne manuscript:

> fader gehalgad sie noma őin tocymaeő ric őin hlaf userne
> daeghuaemlice sel us eghuelc daege Ĵ [f]gef us synna usra gif
> faestlice aec þe [f]gefaes eghuelc scyldge us [f]gef ne usic
> onlaed őu in costunge.

Other Versions—The Rushworth Gloss dating from 975 seems the work of two men: the priest Farman and a scribe named Owun. It is based in part on the Lindisfarne Gospels, but in Matthew and parts of John the rendering reads as continuous prose. Thus, this is the oldest example of continuous Bible translation in English.

The West Saxon Gospels gives a full and readable translation that comes close to modern standards. The author remains anonymous, and the date is uncertain. But one of the earliest surviving copies, at Cambridge University, was presented to Exeter cathedral by Bishop Leofric who died in 1072.

About the same time as the West Saxon Gospels, a brilliant scholar, Bene-

A page from the Lindisfarne Gospels, an illuminated Latin manuscript, dating before A.D. 700. A Northumbrian translation was written between the lines of the Latin in the tenth century, probably at Durham. Compare the elegant lettering of the Latin with the less formal, cursive script used for the Anglo-Saxon glass.

dictine monk, and literary stylist, Ælfric the Grammarian (*c.* 955–1020), wrote the *Heptateuch*, a free, paraphrastic rendering into English of the first seven books of the Bible. Ælfric also wrote a series of saints' lives in English and prepared a number of English-language homilies to aid those clergy who could not handle Latin.

All these translators relied on the Latin Bible, usually the Vulgate but some traces of Old Latin versions show through. Bede, it is said, used a diglot version of the Acts of the Apostles in both Greek in Latin, but this would have been rare. Very few, even among the learned, had a good command of Greek.

3 THE BIBLE IN MIDDLE ENGLISH

When the year A.D. 1000 drew near, some Christians expected the return of Christ to mark the close of the first Christian millennium. Those were hard, difficult times. People would welcome the prospect of new heavens and new earth.

Jesus did not return as hoped, so the people, the Church, and the State settled down to live with each other, and not always in peace.

Murder in the Cathedral

On December 29, 1170, four knights stole into Canterbury Cathedral and murdered the Archbishop, Thomas à Becket. Their King, Henry II, had pleaded, perhaps only in momentary anger but within the hearing of these loyal knights, for someone to rid him of this troublesome priest. So the knights promptly obeyed. Public outcry forced Henry to do public penance at Becket's tomb. Becket was elevated to sainthood.

Why this tragedy? It comes down to a power struggle between Church and State. The Church viewed itself as overseer of Christian civilization. Clergy enjoyed special, protected privileges. Civil law could not touch them; they were held accountable only to ecclesiastical courts. Even Kings, in principle, paid obeisance to the Pope as the arbiter of faith and, in practice, of life. To Henry's dismay, Becket strongly defended the Church's privilege.

Henry had heard of 100 murders committed by clergy. One priest had poisoned his Bishop. One diocese had not received a visit from its bishop for more than a century. Some parish priests drew their living but never showed their face in the parish, hiring stand-ins to provide a minimum of spiritual care. Laxness and immorality abounded.

Henry wanted Becket to clean house. Though they numbered but one-percent of the population, the clergy controlled perhaps one-quarter of England's wealth. If the Church cost him so much money, Henry thought, then it should at least do its job well.

In Becket's ecclesiastical courts, however, erring clergy received, at most, a mere slap on the hand. Becket also dragged his feet on broader, sweeping reforms. He constantly asserted the privileges of the Church. Henry was infuriated.

Not that Henry was a high-principled moralist. These were corrupt times for everyone. Henry thought the Church was stepping on the toes of his own immodest sense of authority and using up financial resources he coveted for his own purpose.

Regardless of whether we come down on the side of Becket or Henry in this clash of Church and State, the episode illustrates a tension that will divide Christian society for many centuries. As the Church involved itself in power politics, numbers of Christians lamented the discrepancy between what the Gospel taught and what they saw practiced. The mood for reform grew, finally culminating in the Reformation. But before the wrenching waves of the sixteenth century would crash down, an Englishman would arise who thought that if the ordinary people could hear and read Scripture in their own language, it would move the Church back to its true, apostolic mission.

BECKET NOT FORGOTTEN

The events surrounding the murder of Archbishop Thomas à Becket play a large role in English literature. Chaucer's "Canterbury Tales" are written with the framework of a pilgrimage to St. Thomas' tomb. Shakespeare dealt with the incident in his play, "Henry II." The 20th-century poet T.S. Eliot dramatized the episode with his play, "Murder in the Cathedral."

The Bible in Sight and Sound

A Bible in English, or any other language, has little value if the owner cannot read it. Books cost a fortune before the printing press came along. Since books weren't readily available, people had little incentive to learn to read. Literacy grows with the availability of written literature. So the Church learned to use visual aids to tell the Bible story. Pope Gregory I in the sixth century clearly understood the value of visuals when he wrote:

> Pictures are used in churches so that those who are illiterate might
> at least read by looking at the walls.

The stained glass windows, statues, and paintings at which we marvel in ancient churches are much more than decoration. They were the Bible of the common person.

The Mass, too, through its pageantry and drama, taught biblical stories as well as providing the vehicle for worship. Lessons were read in Latin, but sometimes paraphrased into English. Sermons, given in the vernacular, would include biblical stories and quotations. The actions of the Mass dramatically portrayed important parts of the Bible, such as the enactment of Christ's sacrifice.

Stained glass windows in churches were used to tell the biblical stories to the masses who could not read. This window from the Abbey of Klosterneuburg, Austria, shows Christ healing a man born blind, John 9.1-41.

For festival days, other dramatic touches would be added. On Good Friday the veil which had concealed the sanctuary since the first Sunday in Lent would be let down. This dramatized the Gospel report that the veil in the Jerusalem Temple was torn in two at the death of Christ (Matthew 27.51). Especially during Easter, antiphonal choral responses began to be acted out with motion and gestures. This developed, by the tenth century, into processions to visit the empty tomb. Two centuries later, the action had developed to the point where many churches were presenting what amounted to a one-act play about the Easter event.

From these simple beginnings sprang the so-called "miracle plays," which became the Bible translation most familiar to the average English person. A miracle play tells a biblical story in dramatic form. They were originally performed in churches by the clergy, but as the number of players increased, lay groups assumed responsibility for presenting the plays.

Different trade guilds—shipwrights, goldsmiths, glovers, and so forth—would stage a play at their own expense. They would construct stages in public places such as the market square. Heaven might be represented by an overhead pavilion, Hell by a fiery dragon. The actors often wore elaborate costumes.

Some plays included comic elements. Noah's wife, in "The Deluge," refuses point-blank to go into the ark with all those smelly animals and has to be shoved aboard by force. Historians estimate that miracle plays were presented at 125 places in England, and the separate plays were stitched into cycles at various locations. There was a cycle of plays given at York and one at Chester.

Taken together, these cycles of miracle plays treat 21 Old Testament incidents and 68 episodes from the New Testament. Written in Middle English, the language of Chaucer, these plays reached the height of popularity in the late fourteenth and fifteenth centuries, then entered into a decline.

The "Morning Star"

John Wyclif (c. 1328–1384), born near Richmond in Yorkshire, has been called "the Morning Star of the Reformation." His thinking influenced Jan Huss (or Hus, c. 1359–1415), a Bohemian reformer, and through Huss, the Moravians and, later, Martin Luther. Wyclif promoted a program of church reform in both doctrine and practice. The centerpiece was a Bible in the language of the people.

This "radical," like Huss and Luther, was primarily a scholar, a university teacher. Only in his last eight or nine years did he turn to active reform. He studied scholastic philosophy and theology at Oxford University. After gaining his degree, he taught at Oxford where, as a popular professor, he addressed crowded lecture halls.

He held three parish appointments as rector: Fillingham (1361), Ludgershall (1368), and Lutterworth (1374), this last post coming by royal appointment. Wyclif, though, spent little time in his parishes. The income they provided funded his university studies.

Wyclif associated himself with the anti-clerical party in England. In 1374 he went to Bruges (in modern Belgium) to represent the English crown in negotiations over payments of tribute to the Holy See. This mission brought him in contact with John of Gaunt, an influential son of King Edward III. Their friendship later served Wyclif well.

A later engraving by an unknown artist shows Wyclif (c. 1330-1384) at work on his Bible translation. Note the hourglass on the table, used to keep track of the time before the invention of the clock.

Beginning in 1377, he launched a series of strong attacks on Church doctrine and practice. Wyclif's ideas will not seem unusual to the heirs of Luther and Calvin, but he formulated them a century and a half before the two great reformers. Wyclif claimed Popes were unnecessary and could be removed for heresy or misconduct. He argued that all property comes from God and the steward who receives a share must render faithful service.

That last point caught the favorable attention of the current government, as it would have pleased Henry II. The English were smarting under the exactions of the revenue-hungry Papacy, operating in splendid, schismatic, and scandalous exile in Avignon, France. The English Parliament had, in 1376, sought to curtail the collection of Papal revenues in England and to prevent payments to absentee Papal appointees. When the Bishop of London and the Archbishop of Canterbury tried to take action against Wyclif, John of Gaunt and other powerful officials shielded him.

Later Wyclif argued for more radical measures, criticizing long-held doctrines such as transubstantiation. He asserted that a lay person could be his own priest, and even officiate at the Eucharist in some circumstances. Scripture, he maintained, rather than the authority of the Church, was the basis for Christian teaching. For him, the visible church was not necessary to salvation, and the cult of relics, saints, and pilgrimages violated true Christianity. Priests and bishops were worthy of honor so far as their character warranted it. Elaborate services, in his view, erected a barrier to true, sincere worship.

Oxford University, second in prestige in northern Europe only to the University of Paris, prided itself on its independence and protected Wyclif's position. His enemies, though, succeeded in replacing or expelling Wyclif's university friends. Wyclif retired to Lutterworth to continue his work.

Wyclif's Bible

Wyclif's Bible was completed in 1382. Other hands may have worked on the translation, but the concept was wholly that of Wyclif. Realizing how important it was for laypeople to read Scripture on their own, he planned a translation of the entire Bible prepared with the average person in mind, for use by ordinary folk. Earlier translations had been made by scholar-monks for their own kind or for the clergy. Wyclif's vision was indeed radical and unique—and dangerous to the established order.

He had help with the actual work. Nicholas of Hereford, whose association with Wyclif caused his excommunication, translated the Old Testament at least as far as Baruch 3.20, one of the books of the Apocrypha which, in the Vulgate order they followed, is grouped with Lamentations at the end of Jeremiah. Perhaps he ended here because he was accused of heresy and had to defend himself in Rome. We do not know who finished the translation. Wyclif's secretary, John Purvey, who assisted with the New Testament, seems a likely suggestion.

How much of the actual work Wyclif did is disputed. Some say he translated the bulk of the New Testament. Others argue for several hands. In the last two or three years of his life, Wyclif's health began to fail, which limited his active participation in the project. In any case, from the outset it was widely recognized as "Wyclif's Bible." His vision, if nothing else, dominated the project.

Purvey, like Hereford, got into trouble for his involvement with Wyclif. Both recanted and disassociated themselves from the reformer. Thus, they could end their lives in peace. Other Wyclif followers who remained loyal met much different ends.

This pioneering Bible version stands as a monument to English letters and church life. From a modern perspective, however, the translators could be criticized for working from Latin to English, without consulting Greek and Hebrew manuscripts. Further, they depended on inferior copies of the Vulgate. But interest in seeking out the best texts was just beginning to develop in scholarly circles, so we cannot fault them overmuch.

Their choice of language, however, was in their control. The English language was developing very rapidly as a literary vehicle, but Wyclif's team elected to use an older style of the Midlands dialect. In scholarly terms, they wrote

THE RISE OF MIDDLE ENGLISH

As French became the language of the learned and upper classes in England, after the Norman Conquest, vernacular literature survived mostly in the remote western end of the island. One unknown cleric lamented:

> Saint Bede was born here in Britain among us and learnedly he translated books by means of which the English people were instructed...Abbot Ælfric...was a scholar and translated [part of the Old Testament]...These taught our people in English...Now is the learning lost and the people forlorn...Those who teach the people now are men of other tongues...

But changes were coming. The Norman kings, who at first resided in France and ruled England like a distant colony, began to look upon England as their main kingdom and settled permanently on the island. The English nobles, once dispossessed, regained their positions of prominence. Thus, Anglo-Norman and English began to mix and from this rose Middle English and eventually, the full richness of the language of the King James Bible and Shakespeare.

The Psalter was the most popular book to be translated in the twelfth and thirteenth centuries. Many lay Christians, especially women, were developing a mystical approach to the faith, perhaps under the influence of the Franciscans. They wanted vernacular Psalters for their meditations and devotions. Several have survived.

One manuscript, the twelfth-century Canterbury or Eadwin Psalter, now at Trinity College, Cambridge, is remarkable. Three of Jerome's Latin translations are presented: the so-called "Hebrew," Jerome's third translation of the Psalter, done from a Hebrew text; the Roman, his first translation, done from the Septuagint, and the Gallican, his second translation from the Septuagint and the one that became standard in the Latin Vulgate version. The "Hebrew" text has an Anglo-Norman gloss, and an English gloss accompanies the Roman version.

Somewhat later, William de Shoreham of Kent (1325) and Richard Rolle of Hampole (1330) translated the Psalms into English. Rolle was a popular mystical, devotional writer. His version of the Psalms apparently gained wide popularity, for many copies have come down to us. But the master of the Middle English Bible is John Wyclif.

in early Middle English at the time when late Middle English was rapidly emerging. This gave their Bible an old-fashioned flavor the day it was finished. It would have seemed a bit archaic to its readers, in much the same way as the *King James Version* strikes modern readers. This linguistic problem only compounded over the years. When printing came to England a century later, no printer sought to publish Wyclif's Bible. By then, people couldn't easily read its brand of English.

The literary style also left something to be desired. It was overly literal, reproducing Latin forms when English demanded otherwise. For example, it often retained the Latin word order and left out parts of the verb *to be*, necessary in English but not in Latin. After Wyclif died in 1384, John Purvey worked on revisions, consulting better Vulgate manuscripts and improving the style of writing by rendering it into more idiomatic English. The revised version was finished around 1395.

While Wyclif's version may have seemed a trifle antiquated to its readers, it appears almost modern to us—when compared with, say, the Lindisfarne Gospels or the Vespasian Psalter. Remember that these two earlier translations were separated from Wyclif by the same time span as stands between us and Shakespeare. Yet we can, without too much difficulty, read Shakespeare. Now compare the samples in the previous chapter from the Lindisfarne Gospels and the Vespasian Psalter with the samples below from Wyclif. You will see clearly how radically English had changed in those four centuries.

Luke 11.2-4, the Lord's Prayer, looks like this in Wyclif's version:

> Fadir, halewid be thi name. Thi kyngdom come to. [Z]yue to vs
> to day oure eche dayes breed. And for[z]yue to vs oure synnes,
> as and we for[z]yuen to ech owynge to vs. And leed not vs in to
> temptacioun.

The phrase "Give to us today our each day's bread" has charm, but it did not survive. Tyndale's "daily bread" became the standard English expression. But that story comes in the next chapter. For now, look at Wyclif's rendering of the opening verses of Psalm 23:

> The Lord gouerneth me, and no thing to me shal lacke; in the
> place of leswe where he me ful sette. Ouer watir of fulfilling he
> nurshide me; my soule he conuertide. He bro[z]te doun me
> vpon the sties of ri[z]twisnesse; for his name. For whi and if
> I shal go in the myddel of the shadewe of deth; I shal not dreden
> euelis, for thou art with me. Thi [z]erde and they staf; tho han
> confortid me.

The expression "The Lord governs me," instead of the "Lord is my shepherd," expresses well Wyclif's own view of the omnipotence of God. "Water of fulfilling" has meaning that is lost in our familiar "still waters." And "my soul he converted" presents us with an illuminating and profound image. Note, too, that Wyclif treats the psalm as prose. An understanding of Hebrew poetry would require serious study of texts in the century or more after Wyclif's death.

This illustration, after a much later painting by W.F. Yeames, shows Wyclif sending forth Lollards or "poor priests" to read his English Bible translation to the eager masses.

The Lollards

Wyclif faced a dilemma. He had prepared a Bible especially for ordinary folk. But in those days before printing presses, each book was written by hand and cost a great deal of money. Further, few people—and not even all the gentry—could read. How then to get the vernacular Scriptures to the masses?

Wyclif had a brilliant solution. He sent forth bands of traveling preachers. He called them by several titles—"poor priests," "unlearned and simple men"—but the adherents they attracted were called Lollards. These itinerant preachers were drawn at first from university graduates and prominent families, but as time passed they came largely from the poor.

The "poor preachers" went forth in russet robes of undressed cloth, with staff in hand and no purse nor sandals. They took food and shelter as it was offered to them. They read the Bible in the vernacular to the illiterate population. They preached, using material Wyclif had prepared. Their sermons emphasized biblical exposition, in contrast to ordinary preaching which often dwelt on miracles and the lives of the saints.

The crowds flocked to Wyclif's "true preachers." The listeners, for the first time, heard the Bible in their own language and they were overjoyed. Even the upper classes and gentry were attracted to the new movement and provided protection for these wandering preachers.

ABOUT EARLY SPELLING

Spelling, at this stage of the English language, depended on the writer. Standardized spelling did not begin to emerge until well into the eighteenth century. Thus, various manuscripts of Wyclif's Bible spell "flesh" as fleisch, fleish, flesch, flesh, flehs, flessh, and even more ways. The pronoun "their" might appear as her, here, ther, their, or thair. (In Middle English, all vowels and consonants would be pronounced.) Wyclif's name, too, is variously spelled: Wycliffe, Wickliffe, Wiclif, and Wycliff.

The established Church, of course, could not tolerate this kind of threat to its authority. The Peasants' Revolt of 1381 was blamed on the Lollards, but probably unjustly. The wandering preachers and their flock were not social revolutionaries. But there was plenty of social unrest to feed the fires of rebellion. Langland's "Piers Plowman," a poem from the period, details many of the social ills. A more likely agitator is John Ball, a "mad preacher" who advocated common ownership of all property and abolition of the distinctions between serf and lord.

Whether the Lollards sparked the revolt or not, the accusation hurt their cause. Loyal supporters among the propertied classes, and they were many, began to fall away. Wyclif lost the backing of John of Gaunt and was declared a heretic twice. Yet he died peacefully at home two years later—so he must have kept some friends in high places.

Outlawing Vernacular Scripture

The Lollard movement survived Wyclif's death, and so did the persecution. Some of Wyclif's followers were burned at the stake. Parliament passed anti-Lollard legislation. Alarmed by a renewal of heresy at Oxford, Archbishop Arundel, in 1408, prepared a Constitution which the Provincial Council at Oxford adopted. It declared in part:

> The Holy Scripture is not to be translated into the vulgar tongue, nor a translation to be expounded, until it shall have

been duly examined, under pain of excommunication and the stigma of heresy.

Parliament put teeth into the ban, declaring that those who read the Scriptures in their mother tongue without authorization would:

forfeit land, cattle, life, and goods from their heirs forever.

That Archbishop Arundel thought the late Wyclif was a dangerous man seems clear from a letter he wrote in 1411 to the Pope:

This pestilent and wretched John Wyclif, of cursed memory, that son of the old serpent [the devil]...endeavoured by every means to attack the very faith and sacred doctrine of Holy Church, devising—to fill up the measure of his malice—the expedient of a new translation of the Scriptures into the mother tongue.

This violent prohibition on vernacular Scripture was much stronger than anything before in the English Church, although prominent, responsible persons, especially of the nobility, could usually obtain permission to own a Psalter or Bible.

Despite the ban, the Lollard movement and the reading of English Scripture continued into the reign of Henry V (1413–1422), who took vigorous measures against the Lollards. The Council of Constance, in 1415, condemned Wyclif on 260 counts of heresy and directed that his body be exhumed and cast from consecrated ground. Thirteen years later, at Papal command, the remains of Wyclif were dug up again, burned, and his ashes cast into the nearby River Swift.

The persecutions and the burnings continued, but they did not stop the Lollard movement. We hear of its revival as late as the reign of Henry VII (1485–1509). After that, the Lollards blend into the mainstream of the English Reformation.

Wyclif Manuscripts

Some 170 copies of Wyclif's Bible have survived to this day. That suggests that many copies circulated in his heyday, for persecutors confiscated and burned copies they found, sometimes along with their owners. Most of these copies represent the later 1395 revision, presumably done by Purvey. Some show signs of further revision, as copyists attempted to further improve the smoothness of this overly literal, somewhat antiquated translation. A few contain passages which seem more like fresh translations than improvements on either version of the Wyclif Bible. Quite likely, a number of translators, whose names are now

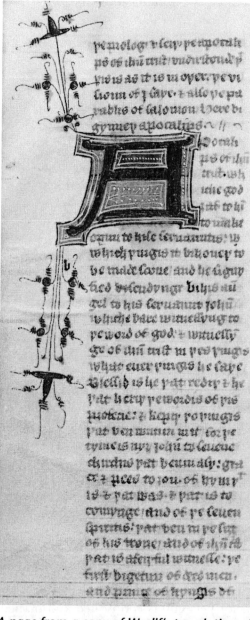

A page from a copy of Wyclif's translation of the New Testament, dating from c. 1330. It shows the opening of the Revelation to John, which Wyclif titled "Apocalypse," a Middle English word from the Greek which means "revelation." Note the lack of verse numbering, which was developed about two centuries later. The large decorative letter and the smaller decorative letters indicate divisions in the text. However, these divisions were not standardized until Bibles were printed. A Bible reader at that time had to rely on memory to find a particular verse or passage of Scripture.

lost, were working in the late fourteenth century and incorporated their work into the body of Wyclif's Bible.

About ten of the surviving manuscripts have glosses added in the margin, to explain a word or a term, and a commentary on the Gospels. They are called the "Glossed Gospels," and appear to be the work of one person, a scholar with access to a good library and, perhaps, connected with Oxford.

Another group of manuscripts contains glosses from a different source. These annotations limit themselves to explaining obscure terms. For instance, in Job 17.3 the Wyclif Bible uses the phrase, "helle is my hous" (hell is my house) which the comment explains this way:

ABOUT GLOSSES

Glosses—marginal notes or notes between the lines—have a long history, going back to Alexandria in the 3rd–2nd centuries B.C. In monasteries, they were used as teaching aids for young novice monks as they set about their studies. Some glosses on Bible translations show that the translator was unsure. The main line might include a Latin-root word or even a transliteration of the Latin. Then a gloss would add the Anglo-Saxon word. Middle English translations tend to let the Latin control the English, and the English glosses reveal the increasing confidence in the English language.

Footnotes in our Bibles serve many of the same functions as medieval glosses, and a modern study edition could be called a highly glossed Bible.

Hell etc.: that is, burying within the earth...in this place and others in this book. "Hell" is a Hebrew word that often signifies "a ditch" or "burying." (*Spelling modernized.*)

Some existing copies are large, well-bound, one- and two-volume copies of the entire Bible done in beautiful script with elegant initial letters. These very expensive editions probably belonged to noble families, who had the necessary connections to own a Bible. One manuscript has an altered date on it, to make it seem as if it were written before the 1408 ban. At the end it has a sentence, "The eer of the lord m.ccc & viij this book was ended," but a fourth c has been erased, changing the date from 1408 to 1308. The owner may have hoped to "grandfather" his copy past the new law by making it seem older than the law.

Other copies of the Wyclif Bible are smaller, less elegant, and written in tiny script. These served a less wealthy audience. They may contain only the key portions of the Bible, a sort of "Reader's Digest" condensation which, with fewer words, allowed faster copying with correspondingly lower cost.

Wyclif's Bible gets quoted frequently in devotional and other writings through the fifteenth century. One hundred years after it appeared, the translation took on a new life in a new language. Murdoch Nisbet rewrote the revised version of Wyclif's Bible in Nisbet's native Scots. Though it never made it into the age of printing, Wyclif's Bible exerted tremendous influence.

Within two centuries of Wyclif's death, his fundamental ideas will dominate the English Church of the Reformation and Scripture will appear in every home at a price lower than Wyclif could ever imagine.

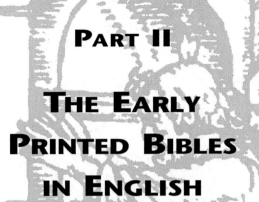

PART II

THE EARLY
PRINTED BIBLES
IN ENGLISH

4 THE PIONEER: WILLIAM TYNDALE

John Wyclif contended with two serious limitations. First, the English language in his day was relatively immature. Wyclif used Latinisms because his English lacked some needed words, expressions and constructions. Second, his textual resources were limited. He relied on the Latin Vulgate and not the best form of it at that. Knowledge of Greek and Hebrew was sparse.

Within 150 years after Wyclif, the situation on both counts changed dramatically as the result of two broad movements in western history: the Renaissance and the Reformation. And this new scholarship became widely available, thanks to a technology called printing.

William Tyndale would be the first Englishman to combine the new learning and the new technology to produce vernacular Scriptures.

The New Learning

A radical change in thought emerged in the western world, as revolutionary as the Copernican understanding of the solar system. The change, underway in Italy in Wyclif's day, came to fruition throughout Europe in Tyndale's era. We call this movement the Renaissance.

Italian scholars came into possession of manuscripts of the classics in their original Greek through trade with Constantinople (modern Istanbul). Constantine I rebuilt this city in A.D. 330 as the seat of the Eastern Roman Empire. After the Germanic tribes overran Rome, culture declined in the west and Greek became a nearly forgotten language. Constantinople, though, continued as a center of Greek language and culture. Scholarship in Greek texts, now crippled in the west, continued to flourish in the east.

Western scholars had known Aristotle, for example, from second- and third-hand sources, through Latin translations of Arabic translations and the works of the Church Fathers. Reading the texts anew in Greek, they discovered that what they had known was both partial in scope and inadequate in translation. A host of previously unknown manuscripts emerged and Italian scholars set themselves to studying and collating these exciting new texts. The fever for learning about classical culture raged through Italy and spread northward in Europe. These apostles of the New Learning were called *humanists*.

A new and essentially revolutionary test of truth emerged from this flurry of scholarship. Previously, it had been enough to ask, "*Who* said it?" The authority of the teacher, such as the Church, sufficed to insure the truth of the teaching. The new test asked, "*What* was being taught?" That is, did the content fit the sources? Could the teaching survive examination, questioning, and testing?

When the Ottoman Sultan Muhammad II conquered Constantinople for Islam in 1453, the New Learning received an unexpected boost. Greek scholars fled the city and went to teach Greek in European universities. Excited by their new insights into the Greek New Testament, many European scholars sought the help of rabbis to bring up their skills in Hebrew for work on the Old Testament. Students diligently compared available manuscripts, seeking to be as faithful as possible to the original languages. It was no longer possible to explain Scripture solely from the Latin Vulgate. (The Vulgate, too, underwent scholarly revisions to establish a standard version since the process of copying over the centuries had corrupted the text. Pope Clement VIII issued such a version in 1592 and it remained the standard Latin version down to modern times.)

The New Learning in England

The 1408 Constitution promulgated by Archbishop Arundel forbidding the making or reading of any unauthorized English translation of the Bible still stood in force. And the Lollards, who survived into the fifteenth century in many villages and towns, still protested this ban and clung to their tattered portions of Wyclif's translation. In many ways, England remained isolated, protected from the controversies and religious discontent that swept the Continent. The country followed its own path and when the Reformation finally came to England it would take on its own distinctive characteristics.

By the beginning of the sixteenth century, England had changed a great deal. After 30 years of dynastic struggle in the War of Roses (1455-85) between the houses of York (with a white rose badge) and Lancaster (red rose), Henry Tudor, head of the house of Lancaster, returned from France to reign as Henry VII, married Elizabeth of the house of York, ended the wars, and established the house of Tudor. The Tudors—the last being Elizabeth I—would transform England by instituting the first truly national, centralized, and efficient government.

The War of the Roses mostly involved the nobility. The struggle destroyed a great number of that class, lending the death blow to the final remnants of feudalism. The middle classes, however, grew in power, influence, and wealth. Since the clergy were identified with the nobility, an anticlerical mood emerged in very respectable circles. Well-to-do merchants, for example, would utter the same criticisms of the clergy as the poor Lollards. In all, the general population simply ceased to look upon the established church as a source of spirituality.

The religious orders which, in earlier days, would periodically revitalize the faith of the people, had fallen into decay. The number of monks and nuns had shrunk by a quarter in the previous three centuries. Monasteries became places that provided good livings for members of noble families; abbots lived as princes. The people needed to look elsewhere for spiritual nourishment and, in keeping with the New Learning, sought strength by returning to the sources, which meant the Bible.

At Oxford, John Colet began to lecture directly from the plain Scripture, without the complicated, often allegorical interpretations favored by medieval scholastics. Colet interpreted the text philologically, that is, by sticking to the text itself, its grammar, and its manuscript history. He was followed by George Stafford at Cambridge. Erasmus, the brightest light of the New Learning, visited these universities and was numbered among the intimate circle surrounding Henry VIII, himself a supporter of New Learning.

ERASMUS

A contemporary painting by Hans Holbein.

The leading humanist of his day, Desiderius Erasmus (c. 1466-1536) was born in Holland, became a priest, and studied at the University of Paris. He devoted himself to Greek and Latin classics and the church fathers. Unlike the humanists of southern Europe, who focussed on pagan and artistic concerns, Erasmus' interest lay in the religious and moral sphere. His overwhelming influence shaped the northern European humanist movement in this direction. He produced an improved Latin Bible based on original Greek texts he had collected, compared, and collated. In 1516, he produced his first edition of the Greek New Testament, which was followed swiftly by other improved editions and became the basic resource for Bible translation into the nineteenth century. While using his wit and learning to denounce clerical abuse and lay ignorance, he remained a tolerant man who recoiled from conflict and sought to preserve the unity of the Catholic tradition.

Monks and friars, who still dominated the universities, attacked the humanism of these "Oxford Reformers." But Henry VIII felt sympathetic to their cause and protected them. Colet later became Dean of St. Paul's Cathedral in London, where he established a school along "modern" lines with stress on Latin, Greek, and the classics.

These enthusiasts of humanism believed their crusade would liberate people from bondage to the past and usher in a new age of enlightenment. Erasmus confessed, in 1516, that he longed for the day when common people could read the Bible, that "the husbandman may sing parts of [the Gospels] at his plow, that the weaver may warble them at his shuttle." They had great confidence in the ability of ordinary people, with sufficient learning, to discover the truth for themselves.

This conviction led to a fresh understanding of the power of the Bible as *autopistos*, a Greek term meaning that Scripture was self-validating and could awaken faith on its own apart from liturgical or ecclesiastical structures. The Scriptures, in a real sense, were alive, and able to build up people for holy living. One Cambridge don, Thomas Bilney, bought a copy of Erasmus' new and elegant Latin translation of the Bible. "I bought it," he admitted, "being allured rather by the cleaner Latin than by the Word of God." But his encounter with Scripture converted him. He became an active reformer and met martyrdom in 1531.

We must remember that, for many people, the reform program did not include adopting the emerging Protestant doctrines. Early humanists, like Erasmus and Henry VIII's close associate, Sir Thomas More, wished to preserve the basic unity of the Catholic church. So would many laypeople.

Book Smuggling

The free interchange of ideas among the masses, made possible by the printed book, was a new concept that caused kings and cardinals to tremble. What sort of mischief could it create? If everyone determined their own doctrine based on their own understanding of the Bible, religious chaos would result. They had a point, and a majority of the population would probably have agreed with them in the beginning.

To control the flow of information, presses were licensed by the king and could print a book only with His Majesty's authorization. This created a major industry in book smuggling. Books banned in England would be printed in Cologne or Basel or Strasbourg. They would be purchased either off the press or at the book fairs that flourished, such as the huge one at Frankfurt (which still operates). The buyers then shipped the books up the Rhine on barges, always on the lookout for hostile church officials. At ports such as Antwerp or Hamburg, they hid the books in bales of cloth and loaded them onto ships heading for the English ports of London, Bristol, or Lynn, near Norfolk. From there, colporteurs or book agents delivered the books on foot to their final buyers, whether university dons or literate merchants and farmers.

This illicit literary network was developed by a mysterious group called the "Society of Christian Brethren," an organization of wealthy and solid individuals, most of them merchants and uniformly anticlerical. Among them were William Petit, Richard Hilles, and Humphrey Monmouth, who later became Tyndale's friend and patron. Historians have described the society as a kind of "Forbidden Book-of-the-Month Club." They were well-organized, with their own accounts and auditors. They smuggled books by the Continental reformers, such as Luther, and later brought in English religious works printed on the Continent—including Tyndale's New Testament. The society also subsidized writers and Bible translators. It was a profitable business, but highly risky. Many colporteurs were arrested. Some were tortured and burned.

"The Captain of Our English Heretics"

The first printed English translation of the New Testament came from the hand of William Tyndale (c.1494–1536; the name is also spelled Tindale or Tindal). It's a story of secret presses, smuggled books, danger—and death.

We know little about the early years of this man whom Sir Thomas More called "the captain of our English heretics." Born in Gloucester 100 years after Wyclif's death, Tyndale attended a grammar school attached to Magdalen Hall, Oxford, and later attended the Hall itself, probably receiving his M.A. in 1515. He studied under the classical scholars Grocyn, Latimer, and Linacre. He likely attended Cambridge also, where Erasmus was lecturing and preparing his edition of the Greek New Testament.

William Tyndale, from a window in the Chapel of Hertford College, Oxford, dedicated in 1994

It is probable that he was ordained sometime around 1520, before returning to Gloucester to assume the duties of tutor to the children of Sir John Walsh of Little Sodbury. That household received many distinguished church leaders, with whom Tyndale often disputed to the despair of the lady of the house. Before long, Tyndale found himself in trouble with the local clergy. Though influenced by humanists—his first translation at Little Sodbury was of Erasmus' *Enchiridion*—he had the spirit of a more radical reformer. The conservative clergy wouldn't have been happy with his view that the lay people need no interme-

THE NEW TECHNOLOGY CALLED PRINTING

The Chinese had forms of printing as early as A.D. 450. But the breakthrough came with the development of movable type, an invention which appeared in Korea a half-century before it came upon the European scene. The later European invention, however, seems to be totally independent, usually credited to Henne Gensfleisch, who assumed the name of Johann Gutenberg (c. 1397–1468). Born in Mainz, Germany, and trained as a goldsmith, he became a partner in a printing firm in the 1430s. There are other claimants, however, to the "invention" of moveable type in Europe: Lourens Janszoon Coster (c. 1370–1440?) of Haarlem seems to have printed a Latin grammar a decade or so before Gutenberg.

Gutenberg cast separate letters from metal, each of uniform height and varying widths. The printer could take these letters, one by one, and arrange them by hand to form words. When he set enough type to fill a sheet, the type was locked in place and the whole unit, called a "form," was placed in the press. The type was inked and pressed against the paper. Then the sheet would be removed for drying and later it would be printed on the reverse side using another form. Since type was expensive, some printers would disassemble the type from the first form, after the desired number of sheets were printed, and use it to set the type for the form that would print the reverse side of the sheet.

Early printers made their own paper. As printing developed into a major industry, so did papermaking.

Gutenberg printed a Latin Bible, which is considered the earliest important printed book. The project probably required several years of work and the Bible came off the press no later than 1455. This two-volume Bible displays excellent workmanship and features hand-done decorations. Some 40 copies of Gutenberg's Bible still exist.

This panel of the Tyndale Window in the Chapel of Hertford College, Oxford, shows Tyndale reading pages from the press. Note how the printer turns the screw which presses the inked type against the paper.

diary between themselves and Scripture, and with his low view of the clerical office. As Tyndale once wrote, "Thou that ministereth in the kitchen, and are but a kitchen page...knoweth that God put thee in that office...[I]f thou compare deed and deed, there is a difference between the washing of dishes and preaching the word of God; but as touching to please God, none at all...."

An English Bible

At some point, Tyndale seized the idea to create an English translation of the Bible. As he said once to a visitor to Little Sodbury, "If God spare my life, ere many years I will cause a boy that driveth the plough [to] know more of the Scripture than thou doest," an echo of Erasmus' sentiment. Tyndale believed in the *autopistos* power of Scripture and the ability of laypeople to interpret Scripture unaided by clergy. He wrote later, "I had perceived by experience, how that it was impossible to establish the lay people in any truth, except the scripture were plainly laid before their eyes in their mother tongue, that they might see the process, order and meaning of the text...."

Tyndale had models to follow for his English translation. Vernacular translations had already appeared on the Continent in Italian, French, German, Catalan, Dutch, German, Slavonic, and even Hebrew.

He eked out a living in London for a year, preaching at St. Dunstan's. Then he found a solid patron, Humphrey Monmouth, who was involved with the "Society of Christian Brethren." A cloth merchant and later an alderman of London, Monmouth represented the rising middle-class of hard-working, literate entrepreneurs whom the humanists considered God's elite (rather than the clergy) and who gravitated in large numbers to the Protestant movement.

Tyndale received a stipend of ten pounds plus room and board in Monmouth's house, where he lived for a year while working on his translation. Monmouth and his associates among London merchants would continue to aid Tyndale for several years. They were the financial backers of the first printed English Scripture.

Living in a merchant's house brought Tyndale into contact with Continental merchants who kept him informed of developments in the European reform movement and supplied him with books and information he needed in his work. Even though he was protected, Tyndale must have felt oppressed by the tense atmosphere in London. He decided to go to Germany, to the free city of Hamburg, leaving behind his dearly beloved country which, as happened, he would never see again.

He later wrote, "[I] understood at the last, not only that there was no room in my lord of London's palace to translate the New Testament, but also that there was no place to do it in all England."

Going to Press

From Hamburg, most historians agree, Tyndale went to Wittenberg where he became familiar with Martin Luther and got caught up in Luther's doctrine of justification by faith. This doctrine, a bedrock teaching of Protestants, asserts that one is made right with God—justified—solely by relying on and trusting in what Jesus Christ did on behalf of the believer. No merit or good work on the part of humans can restore their broken relationship with God. This contrasted with the Catholic teaching that salvation or justification involved both God's mercy in Christ and a person's own good works. Humanist reformers, such as Erasmus and Sir Thomas More, questioned Luther's teaching. If Christ more or less guaranteed your salvation so easily,

SIZES OF BOOKS

Printers gave names to each book size and each size was based on how many leaves were printed on a sheet of paper. A leaf is a sheet printed on both sides, each side being a page. Unlike modern practice, the earliest printed books counted the leaves rather than the pages.

For a big book, called a folio, printers would set two leaves on each sheet, folding it to make the four-page folio. For smaller books, they would print four leaves on a large sheet, fold and trim it, to make an eight-page unit called a quarto. Still smaller is the octavo, with eight leaves per sheet for a sixteen-page unit.

The final dimensions of the book depend upon the measurements of the original unfolded sheet. Based on a 20- by 25-inch sheet, the various sizes, with their names and abbreviations, are:

Folio (f. or fo.) 20- by 12 1/2-inches
Quarto (4to., 4o) 12 1/2- by 10-inches
Octavo (8vo., 8o) 10- by 6 1/4-inches
Duodecimo (12mo., 12o) 6 2/3- by 6 1/4-inches

Sizes ran as small as sixtyfourmo (64mo., 64o) or about 2 1/2- by 3 1/8-inches.

they asked, then why bother with good deeds and caring for the poor?

Tyndale also met a fellow Englishman, William Roye, a talented linguist who was studying at Wittenberg. Roye helped Tyndale get his New Testament into print, but Roye was also an indiscrete boaster, especially after a few beers. And that caused problems.

Work on a quarto edition (see note, "Sizes of Books") began in Cologne in 1525 in the shop of Peter Quentell and was financed by Monmouth and his merchant friends. Why they chose Cologne remains a mystery; it was a very conservative Catholic center. Someone—perhaps the boastful Roye—talked about the secret project in the presence of Cochlaeus, who was an enemy of Luther. Cochlaeus got word to the Imperial Senate. About the time the printer was finishing Matthew and starting on Mark's Gospel, the authorities ordered the work to cease. Tyndale gathered up all copies of the ten sheets that had been printed and fled north to Worms, where he completed the work in 1526 with printer Peter Schoeffer. The same year, an octavo edition of either 3,000 or 6,000 copies came off the press. While the quarto had marginal notes and prefaces, the octavo edition didn't even have chapter headings.

Still, it became a best seller, appearing in England in April, 1526. Some 3,000 copies were smuggled in bales of cloth to England and distributed through Monmouth's underground bookselling operation. The public eagerly bought copies, and the demand continued as an Antwerp printer reprinted large numbers of unauthorized and rather shoddy copies for the English market. Between 1525 and 1528, 18,000 copies had been sold.

Opposition

Tyndale's New Testament hit the market in a Catholic England, eight years before Henry VIII broke with Rome and about the time the king was instituting divorce proceedings against his first wife, Katherine. Luther's teachings were circulating in England and creating disturbances in the church at the time Henry was anxious to keep on good terms with the Vatican. Tyndale's prefaces to the New Testament books amounted to translations of those in Luther's German Bible. The marginal notes also reflected Luther's views. And he followed the order of books in Luther's translation, putting Hebrews, James, Jude, and Revelation at the end. Catholic England was not yet ready for such a Protestant-influenced translation.

WHAT DID A BIBLE COST?

The sponsoring merchants priced Tyndale's New Testament at half a crown, or 2 1/2 shillings. A brick mason, at the time, earned six pence a day, so that New Testament would cost him five days' wages (about $500 in our economy). A half-crown could also buy 60 pounds of beef. Pirated editions from Antwerp soon flooded the market at 13 pence each, or two days wages. In Wyclif's day, the fee for borrowing a manuscript of the Bible for an hour a day over a period of time was the equivalent of five shillings. Thanks to printing, one could own Scripture for half the price of borrowing a copy only a century or so earlier. Today, a brick mason would work perhaps 15-20 minutes to purchase a Bible Society edition of the entire Bible.

But there were other reasons for opposition. Conservatives simply rejected the notion of vernacular Scripture, feeling that the whole idea would destroy morals and faith. The same Cochlaeus who had prevented the printing of Tyndale's work in Cologne expressed his horror and disdain in this way:

> The New Testament translated into the vulgar tongue is in truth the food of death, the fuel of sin, the veil of malice, the pretext of false liberty, the protection of disobedience, the corruption of discipline, the depravity of morals, the termination of Concord, the death of honesty, the well-spring of vices, the disease of virtues, the instigation of rebellion, the milk of pride, the nourishment of contempt, the death of peace, the destruction of charity, the enemy of unity, the murderer of truth.

An engraving depicting Johannes Cochlaeus (1479–1552), by an unknown artist. Cochlaeus opposed the Reformation and interfered with the publication of Tyndale's New Testament.

The learned humanists, who might think Cochlaeus' rhetoric a bit overstated, nevertheless raised scholarly objections to Tyndale's translation. Bishop Tunstall, once a friend, claimed to find 3,000 errors in the translation. (He probably counted the places where Tyndale, using the Greek text, differed from the accepted Latin Vulgate.) Tyndale was more disturbed by the fierce objections expressed by Sir Thomas More, who became the key person in authority to attack his translation. Thomas More criticized Tyndale's work on every imaginable ground—wrong history, poor logic, terrible rhetoric, and even on unacceptable English grammar. He accused Tyndale of merely translating Luther's German Bible. The feud grew bitter with both men stooping to much name-calling.

Was Tyndale's scholarship so inadequate as to merit these learned attacks? A skilled linguist, he worked from Erasmus' Greek New Testament using one or all of the editions of 1516, 1519, and 1522. Erasmus' text wasn't particularly good by modern standards, but it was by far the best available source at the time. Tyndale also consulted the Vulgate, Erasmus' recent Latin version, and Luther's German translation. One biographer asserts boldly that "By the level of his own day Tyndale was a good Greek scholar, fully as good as Erasmus or Luther." He was, as he claimed, working independently, starting afresh with the Greek text: "I had no man to counterfeit," Tyndale said in his own defense, "neither was I helped with English of any that had interpreted the same."

Tyndale's opponents, in the final analysis, viewed his translation as part of the worrisome Lutheran movement. Tyndale's inclusion of Luther's marginal notes and prefaces to the books were as much a basis for their concern as the translation itself. But Tyndale was less interested in making propaganda for the Lutheran cause than in putting a good English Testament into the hands of the people. When Stephen Vaughan visited him, to induce him to return to England with the promise of a pardon, Tyndale told him:

> I assure you that if it would stand with the King's most gracious pleasure to grant only a bare text of the scripture to be put forth among his people...be it the translation of what person soever shall please his majesty, I shall immediately make faithful promises never to write more...[and] submit myself at the feet of his royal majesty, offering my body to suffer what pain or torture yea, what death his grace will, so this be obtained.

The pirated editions which flooded England from the Antwerp press did not contain notes, yet they were still confiscated and burned. In the view of the opponents, the text itself was a tract for the Protestant cause.

They came to this conclusion from the way Tyndale replaced certain terms that had become commonly accepted through the Latin versions. He rendered church (Greek, *ecclesia*) by "congregation;" priest (Greek, *presbyter*) by "senior" or "elder;" do penance (usually Greek, *metanoia*) by "repent;" charity (Greek, *agape*; Latin, *caritas*) by "love;" and in many places, grace (Greek, *charis*) by "favor." We are accustomed to translations using Tyndale's terminology, but at the time his opponents believed that the new terms would undercut the idea of the one universal church, lessen people's respect for the priesthood, and weaken the complex system the church had developed for doing penance for forgiveness.

Some opponents, such as Bishop Tunstall and Archbishop Warham, bought large numbers of copies to burn. Tyndale accepted this in good humor since the extra money would pay for printing later improved editions and awaken public interest. Still, the intense persecution took its toll. About 15,000 copies were printed in the first six editions, but a mere handful survive today. Of the Cologne-Worms quarto, only a fragment—the Gospel of Matthew—has survived, and is in the British Library. Of the 6,000-copy Worms octavo edition, only two complete copies remain, one at the State Library of Würtemberg in Stuttgart, Germany, one at the British Library (lacking only the title page), and one incomplete copy at St. Paul's Cathedral in London.

On to the Old

As soon as he finished his New Testament, Tyndale set to translating the Old Testament from the Hebrew. He worked in Marburg (Germany) on the project from 1527–1531, then moved to Antwerp. He was not able to complete this translation, but the Pentateuch appeared in Marburg in 1530. (*Pentateuch*, a term derived from the Greek, means the first five books of the Bible, Genesis through Deuteronomy, traditionally attributed to Moses; they are also known as the Torah.) The five books were apparently printed separately, for Genesis and Numbers were done in black-letter type and the other three, in roman type. About a year later, Jonah was published in Antwerp. (Only one copy of each survives, both in the collection of the British Library.)

Controversies over his New Testament and the time required for the thorough revision that appeared in 1535, kept Tyndale from seeing the entire Old Testament come off press. He did, however, manage to translate Joshua through 2 Chronicles in manuscript form. That work was finished by John Rogers, a friend and colleague of Tyndale's, who would become another giant of the English Bible.

Living on the Continent proved an advantage to Tyndale. Hebrew scholarship was more advanced there than in England, probably because of the presence of larger Jewish communities. He had available to him decent Hebrew grammar books and dictionaries, as well as the rabbinic Bibles of 1516/17 and 1524/25. Some of his phrasings suggest that he had read Purvey's revision of Wyclif's earlier Bible. Most historians, though, agree that

TYPEFACES

The Generation of Christ

The Generation of Christ

The first typefaces were called black letter, and were patterned after the heavy Gothic scripts that we call "Old English." Soon more elegant and graceful typefaces appeared, called roman, patterned after the cursive forms that had become popular with hand copyists, especially in Italy. In the first decades of Bible printing, printers chose black letter type, which they felt would be more acceptable to the "ordinary reader." Roman-style faces were reserved for classics and scholarly books. The grace and simplicity of roman faces, though, had so many advantages for better page appearance that they eventually became the norm for English Bibles.

Tyndale worked very independently and did not rely on any previous English renderings. As with the New Testament, he very likely consulted Luther's translation into German.

Tyndale wrote, "...the properties of the Hebrew tongue agreeth a thousand times more with the English than with the Latin. The manner of speaking is both one; so that in a thousand places thou needest not but translate into the English, word for word...." There he was wrong; Hebrew structure differs markedly from English. It is a Semitic language while English belongs to the Indo-European family of languages. However, his influence on later translations was such that Hebraisms still abound in our Old Testament translations. We are so used to them that we do not recognize them for what they are. We think of it as "Bible language." ("And it came to pass..." and "He spoke to them, saying..." are examples of "Bible language" that translates the Hebrew literally.)

Tyndale's notes to his Old Testament portions created quite a stir, for they energetically favored the Protestant movement. He emphasized the role of faith and trust in God in determining human conduct. One note at the end of Genesis reads:

> Jacob robbed Laban his uncle: Moses robbed the Egyptians; And Abraham is about to slay and burn his own son: And all are holy works, because they were wrought in faith at God's commandment. To steal, rob and murder are no holy works before worldly people; but unto them that have their trust in God: they are holy when God commandeth them.

With the memory of the German peasant's revolt still fresh in mind and some of the more radical Protestants claiming special divine revelations, it is not difficult to understand how such comments might alarm conservatives in the church.

Tyndale's English Style

It only slightly overstates the case to say that Tyndale set the standard for how the English Bible should read and sound. Scholars estimate that perhaps a third of the 1611 *King James Version* comes directly from Tyndale, and the remaining two-thirds shows his strong influence in style, vocabulary and syntax. In a real sense, the famous 1611 translation can be called a revision of Tyndale's work eight decades earlier.

But his greatest and most enduring contribution was to establish the tradition that our Bible translations should reflect the language and style of everyday speech rather than be literary and formal. Whereas Wyclif had earlier simply transliterated many words from the Latin, Tyndale chose the largest part of his vocabulary from the stock of English words. His was a truly *English* Bible, with very few Latinisms. He grew up in Gloucester and Bristol, where he heard rich currents of English dialects. The English language was maturing rapidly, and Tyndale, in spite of living on the Continent for many years, had an ear finely tuned to the melodies of his blossoming native tongue.

His words flow smoothly, with a rhythm of joy that reveal Tyndale's happiness with the Scriptures. His phrases ring wonderfully when spoken aloud. In a few places he gets wordy: "Emmanuel, which is as much to say by interpretation as God with us." (Tyndale recognized the excess here in Matthew 1.23 and shortened the rendering in his 1534 revision.) He also used some anachronisms; "easter holidays" and "shire town" are often cited. But these blemishes hardly mar the translation's beauty. Consider, for instance, his translation of 1 Corinthians 13, presented here in the original spelling, which essentially became the standard English rendering:

The first chapter of 1 Corinthians from Tyndale's New Testament, dating from c. 1528. Note that the third word, vocacio̅, is Latin-based. In English, it would be "calling." This indicates how the English language was still evolving.

> Though I spake with the tonges of men and angels, and yet had no love, I were even as sounding brasse: or as a tynklynge Cymball. And though I coulde prophesy, and vnderstode all secretes, and all knowledge: yee, yf I had all fayth so that I coulde move mountayns oute of ther places, and yet had no love, I were nothynge. . .

In this passage, as elsewhere, Tyndale translates the Greek *agape* by "love." The Vulgate used the Latin word *caritas*. English translations dependent on the Vulgate rendered this as "charity." Sir Thomas More lambasted Tyndale for dropping "charity" in favor of "love," but Tyndale was correct. Modern translations follow his lead. Thomas More, however, was not merely quibbling at words. He sensed something revolutionary in the change. Love and charity certainly differ. As Protestants dwelt on the meaning of Christian love, they unfolded its essentially radical nature. Love, in the ideal Christian sense, will not stay meekly within the tempered limitations of charity.

In his Lord's Prayer (Luke 11.2-4), Tyndale gave us the enduring phrase "daily bread" (again, in the original spelling):

> Oure father which arte in hevē, halowed by thy name. Lett thy kyngdō come. Thy will, be fulfillet, even in erth as it is in heven. Oure dayly breed geve vs this daye. And forgeve vs oure synnes: for even we forgeve every man that traspaseth vs, and ledde vs not into temptaciō, Butt delliver vs from evyll Amen.

Many beloved phrases from Tyndale's pen continued in later translations, such as "You cannot serve God and mammon" (Matt. 6.24) and "Where two or three are gathered in my name, there am I in the midst of them" (Matt. 18.20).

His Final Work

Tyndale's work on the Old Testament was interrupted by the pressing need to produce an authoritative revision of his New Testament.

Christopher Endhoven of Antwerp was the printer who had pirated Tyndale's work and flooded the English market with unauthorized reprints. This was, of course, long before anyone thought of copyright laws. Endhoven produced three editions in the 1530s which were poorly set and proofread. They contained numerous typographical errors and other mistakes.

George Joye, a close associate of Tyndale's, determined to prepare a corrected reprint of Tyndale's New Testament. It appeared in August of 1534, printed by Endhoven's widow in Antwerp. But Joye had his own ideas about translating the Bible. He altered Tyndale's text considerably, often reverting to the traditional terminology (for instance, using "priest" instead of "senior"). It carried the misleading note that it was the "final" edition of Tyndale's Testament, although Joye did not consult Tyndale.

To protect himself from this spurious "final" edition, Tyndale's revision came off the press of Godfred van der Hagen in the fall of 1534. In this edition, Tyndale included translations of the Old Testament lessons for Holy Communion. He also added marginal notes, put in introductions to the various New Testament books, and changed his rendering of the Greek *presbyter* from "senior" to "elder." This is the true final version of Tyndale's New Testament. (A modern edition was issued in 1938 by Cambridge University Press, titled: *The New Testament*, translated by William Tyndale, 1534, edited by N. Hardy Wallis for the Royal Society of Literature.)

Perhaps 50,000 copies of Tyndale's New Testament had been published. (From 1525 to 1566 this immensely popular work went through 41 editions.) Its liveliness and clarity prepared the way for the English vernacular translations that would follow.

Martyrdom

Meanwhile, Henry VIII had severed his relations with the Roman church in 1534, making himself head of the Church of England. His new wife, Anne Boleyn, supported the idea of a Bible in English. When an edition of his New Testament came off an English press, Tyndale was able to present her with a copy. Perhaps if Tyndale had returned to England, he would have died in his bed. Or perhaps not. In any case, he stayed in Antwerp, living with Thomas Poyntz at English House, a residence established to provide accommodations for English merchants doing business in the bustling city.

On a day in May, 1535, he gave forty shillings to a fellow countryman named Henry Phillips, to whom he had previously lent money. Phillips found a treacherous way to cancel his debts. That evening, Phillips had Tyndale arrested as the translator was leaving for dinner with friends. Tyndale hastily gave his manuscripts and notes to his friend, John Rogers, the chaplain of English House. When his host, Thomas Poyntz, later tried to get Tyndale freed, he too was arrested.

Although Antwerp enjoyed considerable autonomy as a major port and trading center, it lay within the realm of Charles V, the Holy Roman Emperor whose realm was being torn apart by the Protestant revolt. Charles was a committed Catholic with a deep desire to stamp out heresy. Tyndale's arrest was a favor to the Emperor, who had him imprisoned in the Castle of Vilvorde, near Brussels, in the care of the Marquis of Bergen. He would remain there one year and 135 days.

Only one letter from Tyndale's pen comes to us from this period, found in the last century and addressed to the Marquis. It breathes the spirit of a Christian scholar:

> I beg your Lordship and that by the Lord Jesus, that if I am to remain here through the winter, you will request the commissary to have the kindness to send me from the goods of mine which he has, a warmer cap: for I suffer greatly from cold in the head, and am afflicted by a perpetual catarrh [upper respiratory distress] which is much increased in this cell...But most of all I beg your clemency to be urgent with the commissary that he will kindly permit me to have the Hebrew Bible, Hebrew grammar, and Hebrew dictionary that I may pass the time in study...I will be patient abiding the will of God, to the glory of the grace of my Lord Jesus Christ, whose spirit (pray) may ever direct your heart. Amen.

"The Martyrdome of Master William Tindall in Flanders by Vilvord Castle," an engraving in John Foxe's Acts and Monuments of Martyrs (1684 edition). As he is prepared for burning, Tyndale prays, "Lord, open the King of England's eyes."

Thomas Cromwell, Earl of Essex and viceregent to Henry VIII after the fall of Cardinal Wolsey, appealed to him to intercede on behalf of Tyndale. For reasons we do not know, Henry did not. In any case, Charles was not likely to be moved by an appeal from the man who had just scandalously divorced his aunt.

Tyndale acted as his own lawyer during his heresy trial, making an impassioned plea for the doctrine of justification by faith. The outcome held little surprise. Stripping him of his clerical status, the ecclesiastical court handed Tyndale over to the secular authorities for execution. On the morning of October 6, 1536, he was strangled and burned.

His last words were, "Lord, open the king of England's eyes." His prayer would be answered almost before his ashes cooled.

5 THE TRADITION CONTINUES

Had Tyndale lived two or three more years, he would have seen his great dream of the Bible for the people come to pass. For even as he argued his defense at his heresy trial, the Reformation was unfolding in England.

The English Reformation followed its own peculiar course. Unlike Germany, where Luther's theological ideas rallied both sides, England's break with Rome had little to do with doctrine. Historian G.M. Trevelyan wrote:

> The English Reformation, which had begun as a Parliamentary attack on Church fees, and proceeded as a royal raid on Abbey lands, was at last to find its religious basis in the popular knowledge of the Scriptures which had been the dream of Wycliffe. (*History of England*, II, 65)

The story of English Scriptures weaves intimately through the narrative of the English Reformation. A stream of vernacular Scripture versions reflects the ups and downs of contending parties, ultimately flowing into the great literary masterpiece, the authorized *King James Version* of the Bible.

Henry Needs an (Male) Heir

Henry VIII (1509–1547) was a true Renaissance man, talented in music and arts and letters, skilled in sports and hunting, a man both intelligent and self-indulgent. The people loved Henry. He had a sixth-sense for the popular mood, knowing what average people wanted as well as what they would tolerate.

Henry made the common person or "commoner" proud to claim England as home. He had built England's first Royal Navy, an armada of ships designed especially for war and totally under government control. He centralized the governmental bureaucracy and brought England to a position of real strength.

But Henry remembered the bloody dynastic struggles of the War of the Roses. He desperately wanted to secure a peaceful, unchallenged succession. That would require a male heir.

Henry VIII (1491-1547), King of England and Ireland, in a portrait by his contemporary, Hans Holbein

Henry had come to the throne in 1509, at age 18, following the death of his older brother and heir-apparent, Arthur. By a special papal dispensation, he married Arthur's widow, Katherine of Aragon (Spain), the aunt of Charles V who ruled Spain. With Katherine's encouragement, Henry became involved in the conflicts between France and Spain, taking Charles' side but gaining little for his effort. When Charles susequently became Holy Roman Emperor, thus combining two power bases, England suddenly held the critical balance of power between France and the Empire. Relations with Charles chilled and the political usefulness of Katherine's family connections wilted.

Of Katherine's six children, only one survived infancy, a daughter, Mary, whom Henry and his advisors hoped would be useful in forging new alliances through marriage. But Katherine could not have any more children. As the prospects for a male heir disappeared, Henry's interest in Katherine's charms faded.

Meanwhile, Henry had met and was attracted to Anne Boleyn. In 1527, he began seeking a divorce from Katherine on the grounds that the marriage to a brother's widow was not permitted by church law. (It wasn't, but the Pope had made a special dispensation.) Cardinal Wolsey, a masterful diplomat and the king's right hand, sought papal permission for a divorce. The Pope, Clement VII, would normally grant this as a courtesy to a rising monarch but he found himself in a difficult position. Charles V controlled Italy and had armies poised at the gates of the Vatican. The Pope had a very difficult choice to make and Henry was, after all, much farther away than Charles' armies. The mission did not succeed.

Tired of having foreigners determine his future, Henry put financial pressure on the Pope. A series of laws whittled away Papal privileges in England, and payments to Rome ceased. Thomas Cranmer, a lecturer at Jesus College, Cambridge, suggested that Henry ask university faculties to explore the legality of his marriage to Katherine. Cranmer did his job well; the report favored a divorce. Henry skillfully persuaded the Pope to elevate Cranmer to the position of Archbishop of Canterbury. Immediately upon assuming his new office, Cranmer invalidated Henry's marriage to Katherine and crowned Anne (already pregnant and secretly wed to Henry) as queen.

The Pope promptly excommunicated Henry, who then took the next logical step. In 1534 Parliament passed the Act of Supremacy which completed the breach with Rome by making the king head of the Church of England. Henry proceeded to dissolve the monastic foundations, using their assets for several purposes: to pension off the 7,000 or so displaced monks and nuns, to endow educational institutions, to gain the loyalty of the rising gentry by letting them buy these valuable lands at very generous prices, and to enrich his depleted royal treasury.

Thomas Cromwell (c.1485-1540), Earl of Essex and King Henry's chief minister, shown in an 1821 engraving by Andrew Duncan, based on a contemporary portrait by Hans Holbein

Some loyal Catholics—including Henry's friend, Sir Thomas More—would not desert their allegiance to the Pope and paid the price of treason. A protest called the Pilgrimage of Grace swept the northern counties where traditional Catholic sentiments flourished. Some 35,000 people in Lincolnshire and Yorkshire marched in protest. Thomas Cromwell, a layman and lawyer who entered Parliament and became Henry's chief minister, settled the issue with force but avoided excessive bloodshed. It was likely Cromwell's idea to make Henry supreme head of the English church, and now he had secured the king's position. (Thomas Cromwell is not to be confused with Oliver Cromwell who, over a century later, became lord protector under the Commonwealth.)

Tensions

In truth, Henry's bold move pleased most Englishmen. Henry possessed a keen sense of the public mood. He had to, for he lacked a standing army to enforce his will. His split with Rome, at the core, was inspired by nationalist sentiments and the people, swelling with new pride in England, welcomed it.

But almost at once tensions arose. This was a time when Protestant ideas were sweeping the Continent. Luther's striking interpretations were widely discussed in England and, thanks to Tyndale, ordinary folks could read and explore the New Testament on their own. Henry, though, had no great desire to create a Protestant church, nor did many of his subjects. Except for the dissolution of monasteries, which most people felt was long overdue, and some other needed clerical reforms, the new Anglican Church carried on business much as usual.

Henry himself held quite orthodox Catholic beliefs. He had written (or put his name on) a book denouncing Luther's doctrines, for which the Pope had rewarded him with the title "Defender of the Faith." He even burnt a few Protestants who denied transubstantiation, the Roman Catholic understanding of the Eucharist. Numbers of the clergy, and especially the bishops, who shifted their allegiance from Pope to King were willing to accept new leadership but at the same time urgently wanted to keep traditional Catholic teaching and practice.

This tension between Protestant and Catholic traditions within one church shaped the ongoing English Reformation, defined the character of the English Church, and colored the tradition of the English Bible.

The First Printed Complete English Bible

Four years before the break with Rome, a royal proclamation was issued to condemn Tyndale's New Testament and his other writings. Many would go to prison or die for the crime of reading Scripture in their own language. But in the same month, parish clergy were told to read a proclamation which stated that King Henry promised to gather a group of learned men to make an English translation of the Bible.

Nothing came of it then, but now the times had changed. Hugh Latimer, a fervent reformer educated at Cambridge who later became Bishop of Worcester, reminded the king of his earlier promise. The 1534 Canterbury Convocation took up the cause. The upper house of the Convocation, consisting of bishops, abbots, and priors sitting under Thomas Cromwell, asked King Henry to name some learned men for the task:

> [That] the king's majesty should think fit to decree that the holy scripture shall be translated into the vulgar English tongue by certain upright and learned men to be named by the said most illustrious king and be meted out and delivered to the people for their instructions.

Interestingly, the petition itself was first drawn up in Latin. And while it did not exactly authorize an English Bible, it pretty much cleared the way for a vernacular Scripture so long as the bishops approved of it.

The bishops, apparently, could not get themselves organized to make a translation. Anxious to get moving, Thomas Cromwell encouraged the use of a translation done by a friend of his which was already complete and ready to go.

This was the translation of the complete Bible, prepared by Miles Coverdale, and just published in Europe.

Coverdale (c. 1488–1569) was born in Yorkshire, as was Tyndale, and educated at the Augustinian Convent in Cambridge. At Cambridge, he met with Dr. Robert Barnes, prior of the convent, who had gathered a group to discuss Luther's reforms. Coverdale became a reformer and an eloquent preacher. Coverdale developed an interest in Bible translating, although he knew little or no Hebrew and was not supremely proficient in Greek. Early on, he seems to have come under the patronage of Thomas Cromwell, and at Cambridge, got to know Sir Thomas More.

In 1528 he left England, perhaps for his own protection, to go to Germany where, according to most historians, he helped Tyndale with the translation of the Pentateuch. Other historians doubt that Coverdale and Tyndale ever worked together. In any case, Coverdale's life for his first six years in Europe is shrouded in mystery.

Miles Coverdale (1488–1568), from an engraving by J. Jenkins, based on an earlier portrait

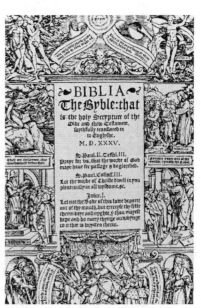

The title page of Coverdale's Bible. Note the use of heavy, black type. The title pages of these early English Bibles were quite elaborate. This one summarizes the biblical story in pictures. Top center, we see the name of God in Hebrew. On the top left are Adam and Eve; top right, Jesus proclaiming the Good News. Down the left side, top to bottom, we see Moses receiving the Ten Commandments and Ezra proclaiming the law in the restored Temple. On the right, Jesus gives the the Great Commission, with a reference to Mark 16, and below that, Peter preaches to the crowds at Pentecost (Acts 2). Along the bottom, the bishops present God's Word to King Henry VIII.

Then in 1534 Jacob van Meteren, an Antwerp merchant, approached him to produce a complete English Bible. He had only published a translation of Campensis' Psalm paraphrases, but he boldly undertook the enormous task and his folio Bible came off the press in fall of 1535. The title page carried no notice of the place of publication. Scholars, by analyzing the typefaces, variously feel that it was published in Zurich, Marburg, or Cologne.

Coverdale managed this monumental task in so short a time by adopting a short cut–he borrowed Tyndale's work and translated the rest from other existing translations. The title page stated that it was translated "out of Douche [German] and Latyn." Though a secondary translation, like the earlier work of Wyclif, at least two-thirds of the Old Testament and all the Apocrypha were Coverdale's own work.

Through his preface to "the Christian reader," Coverdale reveals his essential modesty and his love of Scripture. He confesses his limitations as a translator, but says he was impelled to the work by the lack of English Scripture. "It was neither my labor nor desire, to have this work put in my hand, nevertheless it grieved me that other nations should be more plentously provided for with the scripture in their mother tongue, than we...." He praised those of "ripe knowledge" who would have completed the work they had begun "if they had not impediment"—a clear reference to Tyndale, then languishing in prison, his Old Testament unfinished.

In his dedication addressed to the King, Coverdale wrote that he had "with a clear conscience purely and faithfully trans-

THE ENGLISH APOCRYPHA

The Apocrypha (meaning "hidden writings") consists of those books in the Septuagint, the early Greek translation, which were not accepted in the later Hebrew canon. Jerome's Latin translation based on the Septuagint included them, but since they were noncanonical works he considered them useful for edification but not for developing church dogma. Protestant translators generally positioned the apocryphal books in a separate section, either between the Old and New Testaments or as an appendix following the New Testament. Because of their value as literature from the second temple period in Jewish history, these books are again being translated and included in some Bibles.

lated this out of five sundry interpreters." Who were the "five sundry interpreters" whose work Coverdale put into English? Scholars identify them as Tyndale, for the New Testament, Pentateuch, and Jonah; the Swiss-German translation by Zwingli and Leo Juda, published between 1524 and 1529; the Latin Vulgate; the Latin translation published by Pagninus in 1528, which is very literal in the Old Testament; and Luther's German Bible.

For his New Testament, Coverdale relied on Tyndale with corrections from Luther's Bible. Jonah is pretty much Tyndale intact. In the Pentateuch, he seems to have started with the Zurich translation, aided by Tyndale's text, and referring constantly to his Latin and German sources. The rest of the Old Testament stems from either Luther or the Zurich text. The Apocrypha is his own translation from the Latin. Why Coverdale chose this or that translation as the basis for various parts of his work we cannot say. Perhaps he liked their style. He was not, in any case, a good enough linguist to make a selection based on a thorough understanding of the science and history of language.

Freely Sold in England

Why did Coverdale's Bible get accepted in the same England where the fires that burned Tyndale's New Testament had barely cooled? For one thing, the times had changed. With Henry head of the English church and men such as Cranmer and Cromwell in power, vernacular Scripture at least had a chance.

More important, Coverdale deliberately strove to make his translation acceptable. His dedication to King Henry says he has "neither wrested nor altered so much as one word for the maintenance of any manner of sect...." The translation was Protestant in spirit, to be sure. He moved the books of the Apocrypha, scattered through the Old Testament in the Vulgate, into a separate section. But he was not aggressively Protestant. He showed far less zeal than Tyndale about using new ecclesiastical terms and allowed "penance" and "church" to appear, and he relied on the accepted Latin translations. Nor did he include controversial prefaces and notes. His version was simply less threatening than Tyndale's work, which may explain why Cromwell felt free to sponsor it.

The unbound sheets of his Bible were bought from Meteren by James Nicholson of Southwark for binding and selling. Two versions of this first printing exist. One has front matter in roman type, the other in black letter type. The latter was the one shipped to England. Caution was still necessary when dealing with an English Bible. Nicholson provided a new title page, omitting the clause "truly translated out of Douche and Latyn." "Douche," the early spelling for "Deutsch" or German, could be taken as a reference to Luther and his Bible. But the Germanisms in the text remained. When working from a German translation, Coverdale slipped into forming compounds as is common in German, such as "deadburier," "handreaching," and "righteousnessmaking."

Nicholson issued a revision in 1537 in both folio and quarto editions. The quarto edition carries the notice "set forth with the King's most gracious license," which was not literally true because no official action had been taken to authorize it. The dedication in this edition substituted Queen Jane [Seymour] for Queen Anne [Boleyn], keeping in step with Henry's tumultuous love life. These were the first complete Bibles actually printed in England. In that year and in 1538 the New Testament seems to have been printed separately. Coverdale also issued a slightly changed version in 1538 with the Vulgate in parallel columns. The English printer did such a bad job that Coverdale had to have it redone in Paris.

Two other editions appeared from 1550 and 1553, both printed in Zurich, But the contribution of Coverdale to the English Bible would be felt most fully in his work on the Great Bible.

The Rogers Bible

When Tyndale was arrested in Antwerp, he managed to pass the manuscripts of his unpublished Old Testament work to his friend John Rogers (*c.*1500–1555), chaplain of the English House where they both resided. Tyndale made an excellent choice.

Rogers had graduated from Cambridge in 1525 and served as a junior canon at Christ Church, Oxford, and later as a rector in London. In 1534, he went as chaplain to English House in Antwerp where he met Tyndale. Three years later, Rogers left the Catholic Church, married Andriana Pratt (of whom it was said she was "more richly endowed with virtue and soberness than with worldly treasures"), and became a pastor in the Lutheran center of Wittenberg.

John Rogers (c.1500–1555), from an engraving done in 1620.

With his wife and eight children, he returned to England in the reign of Edward VI. When Catholic Queen Mary ascended to the throne, Rogers was placed under house arrest until he could be burned at the stake, one of the first Protestant martyrs in "Bloody Mary's" reign. He was accompanied to the stake by his wife and now eleven children. The French ambassador, witnessing the execution, observed that his children so comforted him that it seemed more like he was led to a wedding than to his death.

Rogers' Bible plays a critical role in our story because it brought the whole work of Tyndale into the stream of tradition for the English Bible. Basically, Rogers was an editor rather than a translator. He used Tyndale's published work along with the unpublished Old Testament portion in his possession. Some 65 per cent of the Old and New Testament comes from Tyndale. The gaps he filled in with Coverdale's translation.

His English Bible was printed in Antwerp in 1537, but financed and published in England by Richard Grafton and his associate Edward Whitchurch of London. The edition carried a dedication to Henry VIII and 1,500 copies were made. In his petition to Cromwell for the privilege of publishing a Bible, Grafton said he expected the edition would need at least three years to sell out. Apparently Grafton was a bit optimistic. The first reprint came 12 years later, in 1549, and the second reprint came but two years later in 1551. Compared with Tyndale's massive sales, this was small change.

The Bible appeared under the pseudonym of Thomas Matthew, probably to prevent the work from being associated with Tyndale and to be able to market it as a fresh translation. Thus, writers today may refer to it as "Matthew's Bible," or "Rogers'/Matthew's Bible." But it is truly Rogers' work.

John Rogers did quality work with the material he had. He used Tyndale's 1535 revision of the New Testament and Pentateuch with few alterations. Joshua through II Chronicles undoubtedly represent Tyndale's unpublished manuscript of these books. For Ezra through Malachi and the Apocrypha, Rogers used Coverdale's translation. He also used Coverdale for Jonah. Why he did not use Tyndale's translation of that book we do not know. Rogers personally only translated the Prayer of Manasseh, in which he closely followed the French translation done by Olivetan. He also used Olivetan's preface to the Apocrypha.

Rogers corrected the Psalms to conform closer to the Hebrew numbering and he dropped three verses from Psalm 14 not in the Hebrew but found in the Vulgate and in Coverdale. He translated "Hallelujah" as "Praise *the everlasting*," a lovely choice. Still, he paid more attention to Vulgate renderings than did either Coverdale or Tyndale, which helped to make this Bible, dedicated to King Henry and Queen Jane, more acceptable to the English clergy.

Still, one wonders why his notes did not create a furor, as they did with some of Tyndale's editions. Rogers'—or "Matthew's"—Bible contains some 2,000 notes, many from Tyndale and others from Erasmus, Luther, Olivetan, and other continental scholars. The notes were less doctrinally biased than Tyndale's, but still controversial.

Rogers also added some additional material, besides woodcuts, similar to what appears in modern "study Bibles." He included a calendar for daily Scripture readings, chapter summaries, an exhortation on how to study the Bible, a summary of Bible history, and a "Table of Principal Matters" in the Bible, this translated from Olivetan. The "Table" ran for 26 pages and is a combination concordance and dictionary. The comments reflect Protestant sentiments. Under "Meryte" (merit, a major Catholic doctrine) the comment simply says:

> In looking over the Bible, as well the New as the Old Testament, I have not found this word "merit." Merit then is nothing.

Overall, this was the best English Bible to date because most of it drew upon Tyndale and Tyndale translated from the original biblical languages. And since it formed the basis for the Great Bible and ensuing versions down to the *King James Version*, it can be called the Parent of the English Bible.

Rogers' Bible greatly impressed Archbishop Cranmer. "So far as I have read thereof," he wrote, "I like it better than any other translation hertofore made." Cranmer wrote to Cromwell on August 4, 1537, asking him to petition the King for:

a license that the same may be sold and read of every person, without danger of any act, proclamation, or ordinance heretofore granted to the contrary, until such time that we, the Bishops shall set forth a better translation, which I think will not be till a day after doomsday.

Cranmer was despairing of the slow progress of the bishops on their charge of 1534 to create an acceptable translation. Cromwell agreed; he had promoted Coverdale's translation to get around the bishop's road block. The king granted the license and the Rogers' ("Matthew's") Bible appeared with the words on the title page, "Set forth with the King's most gracious license." Thus it became the first "authorized" English Bible.

Thomas Cranmer (1489–1556), Archbishop of Canterbury, in a 1546 portrait by Gerlack Flicke

What an irony of history! Only a year before, Henry had allowed Tyndale to be put to death and now the king endorsed the publication of a Bible largely from the hand of this "chief heretic." The same New Testament which would only months before put the reader in peril of imprisonment or death was now sold and read openly. Tyndale indeed had won; the King's eyes were opened.

Now Bible reading was not only legal but enforced by bishops. Some required every parish church to buy an English Bible. Others ordered their clergy to read a chapter daily in English and Latin. To serve this need, a Latin-English New Testament appeared in 1538. On September 5, 1538, came a royal injunction commanding the clergy to place in every parish church "one book of the whole Bible of the largest volume in English." The parishioners were to pay half the cost, with the clergy footing the rest of the bill. That large-size Bible would soon appear and be called the Great Bible.

Taverner's Bible–A Publishing Venture

Publisher Thomas Bertlelet saw the potential market for Bibles in this freer age and sought a way to intrude on Grafton's government-sanctioned monopoly. All he needed was a Bible translation that wasn't *exactly* like the Rogers' (known as "Matthew's") version from Grafton's press.

Richard Taverner supplied the manuscript. Taverner was a bit of an intellectual rogue, a brilliant mind that would not flow neatly into conventional molds. Born in Brisley, Norfolk, in 1505, he studied at Cambridge and Oxford, where he was briefly imprisoned for reading Tyndale's New Testament. He gained his release because of his musical accomplishments when someone (important?) needed a musician. He went on to study law and joined the circle around Thomas Cromwell, becoming Clerk of the Signet to Henry VIII in 1537. All the while he pursued the study of Greek with diligence.

He chose to become a licensed lay preacher and endured the turmoil of the English Reformation, which included for him an enforced stay in the Tower of London. He would preach now and then before the King and in other places wearing a plain velvet bonnet and a damask gown, with a gold chain about his neck. During Queen Mary's reign, he wisely entered retirement, to emerge again as a preacher under the more comfortable regime of Elizabeth I. She appointed him high sheriff of the county of Oxford, a position he held until his death in 1575.

Besides Greek, Taverner had a passion for Saxon words. His Bible, basically, amounts to a revision of Rogers' work. Knowing nothing of Hebrew, his Old Testament modifications reflect changes in favor of the Vulgate. In the New Testament, however, he stood on firmer ground and made numerous alterations from Tyndale's translation, introducing in the process several Saxon terms to replace Latinisms. In Matthew 24.12, he wrote, "the love of many shall wax cold." Tyndale and Coverdale had, "the love of many shall abate." We owe to Taverner the term "parable" (a Greek root), where Tyndale and Coverdale use "similitude," a Latin root. He also introduced the very familiar term "passover."

Taverner's Bible was published by Bertlelet in folio in 1539, and in the same year the New Testament appeared in quarto and octavo, with a small 12mo edition of the Testament following in 1540 (see note, "Book Sizes," in Chapter 4). A version consisting of the liturgical Epistle and Gospel lessons, accompanied by sermons, came from the press about 1545. The Old Testament was published separately in five parts from 1549–1551. Also in 1551, John Day reissued Taverner's Old Testament in combination with Tyndale's New Testament, as an edition of the Rogers' ("Matthew's") Bible.

No doubt the appearance of the officially sanctioned Great Bible hindered the circulation of Taverner's version. It is in many ways an excellent work, but the circumstances of the time kept it from influencing the English Bible tradition as much as its value would justify.

Others, too, were interested in using as many Anglo-Saxon words as possible in the English Bible. Sir John Cheke, professor of Greek at Cambridge and tutor to Edward VI, tried his hand at translating in non-learned, non-Latin words. (In this effort, one might think of him as the precursor of such modern translations as *Today's English Version* or *Contemporary English Version*.)

He completed Mark and the first chapter of Matthew in manuscript about 1550, but it remained in the library of St. John's College, Cambridge, until it was published in 1843. Cheke used "frosent" instead of "apostle," "freshman" in place of the usual "proselyte," and "crossed" instead of "crucified."

The Great Bible

Now two officially sanctioned Bibles circulated in England—Coverdale's and Rogers' ("Matthew's")—each with its differences in terminology and phrasing. For bishops and others who still worried that vernacular Scripture could unsettle the minds of the laity, this lack of a single scriptural voice appeared ominous. The bishops, though, still could not produce their promised translation. A new translation would skirt the problem of making a difficult choice: Coverdale's work bothered scholars because it was not translated from the original tongues; the Rogers' translation disturbed conservatives because Tyndale's strong Protestant views came through in the notes and prefaces.

The issue had to be settled for the people everywhere were reading the Bible. Middle-of-the-road theologian Edward Foxe commented:

> The lay people do now know the holy scripture better than many of us; and the Germans have made the text of the Bible so plain and easy by the Hebrew and Greek tongue that now many things may be better understood without any glosses at all than by all the commentaries of the doctors.

So a new translation, one without notes, was approved. With the king's permission, Cromwell took charge of the project and enlisted his friend, Miles Coverdale. Even though his own translation had circulated barely two years, Coverdale in a spirit of modest cooperation agreed to work on the new revision, and Grafton and Whitchurch received an exclusive license as publishers. Cromwell himself advanced £400 to print the first 2,000 copies.

Coverdale had not become a masterful linguist overnight, since he published his own secondary translation. This new Bible, too, would rely on secondary sources, but with the explosion of biblical scholarship, much better sources were at hand.

Perhaps on Cromwell's instructions, Coverdale chose to revise the Rogers' ("Matthew's") version rather than his own. He drew upon the 1535 annotated Hebrew-Latin Bible prepared by Sebastian Munster, an excellent source which brought Coverdale much closer to the original Hebrew. He relied on Erasmus for

The heavily illustrated title page of the Great Bible, 1539. Even though it is titled "The Byble in Englyshe," most of the balloons have speakers using Latin, indicating the longing for that familiar language in many circles of the church. As befitting an "official" translation, this page has a patriotic theme. King Henry at the top receives the Verbum Dei (Word of God) from the learned translators. At the bottom, the populace shouts "Vivat Rex," with only one using the English equivalent, "God save the Kynge."

improvements in the New Testament, with the bulk of that text largely borrowed from Tyndale. Coverdale also changed the Vulgate reading at 1 John 5.7, 8.

These new sources influenced Coverdale to drop some of his German idioms and pick up more Latin-root words, although he retained Tyndale's Protestant ecclesiastical terms. Tyndale had used a variety of English words to translate the same Greek or Hebrew term. Coverdale's new revision reduced the variety in favor of more standardization, as he had done in his own version.

FINDING THE BEST ORIGINAL TEXT

A translation of the Bible can never be more accurate than the Greek and Hebrew manuscripts upon which it is based. In the sixteenth century, the science of textual criticism had just begun. This is a complex, painstaking discipline. A person might think, "Find the oldest manuscript, the one closest to the original time, and you have the best." But that is not the case. Biblical manuscripts cluster by families or traditions. Modern analysis identifies a number of these families. A family or tradition means a collection of manuscripts of varying dates which seem to go back to the same original source. Thus a relatively late manuscript may preserve a better text than a document that was copied earlier but from a less reliable source.

Where ancient sources differ, modern translators usually print the other option(s) in a footnote with a comment such as "A few other authorities read..." or "Some early witnesses read...."

1 John 5.7, 8, changed by Coverdale, is one example. The *King James Version* reproduces the text Coverdale received. The Revised Standard Version and other modern translations reflect the changes Coverdale adopted, based on his Greek sources. His textual judgment here, though not picked up in the KJV, is the one almost all modern translators adopt.

The ending of Mark is another example of differences in texts. Some ancient authorities end at 16.8. Other reliable manuscript families offer two different endings: a one verse conclusion, and a longer one that Bibles print as Mark 16.9-20. Mark 16.8 seems like a very abrupt ending, but whether the longer or shorter ending is best remains in dispute. Modern Bibles usually print both options, with explanatory notes.

Another classic problem text is John 7.53—8.11, the story of the woman taken in adultery. This passage appears with many variations of wording in different manuscripts. It also shows up in various places: after John 7.36, after John 21.25, or even after Luke 21.38. Some manuscripts do not include it at all. Modern translations handle the problem in various ways, all intended to separate the passage from the basic text and explain it with a   footnote.

Problems at the Press

But it was not easy to get the Great Bible printed. The problems arose because they chose to use the Parisian printer, Regnault. Perhaps England did not have presses or paper good enough for this job, for the Great Bible was intended from the start to be the official Bible for use in churches. It was put into a large format, with pages measuring 16 1/2 by 11 inches; thus its name, the Great Bible, after its great size. The type and printing are elegant and done on fine paper. The New Testament uses a heavier paper, anticipating that this part of the Bible would get the most use.

The title page carries a fine woodcut, ascribed to Hans Holbein, one of King Henry's favorite artists. It shows Henry at the top, seated on his throne hand-ing a Bible to Archbishop Cranmer, who stands before a group of clergy. Henry also hands a Bible with his other hand to Thomas Cromwell, who is with a group of nobles. Clearly this official Bible intended to promote religious and patriotic loyalty.

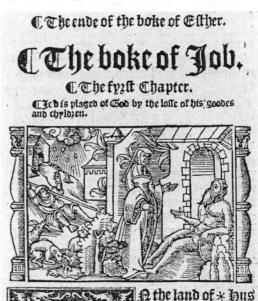

Coverdale omitted the Protestant-toned Table of Principal Matters, the prefaces showing Luther's influence, and the marginal notes. He added in smaller type words and sentences from the Vulgate which were not justified by the original languages, "to content those that herebeforetime hath missed such."

The printing began under the supervision of Bishop Bonner, England's ambassador to France. Bonner took a happy interest in the project. He would wine and dine the printers in his home and spent hours in the print shop. Then in December, 1538, some cold political winds chilled relations between France and

This woodcut illustrates the opening of the Book of Job in the Great Bible. Note that the biblical scene is rendered in a 16th-century setting. Before the 18th century, biblical events were commonly depicted in a contemporary setting.

England. Henry further complicated matters by banning the importation of English books printed abroad.

Coverdale sensed trouble. On December 13th, he wrote Cromwell that he had deposited some sheets with Bonner for safekeeping. On the 17th, the Inquisition (a church tribunal to suppress heresy) descended on the shop, arresting Regnault and confiscating the remaining sheets. The English proofreaders escaped in the nick of time.

Cromwell jumped in to protect the project, in which, after all, he had invested a substantial amount of his own money. French authorities delayed action. Meanwhile, the confiscated sheets were ordered to be burned.

A hat merchant named Anthony Marler came to the rescue. He persuaded the officer in charge of the burning to sell him the sheets for the purpose of wrapping hats for shipping. "Why not make a penny or two for yourself?" he argued to the officer. They struck a bargain and these sheets, with the ones held by Bonner, reached London where Grafton managed to complete the edition with financing by Marler. The title page bore the date April, 1539, but with all the intrigue and delay surrounding the printing, the Great Bible didn't come off the press until months later.

Work began almost at once on the second edition, this time to be done in London. Coverdale had time to revise his translation of Job–Malachi. Cranmer provided an important preface, in which he set forth his vision of the role of the Bible in the life of believers. Because of that preface, the definitive second edition of 1540 is often called Cranmer's Bible. It carried the notice, "This is the Bible appointed to be read in Churches," becoming the first authorized (instead of merely licensed) version.

As the Bible to be placed in every parish church, it was priced rather low at 10 shillings unbound and twelve shillings bound. Tyndale's New Testament alone had cost 2 1/2 shillings and this was a much larger volume, so the price was fair. Still, a copy would cost a skilled laborer a month's wages.

Popular Support

This Bible went through seven editions, six of them with Cranmer's prologue, by 1541, with a total circulation of about 21,000 copies. The third and fifth of these editions carry a notice that they were "overseen" by Bishops Tunstall and Heath, this to disassociate the Bible from Cromwell's name, for he had fallen from the King's favor and been executed in 1541. It was also ironic that Tunstall now endorsed a book that in large part came from the same Tyndale whose translating work he had condemned a decade earlier.

To say that this publicly available Bible swept the nation understates the case. Every parish had a copy, chained to a table for safekeeping. The common people took up Bible reading with enthusiasm. Older people learned to read just so they could read God's Word.

St. Paul's Church in the City of London offered its narthex as a grand gathering place for all sorts of people and businesses. The church put out six copies of the Great Bible to serve the crowds. The babble of people reading aloud and discussing the texts became so clamorous that the Bishop of London issued an order forbidding reading during sermon time, so that worshippers could hear the preacher.

Tyndale would have been immensely pleased that the time of openness to the English Bible had finally come. Unfortunately, it would not last.

6 WRITTEN IN EXILE

The Great Bible embodied all the elements which were to play the major roles in shaping the English Bible tradition—Tyndale's New Testament and Old Testament portions, Coverdale's Psalms, a respectful touch of the Vulgate, and a generally Protestant tone. This tradition accents readability, elegance of meter and measure, and a preference for words of English root.

All the ensuing translations in this tradition, which includes the beloved *King James Version*, can be thought of as revisions of the Great Bible.

The Good Times End

The free range given by Henry VIII to the English Bible did not last long. He had ordered priests to recite and fathers to teach to their families the Ten Commandments, the Articles of Faith, and the Lord's Prayer in English. This instruction reflects what Luther attempted to accomplish with his *Small Catechism*. But Henry never favored Protestantism and was concerned about the success it was having in his church.

In 1539, he asked Parliament to pass the Six Articles as a basic statement of faith for the Anglican Church to replace the earlier Ten Articles. Henry's traditional Catholic sentiments show through clearly. The Six Articles affirm Catholic doctrines and practices such as transubstantiation, communion in one kind (bread only), clerical celibacy, monastic vows, private masses, and oral confession to a priest. The English of Protestant leanings could see a storm was approaching. Hugh Latimer, the Protestant Bishop of Worcester, resigned his office in protest and went into temporary retirement.

Still, Thomas Cromwell and Archbishop Cranmer remained to exert their influence, especially toward freedom for the English Bible. But Cromwell's days were numbered, as it happened, and again Henry's love life plays a large role.

Anne Boleyn, his second queen who gave birth to Elizabeth, also supported the English Bible. But Henry's lusts led his eyes to wander. Around 1535, he spied Anne's lady-in-waiting, Jane Seymour, and became infatuated. Jane would accept no bed but the marriage bed. Jane's stubbornness led Henry to execute Anne for treason. Two weeks later, he and Jane were married. Jane also supported Bible reading. But more to Henry's needs, she produced a male child, who would become Edward VI. Parliament vested succession to her offspring. The throne was secure at last, but Jane unfortunately died twelve days after Edward's birth.

Cromwell now devised a strategic plan for his widower king. He would wed Henry to a Protestant noble, probably from Germany, and thus cement a Protestant alliance. Anne of Cleves was available, sister of one of the most powerful Protestant princes in Germany who was a leader in the Protestant Schmalkaldic League. While Anne exuded powerful political attractions, her physical charms left much to be desired. Henry agreed to the marriage prior to meeting Anne. To this point, he had only seen flattering portrait paintings of her which were designed to sell her as a good match. Upon meeting her he was so put off by her appearance that he tried to break the contract. That wasn't possible, so the couple strode to the altar in January, 1540. The marriage was never consummated and ended in an amicable divorce in July, 1540. Anne continued to live in England.

Cromwell, the matchmaker in this disastrous marriage, fell under Henry's wrath. The King allowed Cromwell's chief enemy, the Duke of Norfolk, to bring charges of treason against him. Cromwell was executed in 1540, the same year of the marriage and divorce, and the same year that Henry, in an earlier more generous mood, had elevated the unfortunate Cromwell to the title of Earl of Essex.

Quite likely, the affair with Anne soured Henry on whatever Protestant sympathies he might have harbored. He withdrew more into the past and that left only Archbishop Cranmer to defend the English Bible and all that stood for.

The Lid Clamps Down

Henry had also lost some of his sensitivity to public opinion. So while the public clamored for the vernacular Scriptures, Henry determined to turn back the clock and stop this unbridled reading and discussion. He wasn't against the use of English in church. Had he lived long enough, he would have put forth a single, accepted translation. What Henry desired was uniformity, consistency, and a decent respect for the religious traditions of the past.

The Catholic-oriented Six Articles and the fall of Cromwell signaled the shift in policy from toleration of some Protestant principles to support for medieval Catholicism. The new trend became evident at the Convocation of 1542. The gathered bishops—most of them leaning to the Catholic side—again discussed plans for a Bible revision based, if at all possible, on the Latin Vulgate, "that Bible which is commonly read in the English Church."

Bishop Stephen Gardiner offered a list of 99 Latin words which "for their genuine and native meaning and for the majesty of their matter" ought to remain in the proposed revision, either in the Latin form or some English equivalent. His list included such terms as *pontifex* (ruler), *baptizare* (baptize), *sandalium* (sandal), *concupiscentia* (lust), and *peccatum* (sin). While such a translation might have pleased the clergy, it would have confused the general reader.

The argument between Latinisms (symbolizing Catholic tradition) and English roots (symbolizing the Protestant perspective) would continue for years. In this instance, Gardiner's proposal was defeated, largely due to pressure from Archbishop Cranmer. Cranmer had the brilliant idea of persuading Henry to refer the issue to the universities. This approach, he was confident, would assure that nothing would get done and would effectively bury the question.

Legal Restrictions

The trend of the 1542 Convocation away from truly vernacular translations based on the original languages became even more ominous the next year when Parliament prohibited reading Tyndale's translation and required all notes in other

STEPHEN GARDINER
(c.1493–1555)

Educated at Cambridge, Gardiner became secretary to Thomas (later Cardinal) Wolsey. Gardiner journeyed to Rome to plead Henry VIII's case for a divorce from Katherine. As a reward, he was made Bishop of Winchester in 1531. Though Gardiner vigorously supported the king as head of the English church, he held very conservative theological views. He thoroughly disliked Thomas Cromwell and likely played a part in his downfall. Under the more Protestant mood of Edward VI's reign, Gardiner was deprived of his bishopric and confined to the Tower for five years. When Catholic Queen Mary I came to the throne, she freed and reinstated Gardiner and elevated him to the important post of Lord Chancellor. He was never popular. Catholics attacked him for supporting royal supremacy over the church. Protestants despised him for his unrepentant commitment to Catholic teaching and practice.

texts to be obliterated. Later they ruled against reading Coverdale's work, too. This marked a return to the policy of fourteen years earlier. Further, Parliament decreed who could and who could not read the English Bible:

> ... [N]o manner of persons, after the first of October, should take upon them to read openly to others in any church or open assembly, within any of the king's dominions, the Bible or any part of the Scripture in English, unless he was so appointed thereunto by the king, or by any ordinary [clergy], on pain of

suffering 100 months imprisonment...*every nobleman and gentle-woman*, being a householder, may read or cause to be read by any of his own family, servants in his house, orchard, or garden, to his own family, any text of the Bible; and also *every merchant-man*, being a householder, and any other persons *other than women*, apprentices, etc., might read to themselves privately the Bible. But *no women, except noblewomen and gentlewomen*, might read to themselves alone; and *no artificers [crafts people], appren-tices, journeymen, servingmen in the degrees of yeoman [independent business person], husbandmen, or labourers*, were to read the New Testament to themselves or to any other, privately or openly, on pain of one month's imprisonment. *(Italics added)*

In effect, the legislation made a class distinction by saying that if you were part of the establishment (*i.e.*, held a title, owned property, or had commercial interests) you could read the Bible. If you belonged to the laboring classes, you simply could not read it, period. Such a policy pleased Henry, who had qualms about the free-wheeling religious discussions generated by the broad availabil-ity of the Great Bible. Still, an order had been issued in 1541, probably influ-enced by Cranmer, to continue the practice of placing the Great Bible in the

A REVOLUTIONARY BOOK

Historically, the institutional church had weighed in on the side of the estab-lished order since becoming the official faith of the Roman Empire under Constantine. Spiritual and humanitarian movements such as the witness of St. Francis notwithstanding, the bishops and the parish priests were largely committed to the feudal ideas that the ranking orders in society are God-ordained and that change amounted to rebellion against the divine order.

This static state of affairs can continue in a Christian society so long as the church controls what the masses will hear. The early efforts of Wyclif to put an English Bible into the hands of common folk unleashed a radical social move-ment, known as the Lollards. This movement continued to draw inspiration from Scripture through nearly 150 years of persecution and harassment.

The Reformation, with its outpouring of vernacular Scriptures, happened at a time when the old feudal order was breaking down. Those with a stake in the existing order tried their best to preserve the old system; thus, Henry's eco-nomic classification of who could and could not read the Bible. Those without a stake had little to lose. They gladly clutched at any scriptural straw that would justify a new social arrangement.

The Bible has given many people a fresh vision of a just social order and has inspired many social and political innovations down to our time.

churches. And this order was not rescinded. The English Bible bothered Henry less than its uncontrolled circulation among the unlettered and oppressed. He sensed, perhaps, the revolutionary potential of vernacular Scripture in the hands of the people.

Except for the vehement Protestants among them, the English people accepted, and some even welcomed, the new legislation. There lingered among the people a fond sentiment for the old ways, and they welcomed this restraint on those radicals who were finding in the Bible support for anarchistic ideas.

Translations Cease

Between 1540 and 1557, no new versions of the Bible appeared, although Tyndale's New Testament, and the versions of Coverdale, Rogers ("Matthew"), and Taverner, along with the "official" Great Bible, were reprinted many times.

How could the Bible continue to be printed when legislation forbade its reading by so many? In truth, the prohibitions that Henry pushed through Parliament were never strongly enforced. Nor were the fundamental Catholic doctrines of the Six Articles. Many people wanted the traditional expression of faith, but large numbers were responsive to Protestant ideals. Those with Protestant leanings supported the king's continuing program of seizing church property and endowments. This made Henry hesitant to offend the Protestants beyond their endurance.

Henry died in 1547, but before his death, he arranged for a council of regents to assist young Edward VI, Henry's son by Jane Seymour, who ascended to the throne at age 9. The council was headed by Lord Protector Edward Seymour, Edward's uncle, who became duke of Somerset. He, like most of the regents, favored Protestantism and moved the English church with measured caution in that direction. The dissolution of monasteries and the destruction of relics, begun by Henry VIII, continued. The 1549 Act of Uniformity required the use of the first Book of Common Prayer, largely written by Archbishop Cranmer, with Psalms from the Great Bible. It breathed the Protestant spirit and showed some Lutheran influences. This book deepened the conflict between the Catholic and reform element in the church. Rebellions erupted in the western counties.

Socially, England was beset by the inclosure controversy. This involved fencing off sections of land which traditionally were held in common for village tenants to cultivate. Inclosure favored the profitable sheep-raising industry, desirable to the gentry, but generated deep resentment in the peasant farmers who now had no land to farm on their own. Somerset tended to side with the disgruntled peasant farmers. This led to his downfall in 1549 at the hands of the gentry and his execution in 1552.

He was replaced as Lord Protector by his rival, John Dudley, who later became duke of Northumberland. Dudley oversaw parliamentary acts which established Protestant ascendancy. Catholics were removed from the council of regents that advised young King Edward. Consequently, the second Act of Uniformity and the second Book of Common Prayer were even more Protestant.

The frail Edward, now dying of tuberculosis, had to decide who would be his successor. Next in line stood Mary, his half-sister born of Katherine. But Mary was a committed Catholic, so Dudley persuaded Edward to confer the succession on equally young but Protestant Jane Grey, the granddaughter of Henry VIII's sister and wife of Dudley's youngest son.

Edward died at age 15. Thus, on July 10, 1553, Lady Jane Grey, also age 15, ascended the throne. She reigned only nine days. The populace wanted Mary and when Northumberland's army deserted him, the Lady's cause was lost. The next year, she, her husband, and her father were executed. Her's was the briefest reign of any English monarch.

Bloody Mary

Edward's half-sister, Mary I, daughter of Katharine, assumed the throne in 1553. Filled with resentment over the shabby treatment Henry dealt to her mother, she led a Catholic restoration insofar as she could. The second Book of Common Prayer and other parliamentary legislation remained in place. She could not give up royal supremacy and return the English to the Pope. But she could restore Catholic worship and bring the nation again into closer communion with Rome. For that purpose, she restored to his offices the out-of-favor Bishop Gardiner and charged him with the responsibility of restoring Catholic spirit and practice to the Church of England.

Mary Tudor (1516-1558), Queen of England 1553-1558, in an engraving by an unknown artist. Her persecutions of Protestants earned her the unfortunate title of "Bloody Mary."

What followed was a blood bath of persecution in which at least 300 martyrs to the Protestant cause perished. Among them were Rogers and Archbishop Cranmer. Coverdale was held under loose arrest and was spared only because his wife's Danish connections brought Christian III of Denmark to plead his cause. Martyrdom embraced clerics and laity alike, from the richest noble to the poorest peasant. These persecutions earned the queen the title, "Bloody Mary."

The creation of martyrs often promotes their cause and Mary's reign of terror only fanned the flames of reformation. John Foxe chronicled the persecution. His huge work, in some editions running to eight volumes, was kept beside the Bible in many English homes down to Victorian times. Ultimately, Mary's persecution had the effect of diminished Catholic influence in the eventual church settlement under Elizabeth I.

Mary's unpopularity was also due in part to her marriage to Phillip II of Spain. Through this union, she had in effect, subsumed English policy to that of Spain. Her brutal efforts to restore Catholicism were generally hated, and her cozy relationship with England's historic rival, Spain, further eroded her public support.

Mary's policies certainly promoted foreign travel. To escape persecution, humanists and Protestants alike fled to the Continent. The former drifted south to Italy. The latter went to Germany, or more likely at this time, Switzerland where John Calvin and his associates were experimenting with a civil government based on their understanding of biblical law and instructions.

Among those who went into exile were five bishops, five deans, and fifty leading clergymen. They joined the exiles in Frankfort, but dissensions arose over questions of vestments and liturgy. The more non-conformist among them then moved on to Geneva. This group included John Knox who later brought Protestantism to Scotland.

The Geneva Bible

The group that went to Geneva included several skillful biblical scholars who devoted themselves to Bible translation "for the space of two years and more, day and night." Among them was William Whittingham, John Calvin's brother-in-law, who said Geneva was "the store of heavenly learning and judgment...the place where God hath appointed us to dwell." For Bible translators, that rang true since Theodore Beza, the finest biblical scholar of the time, worked

NONCONFORMISTS

Nonconformist is the term to describe Christians who would not conform to the liturgy, worship practices, dress, or doctrines of the established Church of England. The Anglican church maintained liturgical worship, with altars, vestments for the priest, chants, hymns, candles, and other traditional worship practices. Most nonconformists sought a simpler style of worship. Many also wanted to uplift the emotional, feeling side of religion and a personal experience of salvation. They favored the theological approach of John Calvin over that of Martin Luther. From the nonconformists movement came the Puritans, the Pilgrims, and later, the Congregationalists and the Methodists.

The generacion of Christ.   2

THE HOLY ªGOSPEL
of Iesus Christ, ᵇaccording to Matthewe.

THE ARGUMENT.

IN this historie written by Matthewe, Marke, Luke, and Iohn, the Spirit of God so gouerned their hearts, that although they were foure in nomber, yet in effect and purpose they so consent, as thogh the whole had bene composed by any one of them. And albeit in stile and maner of writing they be diuers, and sometime one writeth more largely that which the other doeth abbridge: neuertheles in matter and argument they all tende to one end: which is, to publish to the worlde the fauour of God towarde mankinde through Christ Iesus, whome the Father hathe giuen as a pledge of his mercie & loue. And for this cause they intitle their storie, Gospel, which signifieth good tidings, for asmuche as God hathe performed in dede that which the fathers hoped for. So that hereby we are admonished to forsake the worlde, and the vanities thereof, and with moste affectioned hearts embrace this incomparable treasure freely offred vnto vs: for there is no ioye nor consolacion, no peace nor quietnes, no felicitie nor saluacion, but in Iesus Christ, who is the very substance of this Gospel, and in whome all the promises are yea, and amen. And therefore vnder this worde is conteined the whole New testament: but communely we vse this name for the historie, which the foure Euangelists write, conteining Christs coming in the flesh, his death and resurrection, which is the perfite somme of our saluation. Matthewe, Marke, and Luke are more copious in describing his life and death: but Iohn more laboureth to set forthe his doctrine, wherein bothe Christs office, and also the vertue of his death and resurrection more fully appeare: for without this, to knowe that Christ was borne, dead & risen againe, shulde nothing profite vs. The which thing notwithstanding that the thre first touche partely, as he also sometime intermedleth the historical narration, yet Iohn chiefly is occupied herein. And therefore as a moste learned interpreter writeth, they describe, as it were, the bodie, and Iohn setteth before our eyes the soule. Wherefore the same aptely termeth the Gospel writ by Iohn, the keye which openeth the dore to the vnderstanding of the others: for whosoeuer doeth knowe the office, vertue and power of Christ, shal reade that which is written of the Sonne of God come to be the redemer of the worlde, with moste proffit. Now as concerning the writers of this historie, it is euident that Matthewe was a Publicane or custome gatherer, and was thence chosen of Christ to be an Apostle. Marke is thoght to haue bene Peters disciple, and to haue planted the first Church at Alexandria, where he dyed the eight yere of the reigne of Nero. Luke was a phisition of Antiochia and became Pauls disciple, and felowe in all his traueils: he liued foure score and foure yeres, and was buryed at Constantinople. Iohn was that Apostle whome the Lord loued, the sonne of Zebedeus, and brother of Iames: he dyed thre score yeres after Christ, and was buryed nere to the Citie of Ephesus.

CHAP. I.

1 The genealogie of Christ, that is, the Messias promised to the fathers, 18 & he was conceiued by the holy Gost, and borne of the virgine Marie, when she was betrouthed vnto Ioseph. 20 The Angel satisfieth Iosephes minde. 21 Why he is called Iesus, and wherefore Emmanuel.

*He sboke of the generació of IESVS CHRIST the ᵈsonne of ᶜDauid, the sonne of Abraham. *Abrahã begate Isaac. *And Isaac begate Iacob. And *Iacob begate Iudas and his brethren. *And Iudas begate Phares, and Zara of Thamar. And *Phares begate Esrom. And Esrom begate Aram. And Aram begate Aminadab. And Aminadab begate Naasson. And Naasson begate Salmon.

5 And Salmon begate Booz of ᵍRachab. And *Booz begate Obed of Ruth. And Obed begate Iesse.

6 And *Iesse begate Dauid the King. And *Dauid the King begate Solomon of her that was the wife of Vrias.

7 And *Solomon begate Roboam. And Roboam begate Abia. And Abia begate Asa.

8 And Asa begate Iosaphat. And Iosaphat begate Ioram. And Ioram begate Ozias.

9 And Ozias begate ʰIoatham. And Ioatham begate Achaz. And Achaz begate Ezecias.

10 And *Ezecias begate Manasses. And Manasses begate Amon. And Amon begate Iosias.

11 And *Iosias begate Iacim. And Iacim begate Iechonias & his brethren about the time they were caryed away to Babylon.

12 And after they were caryed into Babylon, *Iechonias begate ¹Salathiel. *And Salathiel begate Zorobabel.

Marginal notes (left, top): * This worde signifieth the good tydinges, and is taken here for the storie which conteineth the ioyful message of the comming of the Sonne of God promised from the beginning b That is, writen and taught by Matthewe.

Marginal notes (left, near text): Luk.3.23. r This is the rehearsal of the progenie whereof Iesus Christ is sprog according to the flesh d So called, for that he came of the stoke of Dauid e These two are first reheatsed, because Christ was especially promised to come of them and their sede, and therefore Christ communely was called the sonne of Dauid, because the promes was more euidently confirmed vnto him. *Gen.21.2. *Gen.25.24. *Gen.29.35. *Gen.38.27. f By incestuous adulterie, the which shame setteth forthe his great humilitie, who made him self of no reputation, but became a seruant for our salutie: yea, a worme and no man, the reproche of men, and contempt of the people: and at length suffred the accursed death of the crosse. *2.Chron.2.5. 1esa.4.18.

Marginal notes (right): g Rachab and Ruth, being Gentiles, signifie that Christ came not onely of Iewes, and for them, but also of Gentiles, and for their saluation. Ruth 4,18. 1.Sam.16,1. & 17,12. 2.Sam.12,24. 2.King.11,43 1.chro.3,10. h He nathe omitted thre Kings, Ioas, Amasia, Azaria, abbridging the nomber to make the times fourtene generations. 1.King.20,21 & 21,11. 2.King.23, 34.& 24,1. 2.chro.36,4. 1.King.24,6. 2.chro.36.9. i After the fourtene generations...

captiuitie, the rial royal was appointed vnto him: so that notwithstanding that they were as slaues for the space of seuentie yeres, yet by the prouidence of God the gouvernement remained in the familie of Dauid, where it continued til the coming of Christ. *1 Chro 3,17.esa 4,2. & 5,3.

AA.ii.

The first chapter of Matthew, from the first edition, 1560, of the Geneva Bible. Note the use of roman type, the setting of each verse as a separate paragraph, the introduction which outlines the argument of the book, and the explanatory notes in the margins. The marginal note at top left, for instance, explains the meaning of the word "gospel" as "the joyful message of the comming of the Sonne of God...."

there preparing his excellent Greek and Latin versions. It was in Geneva, too, in 1535, that Olivetan had translated the standard French version which had been used by Rogers.

The first results of their work came from William Whittingham. It was a small New Testament, elegantly printed with ornamental capitals and headpieces and which came off the press of Conrad Badius in 1557. (Coverdale, who was in Geneva at the time, may have assisted as well.) This translation incorporated some innovative features:

- It was the first English Scripture to be printed in roman type. As people discovered that they could read roman type much easier than the earlier black letter type, roman became the standard type for English Bibles.

- It adopted verse divisions for the first time in an English Bible, printing each verse as a separate unit. The verse division for the New Testament first appeared in the fourth edition (1551) of Stephanus' (also called E(s)tienne) Greek Testament, on which Whittingham relied. Earlier versions simply offered the chapter divisions which were worked out in 1228 by Stephen Langton or, as some claim, by Hugues de St. Cher in 1262 and used in Latin versions.

- Whittingham's Testament used italics to display English words not in the original Greek but necessary to make sense in English, an idea he adapted from Beza's 1556 Latin translation.

THE GENEVA BIBLE TRANSLATORS

William Whittingham (1524–1579) was, at age 23, a senior student at Christ Church, Oxford. In Geneva in 1559, he succeeded John Knox as pastor of the English church but returned to England the next year where in 1562 he was made Dean of Durham cathedral. Besides translating the New Testament, he also translated part of the metrical Psalm collection done by Sternhold and Hopkins. Some early Calvinists rejected hymns by human authors and sang instead metrical versions of the Psalms.

Less is known of Anthony Gilby. He was educated at Christ's College, Cambridge. When he returned to England under Elizabeth I, he took the vicarage of Ashby de la Zouch. He died in 1584.

Thomas Sampson (1517–1589) seems to have been the most radical in his reform views. Educated at Cambridge, he had served as Dean of Chichester cathedral during Edward VI's reign until he fled when Queen Mary came to power. After returning to England he became Dean of Christ Church, Oxford, in 1561, but lost that office four years later for nonconformity.

- The version supplied a system of marks to indicate variant readings among Greek manuscripts.

This New Testament would be revised and joined with a fresh translation of the Old Testament, chiefly the work of Anthony Gilby and Thomas Sampson, in 1560 to form the milestone version called the Geneva version. It is also called the "Breeches Bible" for the way it followed Wyclif in translating Genesis 3.7: "They sewed fig leaves together and made themselves breeches." (Other versions of the time used "aprons.")

The first small quarto edition, addressed to Queen Elizabeth and the Brethren of England, Scotland, and Ireland, and featuring woodcut illustrations borrowed from a French Bible, appeared with this title (spelling modernized):

> The Bible and Holy Scriptures Contained in the Old and New Testament. Translated according to the Hebrew and Greek and conferred with the best translations in divers languages. With most profitable Annotations upon all the hard places, and other things of great importance as may appear in the Epistle to the Reader. At Geneva. Printed by Rouland Hall. M.D.L.X.

The members of the English congregation at Geneva stood the expense of the printing. One of the church members most actively interested in the printing was John Bodley, father of the founder of the Bodleian Library in Oxford.

This vastly popular translation was destined to go through some 140 editions. Errors that show up in certain editions give them nicknames among book collectors. The second edition, for example, has "place makers" instead of "peace makers" at Matthew 5.9. This earned it the name Placemaker's Bible. A later edition in 1598 printed "Jesus Church" for "Jesus Christ" at 1 John 5.20, and this is called the Jesus Church Bible. A 1609 edition, called the Judas Bible, has "Judas" instead of "Jesus" in John 6.67.

The Geneva Style

The New Testament portion of the Geneva Bible was based on Whittingham's 1557 version, itself drawing heavily on Tyndale's, but giving somewhat more attention to Beza's 1556 Latin translation. They used Stephanus' Greek text. The Old Testament was based on the Great Bible. The Pentateuch and historical books of the Great Bible largely reflected Tyndale, so they required the least drastic revision. Gilby and Sampson, aided perhaps by Coverdale, worked on the Old Testament, drawing upon several sources: Pagninus' Hebrew-Latin Bible (1528) and the Latin translation of the Old Testament by Sebastian Münster (1534/35), plus the Latin version begun by Leo Juda and finished by Theodorus Bibliander, first published in 1543, and a Latin version done by Castellio (1551). These were checked against Olivetan's French Bible. For the Apocrypha, they used Beza's Latin version along with a Latin translation by Claudius Baduellus (or, Baduel), based on an early printed edition of the Bible called the Complutensian Polyglot and published in 1557. Both were vigorous in style and careful in scholarship.

European scholars had made major strides in their understanding of Hebrew since the early 1500s. The Geneva translators reflect this new respect for Hebrew in the way they translated certain names, to pattern them after a more accurate Hebrew pronunciation: Izhak for Isaac and Iaakob for Jacob.

Their stress on accuracy, moreover, led them to a greatly improved translation of a notoriously difficult and probably textually corrupt passage, Job 19.25b where Job envisions his Vindicator or Redeemer. The Great Bible renders it, "I shall rise out of the earth," while the Geneva version reads "he [my Redeemer or Vindicator] shall stand on the earth," a reading which is followed by the modern *NRSV*.

A number of other phrases familiar to readers of the *KJV* and some later versions come from the Geneva Bible: "a little leaven leaveneth the whole lump," "cloud of witnesses," and in 1 Corinthians 13, "we know in part and we prophesy in part," "childish things," and "in a glass darkly." The Geneva Bible translation of Psalm 23 (printed here in the original spelling) gives an indication of the many ways this version influenced the 1611 King James Bible:

> The Lord *is* my shepherd, I shal not want.
>
> He maketh me to rest in grene pasture, & leadeth me by the stil waters.
>
> He restoreth my soule, & leadeth me in the paths of righteousnes for his Names sake.
>
> Yea, thogh I shulde walke through the valley of the shadow of death, I wil feare no euil: for thou art with me: thy rod and thy staffe, they comfort me.

The Geneva translators strove for a version that everyone could read, that "both the learned and the others might be holpen." To achieve that aim they, like their predecessors, used marginal notes. These were less doctrinally biased than in earlier English Bibles. Even though the translators worked in the heart of John Calvin's territory, they downplayed their Calvinist sympathies. Tyndale's notes were completely rewritten. More stress was put on explaining obscure phrases and terms, providing helpful historical and geographical notes, and showing variant readings from other manuscripts. Still, they managed a few Protestant barbs, such as the note at Revelation 9.11 identifying the Pope as the "angel of the bottomless pit" and the "anti-Christ."

This was, without a doubt, the best English version available in its day. Though never specifically authorized by Queen Elizabeth, her strong Protestant sympathies did nothing to hinder its circulation. The Bible appeared just before the Pope's jurisdiction in Scotland was abolished and the Scottish Reformation triumphed. The Scottish Parliament passed a law that every householder above a certain income must purchase a copy of the Geneva Bible. It spread as widely in England, where it became the standard household Bible.

This was the Bible of Oliver Cromwell, the Puritans, the Pilgrim fathers and their Mayflower Compact, John Bunyan, Shakespeare, and even King James. In fact, the Geneva Bible continued to be the most popular version of the Bible for a generation after the *King James Version* came out in 1611. It contributed heavily to the situation which historian John Richard Green says began in Elizabeth's reign:

> England became the people of a book, and that book was the Bible. It was as yet the one English book which was familiar to every Englishman; it was read at churches and read at home, and everywhere its words, as they fell on ears which custom had not deadened, kindled a startling enthusiasm.

The popularity of this version received a boost from the innovations it took over from Whittingham's earlier Testament: roman type and separate verses. It was printed in the smaller quarto size, making it easy to hold in the hand, unlike the huge Great Bible which was a pulpit Bible intended for church reading. The smaller size also made the Geneva Bible more affordable.

Two other features of this Bible became the standard for the English Bibles to follow: the placement of the Apocrypha between the Testaments (except for the Prayer of Manasseh which slid between 2 Chronicles and Ezra) and the sequential arrangement of the various biblical books.

The rabid interest in Bible reading had an interesting economic spinoff: the sale of spectacles zoomed, with the best and cheapest eyeglasses coming from Germany.

Laurence Tomson (1539–1608) published a revision of Whittingham's Geneva New Testament in 1576. Tomson was skilled in twelve languages and served as secretary to Queen Elizabeth's counselor, Sir Francis Walsingham. He claimed to base his revision on Theodore Beza's Greek Testament, although he seems to have relied heavily on Beza's Latin translation. He added a commentary so "that there is not one hard sentence, nor dark speech, nor doubtful word, but is so opened and hath such light given to it that children may go through with it, and the simplest that are, may walk without guide, without wandering and going astray." In many later editions of the Geneva Bible, Tomson's version was substituted for Whittingham's 1560 Testament.

With the Geneva Bible we have a true "people's Bible"—written in vigorous English, exhibiting careful scholarship without sounding pedantic, and widely available. But it wasn't quite right for official church use, and that takes us to the next stage in the development of the English Bible.

7 A VERSION FOR EACH SIDE

Queen Mary I died in 1558. From a religious viewpoint, her reign was a temporary departure from the general trend toward Protestant views that had begun with Henry. Few non-Catholic English enjoyed the idea of her marriage to the King of Spain. But Catholics found hope in her reign, and there were many with Roman-oriented sympathies in England. When Mary died and Elizabeth moved into power, the Protestant majority returned from their exile and a new era of the English Bible began. It resulted in two new English versions, one by the bishops of the Church of England, the other by Roman Catholics.

Good Queen Bess

Elizabeth I's reign from 1558 to 1603 marked the Golden Age of England's political and cultural life. She inherited a country torn by religious strife, massively in debt, and a failure at war. At her death 45 years later, England had become a force in the world, with a powerful navy and a rich culture. The Elizabethan era produced such notables as William Shakespeare, Edmund Spenser, Francis Bacon, Francis Drake, and Walter Raleigh. In her reign, too, the Protestant movement became firmly established.

During Mary's rule, Elizabeth—daughter of Anne Boleyn and half-sister to Mary—had been imprisoned for fear she would become a rallying point for Protestants. In this period, she gained what freedom she enjoyed by adopting Catholicism at least outwardly. And in truth, she never lost her taste for the traditional pageantry of worship, although one of

Elizabeth I (1533-1603), Queen of England 1558-1603, from a portrait hanging in the Great Hall at Warwick Castle

her first acts as Queen was to re-establish Protestantism through the 1559 Acts of Supremacy and Uniformity. The Pope promptly excommunicated her, as an earlier Pope had excommunicated her father. Rebellions by the Catholic nobility of Northumberland and Westmorland, plots to murder her and to place Catholic Mary Queen of Scots on the throne, and Jesuit intrigues helped to sharpen her distrust of Catholics. While her oppression of Catholics deepened as her reign went on, her policies toward Catholics never went to the murderous lengths her half-sister Mary took against Protestants.

Elizabeth, like her father, wanted absolute power. She wanted religion clean and neat and under her sway. The Church of England would be the only church for all English people. As such, it would be a broad church, with elements to please both those of Catholic and Protestant sentiments. This Elizabethan Settlement became embodied in the 39 Articles of 1567.

But if Elizabeth had to keep the fervent Catholics at bay, she soon had trouble with a rising movement of ultra-Protestants called Puritans. The Puritans wanted to purify the Church of England along Calvinist lines. Doctrinally, Puritans followed Calvin's ideas of predestination and salvation of the elect. In liturgical matters, they rejected pomp and ceremony, vestments and elaborate music. In church government, some sought a presbyterian form while others wanted a congregational polity, but both parties united in their opposition to the control of bishops.

The Elizabethan Settlement steered a middle course of compromise. The 39 Articles included both Catholic and Calvinist elements. The historic episcopate remained. Church rituals drew upon earlier traditions, but in a simplified form and with room to move either in a more "high church" or "low church" direction. That compromise did not satisfy the Puritans who began in London as early as 1567 to meet in small dissenting groups apart from the established church to follow the practice of the church in Geneva. The spirit and tone of the extremely popular Geneva Bible certainly contributed to this separatist movement.

The Bishops' Bible

Elizabeth had restored the official authority of the Great Bible for church use. The people, however, were reading the Geneva Bible. Again, England faced the problem of two different but concurrent translations.

CHURCH GOVERNMENT

Forms of church government, or polity, were a major controversy as the Reformation unfolded. The issue revolved around who had the power to call ministers, discipline clergy, control finances, and oversee ministry. Roman Catholics and some Protestants favored the traditional *episcopal* form in which certain clergy called bishops exercise complete authority over parish clergy and parish life. Other Protestants favored one of two forms:

Congregational—The local assembly of believers gathered in a congregation has complete authority over its affairs. Clergy have no more power than the laity.

Presbyterian—Authority over congregations resides in a presbytery, consisting of teaching elders (ministers) and ruling elders elected as representatives of the congregations in the presbytery.

The Geneva Bible was an independent venture, with John Bodley holding a seven year printing monopoly granted him in 1561. In 1566, he asked for a renewal. Matthew Parker, Archbishop of Canterbury, delayed his application. Parker recognized the superiority of the Geneva Bible over the Great Bible, but he felt its annotations made it unsuitable for official church use. He finally offered to renew Bodley's franchise on terms Bodley could not accept. Parker then, in 1564, set in motion plans to create a revision done by bishops—the kind of translation proposed in Cranmer's time but which never came to pass.

The aim of Parker's proposal was to produce an official Bible which would displace the Geneva Bible. Parker chose to parcel out the work to several translators who would work independently, with him serving as editor-in-chief. He also revised Genesis, Exodus, and parts of the New Testament. Perhaps eight of the translators were bishops, which is why it became known as the Bishops' Bible.

MATTHEW PARKER
(1504–1575)

Born in Norwich, he took his B.A. from Corpus Christi College, Cambridge, in 1525 and then was ordained a deacon and finally a priest in 1527. During his studies, he fell under the influence of Luther and other reformers. In 1535 he became chaplain to Anne Boleyn and a bit later to Henry VIII. After attaining a D.D. in 1538, he moved on to become master of Corpus Christi College and, one year later, vice-chancellor of Cambridge. Edward VI presented him with the deanery of Lincoln but Queen Mary stripped him of his offices, although he managed to remain in England. He lived in obscurity until 1559 when Elizabeth elevated him to Archbishop of Canterbury and charged him to sustain the religious settlement she endorsed against the opposition of the Puritans. A man of high morals, deep piety, and excellent scholarship, he left his fine collection of ancient manuscripts to Corpus Christi College. In 1562 he revised the 39 Articles. A fine churchman, he displayed little fire or enthusiasm for "popular" reformation.

The Record Office in London has preserved a list of the bishops and others to whom he assigned parts for translation. Their initials were to appear at the end of their respective sections, but some errors crept in and the initials in the Bible do not correspond exactly to the list of assignments. Parker, as editor-in-chief, also supplied guidelines to his translators which reveal the style of Bible he had in mind. The guidelines can be summarized as follows:

- Follow the Great Bible, except where it varies from the Greek and Hebrew texts.

- Avoid notes of a doctrinal or controversial nature.

- Mark genealogies "and other such places not edifying" in some way so the reader can skip over them.

- Drop those terms used in the Great Bible which offer any "offense of Lightness or obscenity."

- Print the New Testament on thicker paper than the Old, because it will be read more.

The revisers-translators sought a readable text in the language of the common people. When the Bishop of Ely submitted his section, he added this note:

> I would wish that such usual words as we English people be acquainted with might still remain in their form and sound, so far forth as the Hebrew will well bear, inkhorn [scholarly] terms to be avoided.

The Bishops' Bible generally represents a revision of the Great Bible. The plan of assigning sections to different work groups became a common practice in later translations down to the present time. The process, though, requires careful coordination. Apparently, Parker did not bring the groups together to compare notes, nor did he impose a uniform style on the various sections. Thus the translation lacks consistency in its pattern of changes from the Great Bible.

While translators followed Parker's instructions to avoid controversial, doctrinal comments, they did add notes to clarify the text. They ended up taking over some two-thirds of the New Testament notes in the Geneva Bible, as well as its verse divisions. The note at Psalm 45.9, here in modern spelling, explaining the name "Ophir" is interesting:

> Ophir is thought to be the Island in the west coast, of late found by Christopher Colombus: from whence at this day is brought most fine gold.

Parker only intended slight alterations to the Great Bible, but some workers went beyond this plan to do more extensive revisions. Overall, the revisers knew Greek better than Hebrew and their work on the New Testament is better than on the Old. Some of their changes were eventually incorporated into the *King James Version*. Still, they used an older version of the Lord's Prayer, chose "charity" in 1 Corinthians 13, and generally adopted less accurate language than some earlier translations.

The Bishops' Bible was completed and published in 1568. Parker had appealed to Queen Elizabeth for authorization which, for some unknown reason, did not come. Nevertheless, the episcopal endorsement of this version made it, in effect, the second version "authorized" for church use, after the Great Bible. The title page of the beautifully printed large folio first edition, from the press of

THE PROBLEMATIC PSALTER

The Psalter had long formed the basis for devotion in the church, especially in the daily offices of the monasteries and parish churches. Jerome, in about 392, translated the Psalms into Latin from a version of the Septuagint and put them into his Vulgate Bible. One of Jerome's psalm translations became known as the Gallican Psalter, because it became popular in Gaul, and remained the norm for Western Europe for centuries. Italian churches used another of Jerome's translations, the Roman Psalter, down to the time of Pius V (1566–1572) when it was replaced by the Gallican Psalter in all Italian churches except St. Peter's in Rome. Traditionally, the Roman Psalter was thought to be a pre-Vulgate translation by Jerome, closer perhaps to the Old Latin versions. Latin manuscripts could easily mix the two Psalters, leading to a corrupted Latin text.

When translators began working with the classic Hebrew Masoretic text, they discovered more complexities. The Septuagint, the basis for existing Latin translations, numbered some Psalms differently than the Hebrew, included additional verses, and showed other marked variants. The Great Bible, based on Coverdale's translation, had printed the variations found in Latin but not in Hebrew in a different typeface to distinguish them for the reader.

The first Book of Common Prayer printed in 1549 included the Psalter from the Great Bible but without marking the Latin variants in any way. The Book of Common Prayer services called for reading through the entire Psalter each month, so the people soon took the Great Bible Psalms to heart—with all the Latin additions. When the Bishops' Bible went back to the Hebrew form and numbering, many people resented this change in Psalms that had grown familiar to them over a generation.

Public opposition grew so vocal that later editions of the Bishops' Bible had to include both versions of the Psalms. Interestingly, the popular Geneva Bible Psalms followed the Hebrew text and numbering. People comfortable with one version for home reading objected to that same approach when applied to public worship. The psychology of private and public worship seems to differ, down to the present day. People who happily use modern English Bible versions for personal reading and study may still object to modern English in their liturgy, public prayers, or the church reading of Scripture, preferring the stately thees-and-thous of the past.

Richard Jugge in London, was essentially accurate when it stated, "cum privilegio regiae majestatis" [with royal permission or privilege].

A quarto edition in 1569 corrected many of the misprints that cropped up in the 1568 Old Testament, but made few corrections to the New Testament. These corrections appear in all subsequent editions of the Bishops' Bible, except for the folios of 1572, 1574, and 1578. The 1572 folio has further revisions to the New Testament text and prints the Psalms from the Great Bible in black letter type in parallel columns with those of this revision in roman type. After 1573, all editions except for one carry the dual Psalter, and the 1572 version of the New Testament appears in all later editions. Between the 1568 and 1602, the Bishops' Bible went through 17 editions of the complete Bible and 14 editions of the New Testament.

The folio editions of the Bishops' Bible carried woodcut illustrations of mediocre quality. The first folio edition and the second edition of 1572 borrowed elaborate initial letters from a previous printing of Ovid's *Metamorphoses*. This peculiarity probably resulted from an effort to economize.

The Canterbury Convocation in 1571 ordered every bishop and archbishop to have a copy of this Bible in his home, made available to servants and visitors. Each cathedral was required to have one, and parish churches were urged to get one if at all possible. Between 1568 and 1611, this was the version generally used in churches. But the Geneva Bible remained the favorite for home and personal use and far outweighed the Bishops' Bible in both popularity and longevity.

The Rheims-Douai Bible

Protestants who had fled to Germany and Switzerland during Queen Mary's persecutions now, with Elizabeth on the throne, moved back to England. And numbers of Catholics departed to the Catholic Low Countries, modern Belgium and the Netherlands.

Rome, even at this late date, displayed nothing of the Protestant enthusiasm for vernacular Scripture. But the situation was changing. English-speaking Catholics were a shrinking minority. They were surrounded by Bible-reading, increasingly Protestant Church of England people, yet they had no approved English Bible of their own. Theological issues so captured the imagination of people in the sixteenth century that they discussed such questions as part of daily conversation. Protestants could argue from their Bibles and quote their notes. Catholics had nothing to help them. So for the sake of the Catholic minority and in the hope of somehow bringing England back to the Catholic church, church leaders decided the time had come for an approved Catholic English translation with proper notes.

The entrance to the great Cathedral at Rheims, built in the 13th century, showing the central and right doorways. In this town, the English New Testament prepared for Roman Catholic readers was completed.

In 1568, Cardinal William Allen founded a college at Douai, France, for the purpose of training sons of English Catholics. Allen thought the English were Roman at heart and that the Reformation was a minor disturbance that would soon disappear. He hoped to train missionary priests to bring England back to Catholicism. His enthusiasm, however, clouded his political judgment. When the Spanish Armada threatened to invade and conquer England in 1588, he supported the Catholic Spanish side. Elizabeth's defeat of the Armada brought one of the high moments of English history. Allen's support for the enemy did little for the Catholic cause in England.

Students at Douai pursued a strong course in biblical studies. But, Allen wrote in 1578, they labored under a burden when:

> ... preaching to the unlearned and are obliged on the spur of the moment to translate some passage which they have quoted into the vulgar tongue. They often do it inaccurately and with unpleasant hesitation... Our adversaries on the other hand have

at their fingers' ends all those passages of scripture which seem to make for them, and by a certain deceptive adaptation and alteration of the sacred words, produce the effect of appearing to say nothing but what comes from the Bible. This evil might be remedied if we too had some Catholic version of the Bible, for all the English versions are most corrupt.

It may be difficult for people today to realize how intensely people felt about religion in the sixteenth century. One gets an idea of the fervor behind Protestant and Catholic feelings from two book titles of the day.

WILLIAM ALLEN
(1532–1594)

Allen was educated at Oxford and served as Principal of St. Mary's Hall, Oxford. He was also Canon of York. When Elizabeth came to the throne, he resigned these offices and moved to Louvain in modern Belgium. He made one trip to England, but was forced to flee. Allen then devoted his energies to stopping the English Reformation. Created a Cardinal in 1587, he was promised the post of legate to reconcile England to Rome if the Spanish Armada were successful. He was known for his biblical studies, at one point assisting Cardinal Carafa in preparing a new edition of the Septuagint. Allen died in Rome.

The first comes from Gregory Martin, who wrote it after he finished his work as the major translator of the Rheims New Testament:

> A DISCOVERY of the Manifold Corruptions of the Holy Scriptures by the Heretics of our days, specially the English Sectarians, and of their foul dealing herein, by partial and false translations to the advantage of the heresies in their English Bibles, *printed at Rheims by John Fogny*, 1582.

He was answered promptly by Protestant apologist William Fulke with a book bearing this blunt title:

> A Defense of the sincere and true Translation of the Holy Scriptures into the English tongue, against the manifolde cauils [cavils; complaints] and impudent slaunders of Gregorie Martin, *at London, Imprinted by Henrie Bynneman, for George Bishop, 1583.*

The Plan of Work

Though Allen conceived the project of an English Catholic translation, he had some misgivings, as he wrote to the Pope:

> ...If his Holiness will permit [we] will endeavor to have the Bible faithfully, purely and genuinely translated according to the edition approved by the Church—perhaps indeed it would have been more desireable that the scriptures had never been translated into barbarous tongues; nevertheless at the present day, when either from heresy or other causes, the curiosity of man, even of those who are not bad, is so great, and there is often such need of reading the scriptures in order to confute our opponents, it is better that there should be a faithful and catholic translation than that men should use a corrupt version to their peril or destruction, the more so since the dangers which arise from reading certain more difficult passages may be alleviated by suitable notes.

The actual work on the New Testament fell to Gregory Martin, formerly of St. John's College, Oxford. At this time, 1578, Martin was lecturer in Hebrew and Holy Scripture at the Douai-Rheims College. He worked on the project for three years and the New Testament was printed in 1582. The Old Testament was finished about the same time, but lack of funds delayed its printing in two volumes until 1609–1610. The work then underway on the *King James Version* probably spurred publication of the Douai Old Testament.

Initial work began in Douai, France, but the college had to move for political reasons to Rheims, where the New Testament was completed. It was published in a quarto edition by John Fogny of Rheims. In 1593, the college returned to Douai where it was operating when the Old Testament appeared. For that reason, the convention arose of referring to the Rheims New Testament and the to the Douai Old Testament, using Rheims-Douai Bible to refer to the complete work.

Tyndale sought to "cause a boy that driveth the plough" to read and know the Bible. This translation began with the opposite premise, as the Preface to the New Testament states:

> ...Which translation we do not for all that publish, upon erroneous opinion of necessity, that the holy Scriptures should always be in our mother tongue, or that they ought, or were ordained by God, to be read indifferently of all, or could be easily understood of every one that readeth or heareth them in a known language...or that we generally and absolutely deemed

it…more agreeable to God's word and honour or edification of the faithful, to have them turned into vulgar tongues, than to be kept & studied only in the Ecclesiastical learned languages…

Nor did the translators assume that the Bible should be in the hands of every

husbandman [farmer], artificer [craftsperson], apprentice, boys, girls, mistress, maid, [or] man…[nor used for] table talk, for alebenches [taverns], for boats and barges, and for every profane person and company.

The translators continue in the Preface to say that they closely followed the

old vulgar approved Latin [the Vulgate]: not only in sense…but sometimes in the very words also and phrases, which may seem to the vulgar Reader, and to common English ears…rudeness or ignorance…

And strangely indeed did this translation read for it amounted to a literal translation of the Latin Vulgate with only occassional references to Greek and Hebrew manuscripts. We have seen how disputes over Latin-based versus English-based words reflected the Catholic-Protestant struggle over translations. This unimpeded Catholic translation used a great number of Latinisms.

Consider Philippians 2.7. Tyndale, Coverdale, the Great Bible, and the Geneva Bible read "he made himself of no reputation" (modern versions have "he humbled himself" or "he emptied himself"). The Rheims Testament has "He exinanited himself." "Exinanite" is pure Latin, a transliteration of "exinanivit;" it was never an English word. At Matthew 21.20, the Rheims version reads, "How is it withered incontinent?," where the Protestant-oriented versions had, "How soon is the figge tree withered away?" For Amos 2.13, the Douai reads, "Behold I will screake under you as a wayne schreketh loden with hay." (The *King James Version* renders this verse, "Behold, I am pressed under you, as a cart is pressed *that is* full of sheaves.") The version also restored the ecclesiastical terms dear to Catholics, such as "penance" and "host" and "priest." When all was said and done, it was unlikely that the ordinary farmer would read such foreign-sounding English prose.

Some scholars consider the Psalms in the version to be the weakest English renditions, lacking as they do any real sense of English rhythms. Psalm 23 (Psalm 22 in Vulgate numbering), verses 1-4 read, in the original spelling:

OVr Lord ruleth me, and nothing shal be wanting to me: in place of pasture there he hath placed me.

Vpon the water of refection he hath brought me vp: he hath conuerted my soule.

He hath conducted me vpon the pathes of iustice, for his name.

For, although I shal walke in the middes of the shadow of death,
I wil not feare euils: because thou art with me.

Thy rod and thy staffe: they haue conforted me.

Compare this with Wyclif's translation (page 36), which it resembles, and contrast it with the vigorous English style of the Geneva version (page 91).

The choice of the Vulgate as the basis was deliberate, although it represented a return to translation norms of an earlier generation. The Preface explains that the Vulgate was preferred for its antiquity and long use, its connection with Jerome and Augustine, its approval by the Council of Trent, and its accuracy and superiority even to the Greek and Hebrew text.

Good Scholarship

For all its weaknesses in English style, the Rheims-Douay version displays considerable scholarship. Because the translators used the Vulgate—and were able to consult the newly revised Clementine Vulgate which sought the original Vulgate text—it has some readings which today's scholars consider superior to those of Tyndale, who used Greek sources heavily. Jerome lived, after all, over one thousand years closer to the time of the New Testament than Tyndale or the King James Bible translators. They only had access to relatively late Greek manuscripts. Thus, some Vulgate readings, reflecting earlier and better Greek manuscripts, are more accurate. This was discovered mainly in the nineteenth century when several very old Greek manuscripts came to light, agreeing in many places with the Vulgate.

One example of the improved reading of the Vulgate can be seen at Matthew 6.13, in the doxology at the close of Matthew's Lord's Prayer, "for thine is the kingdom, the power, and the glory." It appears in the *King James Version* because the Greek manuscripts they consulted included it. Later discoveries showed that the best Greek manuscripts omit the Matthean doxology. Many modern translations agree with this approach and include the final doxology only in a footnote.

Martin and his colleagues also made good use of the Greek manuscripts they consulted. They were sensitive, for example, to the powerful Greek definite article, which is missing in Latin, and to the force of Greek tenses. They often follow the word order of the Greek, when it was carried over into the Vulgate Latin. This frequently leads to forceful, if somewhat awkward, phrasing in English.

The Douai Old Testament appeared too late to exert much influence on the King James translators, but they apparently read and studied the Rheims New

Testament. Some scholars attribute the increase in Latinisms in the *King James Version* over the Bishops' Bible, at least in part, to the Rheims New Testament and its commitment to the Vulgate tradition. The channel of influence may have been the Protestant Fulke's answer to Martin's book. Fulke printed the Rheims Testament in parallel columns with the Bishops' Bible and took on Martin point by point. The parallel-column format made it easy to compare the two versions. Still, all things considered, the influence on the King James translators by the Douai-Rheims version was not of major importance.

The Old Testament, with fewer and milder doctrinal notes, came off the press of Lawrence Kellam in 1609-10. As in the Vulgate, the books of the Apocrypha were interspersed through the Old Testament rather than gathered in one place, as had become common in Protestant versions. A second edition of the New Testament was printed in Antwerp in 1600 in pocket size and reissued in 1621 and 1633. The availability of such a portable and relatively affordable edition can be taken to indicate an increase in Bible reading among Catholics. The Old Testament was published later in Rouen in 1635.

Revisions

Revisions of the version generally strove to improve the flow and style of the English; after 1611 revisions adopted more and more of the phrasing and style of the *King James Version*. Other translators despaired of revising the original Rheims-Douai version and simply started afresh.

Father Cornelius Nary, an English scholar at the University of Paris, was one of those who thought the Douai was "in a number of places...unintelligible." He made an original translation which received official approval and was published in Dublin in 1719. His revision of the New Testament makes more use of the Greek and he has a fine English style.

Robert Witham, head of the Seminary at Douai, also published an original version of the New Testament in England in 1730. Witham thought Nary was too eager to follow the lead of Protestants and chose to return more to the Latin Vulgate. His version cannot match that of Nary for style and readability.

Of those who chose to revise the Rheims-Douai version, the most important figure was Bishop Richard Challoner, a scholar at Douai. In 1749 he issued his New Testament, followed by the whole Bible in 1750. He continued to revise the work until his death in 1781.

Bishop Richard Challoner (1691–1781), in an early engraving

The phrasing of the *King James Version* exerted enormous influence on Bishop Challoner. He became, in effect, the basic translator-reviser of the English Catholic Bible.

But his work did not meet with universal approval. Cardinal Newman, a leading Catholic thinker in the 19th century, said that especially in the Old Testament Challoner's revision was "little short of a new translation, nearer to the Protestant than it is to the Douai." The Cardinal added his lament that "at this day the Douai Old Testament no longer exists as a Received Version of the Authentic Vulgate." In truth, no translation of the Vulgate was ever officially "received" or approved by the Roman Catholic church.

Father Bernard MacMahon further revised Challoner's work (New Testament, 1783; entire Bible, 1791). Approved by Archbishop Troy of Dublin, this revision got the nickname "Troy's Bible." Scholars generally conclude that MacMahon was in over his head for this task. His judgments and scholarship were poor. But his version became popular in Ireland where the Catholics were making advances, as well as in other English-speaking lands. Due to its support from the Irish hierarchy, MacMahon's version circulated on equal footing with earlier editions of Challoner's work, although the latter were clearly superior.

The first Roman Catholic Bible printed in the United States was a large quarto edition based on Challoner's second edition of 1763-74 and published in 1790 by Carey, Stewart and Company of Philadelphia. (This was also the first English quarto Bible of any kind published in the United States.)

Archbishop Francis Patrick Kenrick of Philadelphia further revised the New Testament, publishing the Gospels in 1849 and the rest of the New Testament in 1851. The Old Testament followed in four volumes, issued between 1857 and 1860. In 1862 he published a second, revised edition of the New Testament with fresh notes. Kenrick's work reveals some independent judgments. For example, he translates the Vulgate *poenitentiam agite* alternately as "repent" and "do penance."

The Rheims-Douai Bible in one or the other of its later revisions remained the staple Scripture for American Roman Catholics until the 1940s. Official commitment to the Vulgate as the basis for Bible translation eventually faded and Catholic scholars have since emerged as a major creative force in Bible translations and biblical studies. The shift began in 1890 when a French Dominican founded a school in Jerusalem for biblical studies. That story will be told later in Chapter 13.

8 HIS MAJESTY'S VERSION

Something wonderful departed England with the passing of Queen Elizabeth. She had laid important foundations on which her successor could build an even greater state, but a less worthy monarch followed her. History would remember his name best not for what he did for England, but for a Bible translation he sponsored: the King James Bible.

End of an Era

When Elizabeth I died in 1603, she left her kingdom at the height of its political and cultural glory. England was now a power in Europe, having defeated the Spanish Armada. The island kingdom was embracing the globe. Drake had sailed around the world and Raleigh had made the first attempts to colonize America. English literature flowered as never before or perhaps since. This was the era of Shakespeare, Marlowe, Bacon, Spenser, and more. These great poets and writers gave to the English language such vigor and power and grace that one may almost say they invented the language.

On the religious side, Elizabeth had secured the independence of the English church from Rome. The threat to royal supremacy in the Church of England now came from within. The Puritan movement grew stronger and more vocal, fed by its desire for more radical church reforms in doctrine and practice along Calvinist lines. The current Bible translations symbolized the warring parties: the Puritans fed by the "ultra-Protestant," Calvinist-toned Geneva Bible, and the loyal Church of England supporters nourished on the Bishops' Bible (or the Great Bible) in their churches. Puritans more and more gathered into covenant groups for worship and study apart from the established church. Conformity became a major issue. Add to the mix a Catholic minority also with their own Bible, and the confusion becomes apparent. This is the sort of disunity and conflict that a church which hopes to be the sole established church of the nation seeks to avoid. Royal prerogatives were involved, too. Since the monarch headed the church, religious dissent meant some degree of disloyalty to the sovereign.

James I, son of Mary Queen of Scots and descendent of Henry VII, assumed the throne after reigning 36 years as James VI of Scotland, having come to the throne as an infant. His ascension to the throne marks the beginning of the House of Stuart. Since Elizabeth died unmarried and childless, the English worried about her succession. They were grateful when arrangements were made with James, thus avoiding a civil war. The agreement implied that James would pursue Elizabeth's policies.

James I (1566–1625), King of Scotland from 1567, King of England from 1603. Though a man interested in literature and letters, once he became King of England he did not always recognize the differences between England and the Scotland from which he came. The English church differed from the Scottish kirk. The English Parliament was an active, powerful body, while the Scottish Parliament was a "court of record."

The Puritans expected a great deal from James, since he came from a Calvinist background, but they were to be disappointed. At the Hampton Court conference, James shouted "no bishop, no king" and threatened to harass all who did not conform to the established church. Thus, the Puritans, like many others, ended up as his foes, which may explain why they were hesitant to embrace the Bible translation James sponsored.

James was a scholarly man with Protestant leanings, the result of an intense education under his tutor George Buchanan. Buchanan, the greatest of the Scottish humanists, was a noted Latinist and a supporter of the Reformation of the Scottish Church, having been Moderator of the General Assembly of the Church of Scotland. James had by age 20 written sonnets, tried his hand at paraphrasing some Psalms, and rendered a paraphrase of the Revelation of St. John. He had hoped that the Church of Scotland might adopt his metrical Psalms, but they preferred to sing the ones from Geneva.

James was bookish, uncertain, and somewhat shifty. He was the only fervent pacifist to sit on the English throne. In addition, he was effeminate in manner, a spendthrift, and intensely vain. During his reign he totally neglected the splendid Royal Navy developed by Henry and Elizabeth. England was becoming a maritime power without a navy. James also believed passionately in the divine right of kings and held exalted views of royal prerogatives. One modern biographer termed him "the wisest fool in Christendom."

Scotland, where James had been king since he was one year old, was a different world from England. Parliamentary democracy had not progressed as far as it had in England, where the House of Commons had evolved into a force with which the monarch would have to reckon. A Scottish king held the throne by balancing off competing factions of nobles and clan leaders. The Scottish Parliament held little power. James had seen democracy in action when working with the Kirk (Church of Scotland) and he didn't like it. "A Scottish Presbytery," he said once, "agreeth with a monarchy as God with the Devil...Then Jack, Tom, Will and Dick shall meet and at their pleasure censure me and my council."

Religious Conflict

On his way from Edinburgh to London to assume his new duties, James was presented with a petition bearing about 1,000 signatures, the so-called "Millenary Petition" which outlined the grievances of the Puritan-minded clergy against the established Church. (It is important to remember that at that time no one could worship God legally outside the established church. Dissenters had to work within the church to change it enough to accomodate their interests.)

Puritans placed great hope in James, since he liked Calvinism. They were soon disappointed. Although James embraced many of the Puritan doctrines, he despised democratic, free church organizations and saw them as a threat to his absolute royal power. He also acted deceitfully to obtain political favor, fawning over enemies who could hurt him, while taking the alliances of friends for granted. (Later, James would behead the folk hero Sir Walter Raleigh to appease the ambassador from hostile Spain.)

In one of his first acts, James liberalized the Elizabethan restrictions on Catholics. At the time, Catholics were, with some reason, perceived as the advance forces of the enemy, Spain. When an alarming number of Catholics emerged, indicating that Rome had more allegiance in England than was thought, popular panic caused James to retract his liberal policies.

As the clamps screwed down once again, several leading Catholic families who supported the policies of the Jesuits, eager to return England to Rome at any cost, plotted to assasinate the king. And, because of the great power it held, they wanted to destroy Parliament as well. They planned the blow for November 5, 1605, when James would attend the opening of Parliament.

Aided by military engineers who had fought for Spain in the Netherlands, the plotters placed 36 barrels of gunpowder under the House of Lords. Their scheme came to light in October through a mysterious letter and the conspirators, including some Jesuit priests, were rounded up and executed. The plot undermined the fortunes of Catholics in England. For nearly 200 years afterwards, the English clung to a powerful distrust of Catholicism. The English still celebrate Guy Fawkes Day on November 5, burning effigies of Fawkes, one of the plotters, to celebrate the suppression of the Gunpowder Plot.

Meanwhile, the Puritan faction wanted a hearing. A conference was called at Hampton Court in January, 1604. James attended, and four Puritans were summoned to meet with nine bishops, seven deans and archdeacons, and five ecclesiastical lawyers. The Puritans were willing to temper some of their earlier demands, such as the abolition of bishops. James, it is said, gave a five-hour speech on the evils rampant in the church. One attending bishop wrote, "On that day his majesty did wonderfully play the puritan." But that was the first part of the speech. Toward the end, he lambasted the Puritans. He announced, "I will make them conform or I will harry them out of the land, or yet do worse." The result was a standoff. The Puritan pleas made little impact and the clerics despaired of the Puritan inability to "listen to reason."

A New Translation

When the conference seemed to come to a draw, John Reynolds, President of Corpus Christi College, Oxford, and spokesperson for the Puritan delegation, came up with a suggestion. He complained about the biblical translations used in the Book of Common Prayer. He then "moved his Majesty, that there might be a new translation of the Bible, because those which were allowed in the

Corpus Christi College, Oxford, as seen today

reigns of Henry the eighth and Edward the sixth, were corrupt and not answerable to the truth of the Original" (spelling modernized). Most likely, Reynolds raised the issue for the sake of argument over the Scriptures used in the Book of Common Prayer, which were drawn from the Great Bible, intending that these passages might be revised. As for the whole Bible, he was quite happy with the Geneva version.

Bancroft, Bishop of London, amended the motion to exclude controversial notes and the king agreed, since he disliked the Geneva notes. James then

> gave this caveat (upon a word cast out by my Lord of London [Bancroft]) that no marginal notes should be added, having found in them which are annexed to the Geneva translation (which he saw in a Bible given him by an English Lady), some notes very partial, untrue, seditious, and savoring too much of dangerous and traitorous conceits. As for examples, Exod. 1.19 where the marginal note alloweth *disobedience to Kings*. And 2 Chron. 15.16, the note taxeth *Asa* for despising his mother, *only* and *not killing her*. [Spelling modernized; italics added]

Reynolds must have been amazed. The conference agenda had nothing to do with Bible translations, yet this was the major outcome of the meeting. But the translation proposal had struck the heart of bookish, literary James, himself keen on biblical translation. He would take more delight in shepherding a magnificent new translation than he would in building a palace, and certainly more joy than in maintaining a powerful fleet. Bancroft protested, "If every man's humour should be followed, there would be no end of translating." But His Majesty's excitement was intense. He determined not only to allow a translation, but to be the motive force behind it, an idea which did not please the bishops in attendance.

The Preface to the ensuing translation gives a hint of the mood of the meeting. "And although [the motion to prepare a new translation] was judged to be but a very poor and empty shift, yet even hereupon did his majesty begin to bethink himself of the good that might ensue by a new translation, and presently after gave order for this translation."

Thus, in a state of surprise bordering on shock, with an otherwise ineffectual king spurring on the churchmen, the greatest of all English Bible translations began.

The Work Begins

King James delegated much of the work through Bancroft, who represented the then-vacant See of Canterbury, while still taking an active interest in the project. To achieve the goal of a translation acceptable to all parties, James ordered in February, 1604, that the work "be done by the best learned in both Universities, after them to be reviewed by the Bishops, and the chief learned of the Church; from them to be presented to the *Privy-Council*; and lastly to be ratified by his *Royal authority*, and so this whole Church to be bound unto it, and none other" [spelling modernized].

The Dean of Westminster and the Regius Professors of Hebrew at both Oxford and Cambridge were asked to name persons competent for this task. By July 22, 1604, the King could write Bancroft that he had appointed 54 men for the task. Various lists of these scholars give different names, about 50 in all counting every list, but only 47 on any one list. They represented the finest biblical scholarship of their time. Those without specific assignments were invited to contribute their comments and scholarly advice. A call went out to all Bishops to urge their clergy to bring this project to the attention of any parishioner who had the linguistic or scholarly skills to make a contribution.

The group divided into six companies, each company with a center for meeting and a specific part of the Scripture to translate. The centers were Cambridge, Oxford, and Westminster. Each company had its distinguished leaders: the respective Regius Professors of Greek and Hebrew for Cambridge and Oxford, and the Dean of Westminster and the Dean of Chester for Westminster. The work was divided among them as follows.

1. Genesis through 2 Kings (Westminster Company)

2. 1 Chronicles through Ecclesiastes (Cambridge Company)

3. Isaiah through Malachi (Oxford Company)

4. The Apocrypha (Cambridge Company)

5. The four Gospels, Acts, Revelation (Oxford Company)

6. Romans through Jude (Westminster Company)

The plan went like this: In each of the six companies, each member would work on a chapter or chapters individually. Then he would meet with his colleagues so that the whole company might debate the merits of any translation, decide on choice of variant readings, argue disputed points, and come to a consensus of what should go in the final manuscript.

When a company had completed a whole book of the Bible, it was passed to representatives of the other companies for review. If a review company had

A CONSTELLATION OF BRILLIANT SCHOLARS

A scholarly evaluation of the qualities of the revision team and their resources comes from S.L. Greenslade, Regius Professor of Ecclesiastical History in the University of Oxford. (Additional identification of the scholars supplied in brackets.)

> Scholarship, especially Hebrew scholarship, had much improved in England since the mid-sixteenth century. The excellent continental scholars Fagius, Tremellius and Chevalier had been brought over to teach Hebrew at Cambridge, the early dictionaries and grammars upon which Tyndale and his successors depended had been revised or superseded, and there was more knowledge of the cognate languages, Aramaic and Syriac. Increasing familiarity with Jewish commentaries on the Old Testament was an important factor in Bible study and translation. Kimhi, whose Hebrew is straightforward, was widely and directly known, the more difficult Rashi and Ibn Ezra at least at second hand through the commentaries of Mercier. Among the revisers Edward Lively [Fellow of Trinity College] was a good Hebraist (but he died in 1605), [Dr.] Lancelot Andrewes [Dean of Westminster, master of 15 languages, famous preacher and devotional writer, and a high churchman] was regarded as a brilliant linguist, [Mr. William] Bedwell [St. John's College, Cambridge, the father of Arabic studies in England] was perhaps the most distinguished Orientalist of his day. Other good Semitists were [Dr.] Miles Smith [Canon of Hereford, energetic Puritan, and writer of the KJV Preface], [Dr.] John Reynolds [President, Corpus Christi College, Cambridge, great Puritan scholar and teacher of Richard Hooker, the classic exponent of the Anglican position] and Thomas Harrison [Vice-Master of Trinity College]. [Mr. Lawrence] Chaderton [or Chatterton, Master of Emmanuel College and one of the Puritans at the Hampton Court conference; he lived to be an active senior of 103 years] and [Mr. Richard] Kilby [or Kilbye, Rector of Lincoln College and friend of angler Issac Walton] knew the rabbis. Sir Henry Savile, editor of the Eton Chrysostom [and Provost of Eton, a great scholar keen on the new sciences, to whom his wife once said, "I wish I were a book. Then you would respect me."], was eminent among Greek scholars, [Dr. Hadrian de] Saravia's [Canon of Canterbury, born on the Continent of Hispano-Flemish parentage] knowledge of modern languages was a considerable asset. Despite the omission of two of the best contemporary Hebraists, Andrew Willett and the cantankerous [Hugh] Broughton [who had earlier planned an independent translation and done work on several biblical books, the results of which were in the hands of the KJV team], they were unquestionably a strong team.[2]

This painting, by an unknown artist, shows the brilliant company of translators presenting their finished work to James I.

doubts or questions, they passed their concerns back to the original company. (King James was quite insistent on this careful process of review to avoid any idiosyncratic renderings.) Should this process fail to resolve the difference, the matter would wait for the end of the project, when two representatives from each company met to review the entire work. Inquiries on particularly difficult matters were to be directed to outside specialists.

The plan to use separate companies of translators resembles the Bishops' Bible plan to use separate individual translators for different books. The great attention to review and coordination, however, might reflect a concern to avoid the inconsistencies of the Bishops' Bible which lacked a final, sure editorial hand.

The spirit of the translators is reflected in Miles Smith's prefatory "The Translators to the Reader," where he writes:

> Truly (good Christian Reader) we never thought from the beginning, that we should need to make a new Translation, nor yet to make a bad one a good one, (for them the imputation of *Sixtus* [V, Pope 1585–1590 and leader of the Catholic Counter-Reformation] had been true in some sort, that our people had been fed with gall of Dragons instead of wine, with whey instead of milk) but to make a good one better, or out of many good ones,

one principal good one, not justly to be excepted against; that hath been our endeavour, that our mark. To that purpose there were many chosen, that were greater in other men's eyes then in their own, and that sought the truth rather than their own praise. [*Spelling modernized; brackets added.*]

A Great Work

It is not often that a committee produces a monumental work of literature as did this team of scholars. Their translation is still read and loved and admired after nearly 400 years. The 15 rules under which they operated, almost certainly drawn up by Bishop Bancroft, are worth citing. Several rules had to do with organization and procedure, which has been discussed. Others spelled out principles of translation and they are quoted below. (It is interesting to compare them with the summary of the rules for the Bishops' Bible, page 98.)

The Rules to be observed in the Translation of the Bible

1. The ordinary Bible read in the Church, commonly called the *Bishops' Bible*, to be followed, and as little altered as the Truth of the original will permit.

2. The names of the Prophets, and the Holy Writers, with the other Names of the Text, to be retained, as nigh as may be, accordingly as they were vulgarly used.

3. The Old Ecclesiastical Words to be kept, *viz.* the Word *Church* not to be translated *Congregation* &c.

4. When a Word has diverse Significations [meanings or possible translations], that to be kept which hath been most commonly used by the most of the Ancient Fathers, being agreeable to the Propriety of the Place, and the Analogy of Faith.

5. The Division of the Chapters to be altered, either not at all, or as little as may be, if Necessity so require.

6. No Marginal Notes at all to be affixed, but only for the explanation of the *Hebrew* or *Greek* Words, which cannot without some circumlocution, so briefly and fitly be expressed in the Text.

7. Such Quotations of Places to be marginally set down as shall serve for the fit Reference of one Scripture to another.

[Rules 8-13 deal with organizational arrangements already discussed.]

14. These translations to be used when they agree better with the Text than the Bishops' Bible. Tindoll's [Tyndale's], Matthew's [or Rogers'], Coverdale's, Whitchurch's [Great Bible, so-called because Whitchurch printed the fifth edition], Geneva.

15. Besides the said Directors before mentioned, three or four of the most Ancient and Grave Divines, in either of the Universities, not employed in Translating, to be assigned by the Vice-Chancellor, upon Conference with the rest of the Heads, to be Overseers of the Translations as well *Hebrew* as *Greek*, for the better Observation of the 4th Rule above specified. [*Spelling modernized; brackets added*]

Rules 1, 3, and 6 reflect the religious tensions of the times. These decisions were as much a matter of politics as of faith. They were intended to appease the established church party and to keep the new Bible from becoming another Puritan-leaning Geneva Bible.

Rule 2 tried to solve a problem in some earlier translations where, for instance, the name of Isaiah was spelled differently in the Old Testament and the New, or from book to book in the same Testament. The *KJV* translators were careful about this, but several cases of different spellings in the Old and the New Testaments crept in, such as Elias (NT) and Elijah (OT), Greek and Hebrew forms for the same name. But it also meant that they did not feel free to simplify some Hebrew terms for the common reader. Where previous translations, at Genesis 35.8, said that Deborah was buried under a tree which "was called the oak of lamentation," the King James revisers felt compelled to render it as Hebrew, the oak that "was called Allon Bachuth."

Rule 4 strove to avoid rendering words in such a manner as to reflect a new point of view. Consider the Greek *dikaioo* which the *KJV* translators usually rendered as "justify." It lends itself to other renderings: "to make righteous," "to make right with God," "to render innocent," "to make free," and so forth. The translators followed Rule 4 in using the traditional theological term. (Some contemporary translations opt for other renderings, because they feel modern readers are less comfortable with traditional theological terms.) The translators were urged to make their choice among options based on context ("Propriety of the Place") and appropriateness for expressing Christian meaning ("Analogy of Faith").

Rule 5 kept the traditional chapter divisions inherited from the thirteenth century. These were rather arbitrary. The translators could have improved the sense in many places by altering the divisions. For instance, 1 Corinthians 12.31 clearly begins the thought of 1 Corinthians 13. The outline in any commentary will reveal that the thought units of a biblical writing do not follow the traditional chapter divisions. But ever since the Geneva Bible, people were regularly quoting Scripture by chapter and verse reference. Changing the scheme of division would have upset many potential readers.

Rule 7 encourages cross references, by which Scripture can interpret Scripture, an important study aid taken over from earlier versions. The cross-references in contemporary *KJV* Bibles, often appearing in the center column, are not those of the original edition, but rather those of modern publishers.

Rule 14 lists the versions to be consulted officially and used where their renderings are an improvement over the Bishops' Bible. This list clearly shows how all the major translations from Tyndale on ultimately influenced the *King James Version*. Though the Rheims Testament isn't listed, we know that the translators made use of it as well.

Rule 15 opened the door for very conservative and old reviewers, another attempt by Bancroft (and James) to insure this would not become a radical, Puritan revision.

How much did these rules help (or hinder) the translators? To answer that, we must see them at work.

9 PRODUCING THE KING JAMES BIBLE

The translators had a plan of organization and a carefully crafted set of guidelines, as did their predecessors who worked on the Bishops' Bible. We know this remarkable group produced a monumental work which would influence not only the future of English Bible translations but also English literature in all its forms. One wonders, though, if this team realized, as they labored, what a treasure they were producing?

The Translators Go to Work

The vast majority of the translators worked long and hard at their assigned tasks. One example is John Bois, born in Suffolk in 1560, and a Cambridge graduate. It was said that he could read the Hebrew Bible at age six and write the Hebrew alphabet with elegance. He was industrious. As a Cambridge undergraduate, he studied from 4:00 a.m. to 8:00 p.m. He turned from a medical career to pursue the humanities and was assigned, as a Fellow of St. John's College, to the Sixth Company, dealing with the Apocrypha. Bois worked all week at St. John's, returning to his parish on Saturday to prepare for Sunday's sermon. Some university men, his biographer infers, did not take kindly to the appointment of a country preacher to this august group. Dr. Bois was also chosen to be among the select group of company representatives who did the final work on the translation and prepared it for press.

Several of the translators worked far into the night every day of the week, sometimes risking their health. John Reynolds, who first inspired the project and eventually died working on the translation, met regularly on his deathbed with his colleagues to compare notes.

Finding the financial resources for all this intellectual manpower was another matter. As the enthusiastic patron of the project, James could have been expected to foot the bills from the royal purse. Fifty or so key intellectuals, academic and ecclesiastical leaders, would devote years of full-time labor to this project. Under better circumstances, stipends would have been provided for them by the king, but after about a year on the throne, James, ever the spendthrift, had exhausted the royal accounts. Ultimately, James never spent a single farthing on his pet project. True to form, he persuaded Bancroft that although he delighted in the translation more than in the recent peace with Spain, and that he personally would gladly have borne the expense, some of his lords did not find this convenient and advised against financing the project.

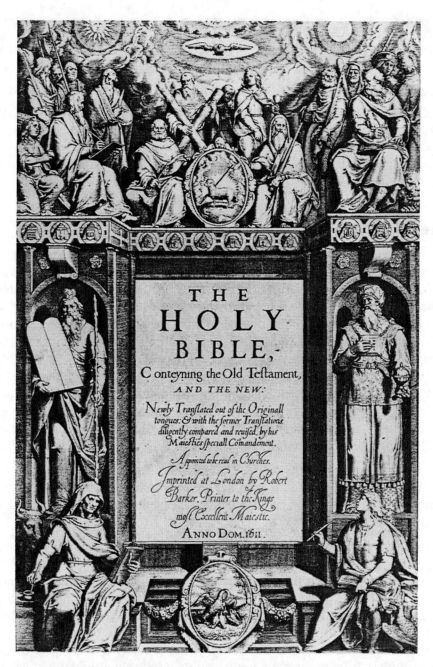

The title page of the first edition, 1611, of the King James Bible is a masterpiece of engraving and printing. The design shows the influence of classical art. At the top of the page, a dove, representing God's Spirit, flows over a grouping of biblical worthies. In mid-center, we see the Agnus Dei or Lamb of God symbol. On the left appears Moses with the tablets of Law. On the right is Ezra, who restored the Temple.

To make ends meet, the translators were forced to improvise. Bancroft was delegated to do the best he could for them. When the companies met in common session at the universities and Westminster, they received their food and lodging from the host institution, so that much was covered. Bancroft then searched for available ecclesiastical appointments that carried an income while allowing the incumbent free time for translation work.

Some translators he persuaded to continue with promises of future appointments or promotions. Bancroft himself was made Archbishop of Canterbury. Lancelot Andrewes became Bishop of Chicester in 1605, Bishop of Ely in 1609, and in 1619 Bishop of Winchester, then the most ancient and richest see in England. Andrewes obtained a justly deserved reputation for hospitality. "My Lord of Winchester," it was said, "keeps Christmas all year round."

Most translators, though, simply took time from their regular appointments. Consequently, many dioceses, parishes, and universities ended up subsidizing the translation. Some of the translators suffered financial loss working on the project.

Some financial support came from private business. At the end of the project, 12 key translators representing the six companies gathered in London to labor for nine months on the final revisions. During this period, they each received three shillings a week from the Company of Stationers, the printers' guild. This cash may have come from Robert Barker, who would print this Bible. At least, he later claimed that he paid £2,500—a staggering sum—toward the revision.

Bois was the only one to take notes at this final revision meeting. They explain in detail how the translators proceeded in their work. These notes were lost from 1688 until 1964, when Professor Ward Allen traced down a handwritten copy among the papers of William Fulham, a seventeenth-century antiquarian and collector, whose papers were in the Corpus Christi College Library at Oxford University.

Preparing the Text

The review process so dear to King James proved a blessing. Each talented translator had a chance to put his comments into the mix. When they met for their review sessions, the translators would keep resource and reference works in front of them. One of their number would read the draft text. Others would argue their points, cite their references, put in their judgments. They took their work very seriously. In modern terms, we might say they had a good system of quality control. The king's personal interest in this project may have motivated them to do their very finest work.

Perhaps the greatest improvement in accuracy came in the Old Testament, because the translators had the advantage of the great strides taken in understanding Hebrew and similar ancient languages since the Geneva version. They also used the following new critical texts well: the Latin Old Testament of Arias Montanus (based on the Hebrew) and the Latin Bible of Junius and Tremellius (from the Hebrew in the Old Testament and the Greek and Syriac for the Apocrypha) published in 1579, Tremellius' Latin version of the Syriac New Testament, as well as the earlier works by Munster, Pagninus, and Beza. Although the translators applied state-of-the-art scholarship to their task, the most advanced scholars of their day still did not fully understand Hebrew tenses and many Hebrew idioms.

The translators also consulted earlier English versions of the Old Testament. The prophetical books show many changes due to the influence of the Geneva Bible. They made fewer changes from the normative Bishops' Bible text when working on the historical and poetical books, but these tend to be independent (based on their own judgment), especially in the Apocrypha. In addition, they referred to several recent translations in various European languages.

In hindsight, we can say that for the Greek of the New Testament they were less fortunate. The major manuscript discoveries in this field were not made until the nineteenth century. Instead, they worked with the best critical editions of the text available at their time. They used Tremellius' Latin version based on the Greek, along with Greek texts prepared by Estienne (also called Stephanus) and Beza. The changes they made in the New Testament translation of the Bishops' Bible were influenced mostly by the Geneva and Rheims Testaments: the Geneva New Testament for interpretation and the Rheims Testament for vocabulary, which used more Latinisms than earlier versions.

The English of the *King James Version (KJV)* pulses with the rhythm and vigor of Tyndale and Coverdale from nearly a century before. Professor Laura H. Wild describes the King James text this way:

> A few of Wyclif's phrases are here [in the *KJV*], but Tyndale is largely responsible for the Bishops' Bible which was used as its foundation. [Through the Great Bible] Coverdale put his delicate touch on [the *KJV*, and] the sturdy tone of the Geneva Text and the sonorous Latinisms of the Rhemish New Testament modified certain sentences. But Tyndale was the genius who penetrated to the very heart of the Scripture, finding priceless treasures, then sent it on its way in English waters like a ship laden with life-giving fruits.[3]

Publication

Finally the book was ready. Since the project began in early 1604, about three years went into preparatory work, two years and nine months into actual translating, and another nine months preparing the final manuscript for the press. Thomas Bilson and Miles Smith put the finishing touches on the version. It came out in 1611, from the presses of Robert Barker, the King's printer.

The title reads: *The Holy Bible, Conteyning the Old Testament, and the New: Newly Translated out of the Originall tongues: & with the former Translations diligently compared and reuised, by his Majesties speciall Commandement. Appointed to be read in Churches.*

The first edition was a large folio (see note, "Sizes of Books," Chapter 4). Each page displayed a double-column type block of 59 lines per column measuring 9 by 14 1/2 inches, printed in fine Gothic black letter. Chapter headings, marginal notes, and other material not in the original text were printed in roman letters. In those times, binding was often done to the customer's order, so the overall size of the page depends on how much the binder trimmed off. Existing copies with wide enough margins for book collectors to identify them as "fine and large" have pages of 10 1/2 by 16 1/2 inches.

The Bible contained some 1,500 pages, measuring three inches thick without binding. The engraved title page depicted Moses on the left and Aaron on the right, with the Evangelists in the four corners. Also worked into the design were the sacred name of God written in Hebrew, a dove symbolizing the Holy Spirit, and a pelican, a symbol for Christ's suffering and the Eucharist.

The New Testament had a separate title page, featuring the traditional emblems of the twelve tribes of Israel down the left side and the symbolic emblems of the Twelve Apostles down the right side. There were in addition the traditional emblems of the four Evangelists: Matthew (an angel) and Mark (a lion) on the top of the page, with Luke (an ox) and John (an eagle) along the bottom.

Some 18 pages of additional matter were added in the front of the book. This material included a dedication to King James: "To the most high and mighty Prince James, by the grace of God, King of Great Britain, France, and Ireland, Defender of the Faith, &c.," designed to flatter a vain monarch. Next came a lengthy and excellent essay, "The Translators to the Reader," probably from the pen of Miles Smith. It is regrettably left out of many modern printings, but it contains the complete rationale for the translation and a great deal of useful information on how the translators handled their task.

The rest of the introductory items were devotional or study aids: a calendar-almanac listing holy days and morning and evening Scripture readings, a condensed almanac for 39 years, a table "to find Easter for ever," several lists of Scripture readings, and a chart of the books of the Bible, including the Apocrypha, with the number of chapters in each.

Within the text, each chapter began with a summary heading and each column carried a running headnote. There were 17,000 cross references and marginal notes. The notes dealt solely with linguistic and textual matters such as alternative renderings or variant readings from other manuscript sources. The interpretative and doctrinal notes of earlier versions were carefully avoided.

A CONSERVATIVE APPROACH

The King James translators strove to meet the expectations of their readers. They had a sober—perhaps somewhat bitter—realization that people resist change in their religious life. They felt that their new translation, coming on the heels of so many others, would present all the change that people could handle. They expressed their attitude in the translators' preface: "For he that meddleth with men's religion in any part, meddleth with their custom, nay, with their freehold; and though they find no content in that which they have, yet they cannot abide to hear of altering" [modernized spelling].

The translators chose to use the chapter divisions of Stephen Langton from the 13th century and the verse divisions developed by Robert Estienne in 1551, which were used in the Geneva Bible. And, like the Geneva Bible, each verse was printed as a separate unit. In time, the wide use of the King James Bible using this format would give more currency to the temptation to deal with the Bible verse-by-verse, without reference to the larger context. This style of setting verses opened a page to the eye by offering more white space (an important consideration with a heavy, blackletter text) and making the text easier to read.

The translators bowed to tradition when they chose blackletter type for their first folio edition rather than the more readable roman type introduced in the Geneva Bible. However, the subsequent editions, in the smaller quarto and octavo sizes designed for home and personal reading, adopted roman type. In these editions words which were necessary for the English sense but not in the original language were printed in italics.

The translators adopted this arrangement in an attempt to be frank and honest about their translation, since previous versions had been heavily criticized by those who claimed certain words or phrases weren't in the original languages. Hebrew, for instance, doesn't use a separate verb "to be," which is essential in English. Thus, Psalm 23.1a reads, "The LORD *is* my shepherd." Some modern readers mistakenly think these italicized words and phrases indicate stress or

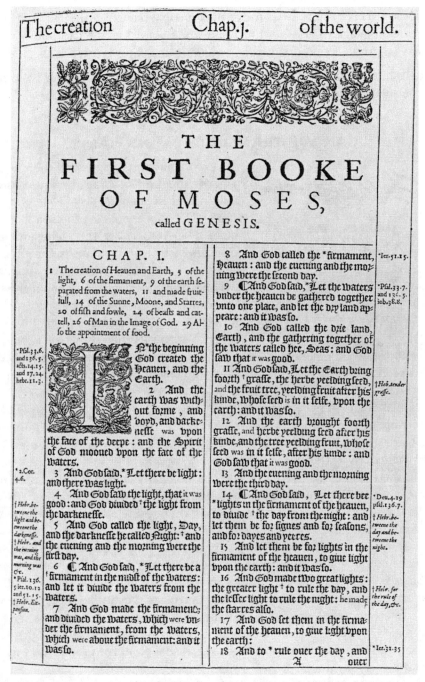

Genesis, chapter 1, from the King James Bible. Note the black-letter type, the verses set separately, the opening chapter summary, the paragraph marker (at verse 6), and the use of roman type for words added by translators. In the margin are cross-references to related verses and notes about translation of certain words.

emphasis. This is not the case. Today most people recognize that *any* translation from one language to another must add some words in order to make sense in the new language. Consequently, few modern translations use this mechanism.

The translators also adopted LORD (in large and small capital letters) to represent the specific name of God.

CAN WE TRANSLATE GOD'S NAME?

God's name in early paleo-Hebrew (above) and the conventional square script (below)

Hebrew manuscripts represent the specific name of the God of Israel by four characters—in our alphabet, YHWH. Jews have refrained from pronouncing the sacred name out of deep respect for the commandment against misuse of God's name. Hebrew is usually written without vowels. Vowel points—dots and short lines written beneath the letters—came to be added in the sixth to seventh centuries A.D. as an aid to liturgical readers. For YHWH they chose the vowels of Adonai, the word meaning Lord in the more general sense. Adonai was the word pronounced by Jews in public worship when they encountered YHWH in the texts.

From about 1520 on, scholars felt that Jehovah represented the best English rendering of this name. However, they were not able to know, from the resources available to them, that in imposing the vowels of Adonai onto the consonants YHWH they were creating a new hybrid term that had never existed. In the 20th century, research into the way early church fathers wrote this name in Greek suggested that the best pronunciation would be Yahweh. Thus, while the American Standard Version (1901) adopted Jehovah, some modern versions, such as the Jerusalem Bible, use Yahweh.

Most modern translations, though, make explicit the practice which the early Christians used when reading from the Septuagint, the Greek translation of the Hebrew Scriptures used by both Jews and Christians in the first century. Rather than translate the sacred name, the early Christians substituted the Greek word *kyrios* (meaning Lord) when they read the Scriptures aloud. To show that YHWH is intended, modern translations use LORD (using large and small capitals). This special typographical treatment keeps the reader from confusing God's name with the everyday use of the word "lord."

Four uses of Jehovah do appear in the text of the King James Bible, however, and three more with Jehovah in a combination form, in those passages where the personal divine name is announced.

Off the Press

The first press run was 20,000 copies, a large quantity for that time. Two separate presses were used, each to produce identical copies. But the printing technology of the time could not produce "identical" editions, since the type used on each press was set separately. Thus, copies from press number one were printed from different type than those from press number two. This led to discrepancies between the volumes printed on the separate presses. Many of these differences are minute, but they appear on almost every page of the separate press runs.

The biggest discrepancy occurred at Ruth 3.15. Bibles printed on one press read, "he measured six *measures* of barley, and laid *it* on her: and he [Boaz] went into the city." Those printed on the other press read, "and she [Ruth] went into the city." Thus the two initial issues are known as the "He Bible" and the "She Bible." This is a case of alternative readings creeping in. Both pronouns are possible, but the translators intended "she." Later printings drew on either the He or She Bible and perpetuated the differences for a long time. (Modern translations are about equally divided in their choice of "he" or "she.")

A misprint, never corrected, has caused bewilderment to many Bible readers. At Matthew 23.24, it reads, "straining at a gnat." How does one strain *at* a gnat? It should have read "straining *out* a gnat."

Into the Churches

The title page of the *King James Version* read, "Appointed to be read in Churches," and the version has come to be called, especially in Great Britain, the Authorized Version (*AV*). In truth, it was never officially authorized by governmental action, nor was its use in the churches required by law. The term Authorized Version is a false claim, especially since both the Great and Bishops' Bibles were authorized in the stricter sense of being required. This was more an "endorsed" version. It soon made its way into churches because printings of the Bishops' Bible ceased after 1602. But in their sermons and writings, many of the *KJV* translators continued to use the Geneva or Bishops' versions.

Not every scholar greeted the new translation with enthusiasm. Some denounced it for relying too much on the Greek Septuagint rather than on the Hebrew. Others accused the translators of blasphemy and called them "damnable corruptors" of God's Word. Puritans especially doubted the integrity of a translation involving so many "high church" people.

Hugh Broughton, the great biblical scholar who was not invited to participate in the translation because of his eccentricity and bad temper, published his vitriolic criticism of the final work. Broughton railed at the timidity of the translators which caused them to place better renderings in the margin rather than in the text. He counted the number of "idle words" and declared that the translators would have to answer for their sloth on the Day of Judgment. Broughton even went so far as to predict that Richard Bancroft, the organizer of the translation and Archbishop of Canterbury, would find his ultimate eternal abode in hell.

The public clung to their love for the Geneva Bible and it took a generation for the *KJV* to replace it in popular affection. Puritans especially loved the Geneva version and when the Pilgrims came to the New World in 1620, it was the Geneva version they chose to bring with them.

A casual look at the publication histories of these two translations reveals the time it took for the historic *KJV* Bible to gain broad acceptance. Between 1611 and 1614, six editions of the Geneva Bible appeared, compared with at least 17 for the *KJV*. By 1644, the trend favoring the *KJV* became clear. At that date, some 15 Geneva editions had come off the press, in contrast to a remarkable 182 editions of the *KJV*.

The quarto and octavo editions of the *King James Version* appeared in 1612, beautiful books that resembled the best Geneva editions. A separate tiny duodecimo edition of the New Testament was printed in 1611, and an octavo version in 1612. As the new Bible caught on, editions multiplied, and so did the variants from the original editions. As early as 1613 one edition already showed more than 300 variants from the original two issues.

Later Revisions

Many people assume that the beloved King James Bible has never undergone revision. This is not correct. Revisions to correct errors were made in 1629 and 1638, but each revision seemed only to add more misprints. Ironically, editions of the Geneva Bible show far fewer errors. It seems that for some reason the quality of work by English printers had begun to decline.

One printing in 1631 listed one of the Ten Commandments as "Thou shalt commit adultery." The authorities fined the printers £300 for this slip, and labeled the edition the "Wicked Bible." An edition of 1653 had at 1 Corinthians 6.9, "the unrighteous shall inherit the Kingdom of God," earning it the label of the Unrighteous Bible.

Cotton Mather, the New England Puritan leader, complained in 1702 of "Scandalous Errors of the Press-work" through which the "Holy Bible itself...hath been affronted." An elegant edition from Oxford in 1717 titled the twentieth chapter of Luke, "The Parable of the Vinegar" [Vineyard], and is known among collectors as the "Vinegar Bible." This edition set a near record for misprints and errors.

THE KING JAMES BIBLE IN AMERICA

Though the Pilgrims brought the Geneva Bible with them from England, by the time printing got started in the colonies, the KJV was in popular circulation. However, publishing of the KJV was restricted to the King's printers in England. As early as 1688, William Bradford of Philadelphia proposed an American edition of the Bible, but the idea was not picked up. Cotton Mather, despairing of printers' errors, labored 15 years on his own American edition but could not find a publisher for it either here or in England. The manuscript is still preserved in the Massachusetts Historical Society.

John Fleming, a printer in Boston, sought 300 subscribers to underwrite "as correct and beautiful an Edition of the Sacred Writings" as any in the world. But he could not raise his quota of subscriptions.

With the American Revolution, the need to seek the King's license for printing the Bible fell by the wayside, but the war posed other obstacles. A committee of the Continental Congress explored the possibility of an American edition and declared that the fledgling States did not have the proper type nor enough paper. So they recommended importing 20,000 Bibles from Holland, Scotland and elsewhere in Europe. Seven colonies favored the proposal; six did not.

An enterprising Scottish printer, Robert Aitken, had come to Philadelphia in 1769. The discussion in Congress inspired him and in 1777 he published the New Testament, with three more editions following swiftly in 1778, 1779, and 1781. Congress then endorsed his plan to print the whole Bible, which appeared in 1782.

Robert Aitken, c. 1734–1802, who printed the first English Bible in America in 1777, in an early engraving.

Congress, however, declined to give him exclusive rights and, despite the recommendation of the Presbyterian Synod to adopt his Bible, Aitken lost a great deal of money on the project. In the next ten years, many other editions appeared from other printers.

Another printer, Isaiah Thomas, devised an unusual scheme to finance his 1791 edition. He set the price at 42 shillings, one half to be paid in advance of printing. For the advance payment, he would accept rye, wheat, corn, butter, or pork, delivered to his stores in Boston or Worcester. The remaining 21 shillings were to be paid in cash upon delivery of the printed Bible. George Washington wrote him a commendation and he received several honorary degrees.

In that same year, Isaac Collins in New Jersey who had in 1788 published a New Testament, brought out an edition of the Bible noted for its scrupulous printing accuracy. Only one broken letter and one wrong punctuation mark crept in; his careful reading of the proofs eleven times paid off.

Other American editions appeared before the end of the eighteenth century: in New York, Hugh Gaine (NT, 1790, Bible 1792) and Hodge and Campbell (1792); in Philadelphia, three editions by William Young (1790, 1791/92, and 1794) and Brown's "Self-Interpreting" Bible (1792).

Parliament passed a bill in 1653 to create a revision committee which finally was appointed in 1657. Unfortunately, nothing came of the project. It remained for the Universities to standardize the text. Both Oxford and Cambridge Universities, in a sense, "owned" the text because of their mutual involvement in its translation. At Sidney Sussex College, Cambridge, Thomas Parris prepared a careful edition which regularized the spelling and punctuation, corrected errors, and emended the text to correct translation mistakes. This edition, of 1762, became known as the Cambridge Standard Edition. In 1769, Benjamin Blayney, Regius Professor of Hebrew at Oxford, introduced another corrected edition which also modernized the spelling. This is known as the Oxford Standard Edition and it is essentially this text of the *KJV* with which we are now familiar.

Most emendations in the various revisions were designed to improve the text. For instance, where the original 1611 edition had "Thou art Christ," at Matthew 16.16, the revised editions had "Thou art the Christ." "He came and worshipped" in Mark 5.6 was changed to "he ran and worshipped." Most of the changes were minor.

Modernized spelling strikes the reader as the most obvious change in the Oxford Standard Edition. Compare Psalm 23.1-6 in a current edition with that of the 1611 edition:

1. The LORD *is* my shepheard, I shall not want.

2. He maketh me to lie downe in greene pastures: he leadeth mee beside the still waters.

3. He restoreth my soule: he leadeth me in the pathes of righteousness, for his names sake.

4. Yea, though I walke through the valley of the shadowe of death, I will feare no euill: for thou *art* with me, thy rod and they staffe, they comfort me.

5. Thou preparest a table before me, in the presence of mine enemies: thou annointest my head with oyle, my cuppe runneth ouer.

6. Surely goodnes and mercie shall followe me all the daies of my life: and I will dwell in the house of the LORD for euer.

Literary Impact

The King James Bible was a translation designed to meet a compromise in the complex ecclesiastical politics of the day. Because it relied on the earlier Bishops' Bible, the language was a trifle out-of-date even as the version went to press, in the same way as Wyclif's translation sounded archaic from the start. Still, we cannot deny the quality of the result. One writer summed up the impact of the King James Bible on our language with these words:

> Not even Shakespeare has more deeply affected English literature than has the *King James Version*. The extent of its influence, which is practically impossible to exaggerate, is well known. Like the man who, taken to see *Hamlet*, remarked later that it was a good play though with too many quotations in it, the most god-less adult whose mother tongue is English cannot fail to find in the Bible much that is already exceedingly familiar. The *King James Version*, having been injected into the stream of the language, has invigorated and enriched all subsequent English prose. There is hardly a book today in decent English that echoes no cadence from it or reflects no phrase. Its effect on English literature was immediate as well as permanent: within a generation or so after its appearance it had shown that it could transform an itinerant tinker such as was John Bunyan into an exemplar of English style.[4]

But the Bible is more than literature. It is God's Word. Compared with the elegant classical Greek, the common idiomatic Greek used in the New Testament sounds rather crude. The stately English of the *King James Version* actually makes the New Testament sound better than it would in Greek. Ultimately, the value of a Bible translation depends upon the accuracy of translation of the best originals.

Tremendous advances in the field of biblical texts would soon cry for a revision of the King James. Lovely and revered as it may be, a 1611 translation simply cannot meet the standards of modern scholarship or reflect current usage in a language that is always changing and evolving. Breakthroughs in textual criticism and the revisions they produced shape the next part of our story of the English Bible.

PART III:

THE MODERN ERA

10 CHALLENGES TO THE KING JAMES BIBLE

The supply of tools for good Bible translating exploded from the late 18th century and into the 19th century. The discovery of older manuscripts and a better understanding of biblical languages led to several independent translations. These set the stage for the first official effort to revise the cherished *King James Version*.

It is useful to make a distinction, even if it is somewhat arbitrary, between two types of Bible translations. Some translations are prepared by a group representing a wide range of Christian interests and are intended for public use in churches. The Great, Bishops', and King James Bibles are examples of this category. We will term these "official" versions. Other translations are developed by one (or a few) scholars who do not work under official ecclesiastical supervision. These translators feel more free to exercise their personal, independent judgments. We will call this category "independent" translations.

This distinction has nothing to do with quality. An independent translation can present readings far superior to official versions. The excellent Geneva version, for instance, was an independent translation, as was Tyndale's masterpiece.

Advances in the Texts

Three very old Greek manuscripts of the Bible were discovered after the *KJV* was completed. These and other discoveries made it increasingly obvious that the source texts available to the King James translators left much to be desired.

The first of these treasures, the Codex Alexandrinus dating from the fifth century, was presented by Cyril Lucar, patriarch of Constantinople, to King Charles I of England in 1627, too late to benefit the King James translators.

Another valuable manuscript, the Codex Vaticanus dating from the fourth century, had long disappeared in the Vatican Library. Knowledge of its existence began to circulate in 1533, but it wasn't until after 1810 when Napoleon carted it to Paris as a trophy of war that scholars could begin to study this important manuscript. Serious work on it didn't begin until the 1880s.

The story of the third great find reads like an adventure tale. Konstantin von Tischendorf, perhaps the greatest expert on biblical manuscripts in his day, played the key role. In May of 1844, this scholar was visiting the Monastery of St. Catherine, at the foot of the traditional Mount Sinai in the Holy Land. In the monastery library, he noticed a basket of old sheets of parchment, molded with

A page from the Codex Sinaiticus recovered in 1859 by Konstantin von Tischendorf (1815– 1874). The leaf shown covers John 2.17— 3.25. This codex includes the entire New Testament and almost all of the Old Testament Septuagint.

age. "The librarian, who was a man of information, told me that two heaps like these…had already been committed to the flames" to provide heat, Tischendorf wrote in his diary. The scholar's excitement betrayed him. The monks sensed he was after something of great value and would only allow him to take 43 sheets home for study.

Tischendorf returned in 1853 but the only trace of this manuscript he could find was a scrap with 11 lines

WHAT IS A CODEX?

The earliest copies of New Testament books, like other ancient writings, were written on papyrus, a material made from reeds. In the third and fourth centuries, the codex (plural, codices) became popular. These manuscripts have separate pages, like modern books, which are sewn or bound together. Until paper became available in Europe, the pages of codices were made of parchment or papyrus. The codex format is associated with Christian literature. The Hebrew Scriptures continued to be written on scrolls.

from Genesis, which had been used for scratch paper. He wasn't discouraged, however, and he came back for a third visit in 1859. One of the monks invited him into his cell for refreshments. As they talked, the monk proudly announced that he had read the Septuagint. Tischendorf wrote in his diaries:

> So saying, [the monk] took down from the corner of the room a bulky kind of volume wrapped in red cloth, and laid it before me. I unrolled the cover, and discovered, to my great surprise,

> not only those very fragments which, fifteen years before, I had taken out of the basket, but also other parts... Full of joy, which this time I had the self-command to conceal from the steward and the rest of the community, I asked, as if in a careless way, for permission to take the manuscript into my sleeping-chamber, to look it over more at leisure. There by myself I could give way to the transport of joy which I felt. I knew that I held in my hand the most precious biblical treasure in existence.

Tischendorf did not exaggerate. This was indeed a precious find. His Codex Sinaiticus contained the entire New Testament (the only early codex to do so) and practically all of the Old Testament Septuagint up through Ezra 9.9. It also included parts of two non-canonical writings, the Epistle of Barnabas and the Shepherd of Hermas. Tischendorf recovered 346 sheets of the manuscript, but no one knows how many sheets of this and other invaluable manuscripts went into the fire to warm the monks on chilly desert evenings.

Tischendorf dated his find to the fourth century and later scholars agree. He managed to get permission to take it to Russia to be copied and eventually he presented it to the Czar. It remained in St. Petersburg (later Leningrad) until 1933, when the Soviet government sold it for £100,000 to the British Museum, where it is now on display.

Along with these and other crucial finds, scholars were making great progress in understanding Hebrew idiom and syntax. Textual critics advanced in their attempts to understand the various genres and types of writings in the Old and New Testaments. Serious scholars could see that even the excellent *King James Version* needed to be revised to reflect these important discoveries.

Independent Translations

Dissatisfaction with the *King James Version* came from many quarters. Ben Franklin considered the version obsolete and even blamed its archaic language for the decline in Bible reading. The great sage and patriot offered some samples of a more readable rendering. This is his version of Job 1.6, 7:

> 6. And it being *levee* day in heaven, all God's nobility came to court, to present themselves before him; and Satan also appeared in the circle, as one of the ministry.

> 7. And God said to Satan: You have been a long time absent; where were you? And Satan answered: I have been at my country seat, and in different places visiting my friends.

Franklin was a deist, as were Jefferson, George Washington, and many other leaders in America and England. Deists took a rational view of religion (in

Europe, the same movement got termed "rationalism"). As highly educated people, they preferred a refined and cultivated rendering of Scripture, and Dr. Edward Harwood of London provided one in 1678 with his *A Liberal Translation* of the New Testament. His version of Luke 1.46-48, part of Mary's song of praise known by its Latin name "The Magnificat," goes like this:

> My soul with reverence adores my Creator, and all my faculties with transport join in celebrating the goodness of God, my Savior, who hath in so signal a manner condescended to regard my poor and humble station.

Benjamin Franklin (1706–1790) thought that the obsolete English used in the King James Version hindered Bible reading.

The rationalist movement led to Unitarianism and, later, Universalism, both powerful forces on the British and American religious scene at the end of the 18th century. Translations from these perspectives include the *Wakefield New Testament* in 1791 for the Unitarian position, and in 1798, the *Scarlett* version of the New Testament for the Universalists.

In a more traditional vein, John Wesley, the founder of Methodism, published a conservative revision of the *King James Version* in 1755 under the title *The New Testament with Notes, for Plain Unlettered Men who know only their Mother Tongue.* Wesley rearranged the text into paragraphs, a practice followed in some modern editions of the *King James Version.* He also made many modifications in the renderings of the *KJV* and a considerable number of these were adopted in the *Revised Version* and the *Revised Standard Version.*

John Wesley (1703–1791), leader in the Evangelical Revival in England and founder of Methodism

Daniel Mace, in 1729, published *The New Testament in Greek and English.* His Greek text took account of the more recently available manuscripts. It marked an improvement over the standard text of the day, and scholars a century later still admired his excellent work on improving the Greek text. Mace, a Presbyterian, used the English of his day in his translation.

Anthony Purver, a Quaker, issued his *New and Literal Translation* in 1764, which came to be known as the "Quaker Bible." His English style was a somewhat flowery. For "hallowed" in the Lord's Prayer, Purver chose "sacredly reverenced." (It is interesting to note that an American Quaker-sponsored revision appeared in 1828 in which passages "unsuitable for a mixed audience" are printed in italics below the text.)

One little known but very deserving translation was published in Philadelphia in 1808. It was the work of Charles Thomson, a tutor at the College of Philadelphia (now the University of Pennsylvania) from 1750–1755, where he received his M.A. Thomson later served as Secretary of the Continental Congress from 1775–1783, and when he retired, he devoted himself to Bible translating. His was the first complete Bible translation done in America. He had purchased a copy of the Septuagint at a book sale and became fascinated by the prospect of making an accessible English translation. He titled it *The Holy Bible, containing The Old and New Covenant, commonly called The Old and New Testament: translated from the Greek.*

Rodolphus Dickinson published his *A New and Corrected Version of the New Testament* in Boston in 1833. He attempted to correct what he thought was the inadequate literary quality of the *King James Version.*

Noah Webster, the great student of language and originator of the dictionary that bears his name, revised the King James Bible in 1833 by incorporating "amendments of the language," which meant updating words that had lost or changed meaning and updating the grammar to conform to modern norms. Webster's was more the work of an historian of word usage and grammar than an effort at serious Bible translation.

Women, too, entered the exploding field of Bible translating. Julia E. Smith published *The Holy Bible…translated literally from the original tongues* at Hartford, Connecticut in 1876. She worked from Hebrew and Greek texts and chose to translate every Greek and Hebrew word with the same English word each time it appeared. She thought this method would make the text more clear.

However, consistent translation could obscure meaning, as can be seen from her rendering of Jeremiah 22.23: "Thou dwelling in Lebanon, building a nest in the cedars, how being compassionated in pangs coming to thee the pain as of her bringing forth." Compare that with the rendering in *Today's English Version*:

> You rest secure among the
> > cedars brought from Lebanon;
> but how pitiful you'll be
> > when pains strike you,
> pains like those of a woman in labor.

All told, the period between 1611 and 1881 was fruitful for Bible translations, with some 70 English translations printed. We noted the contributions of Roman Catholics in Chapter 7. From the Jewish perspective, the major work was done by Isaac Leeser. In 1853 at Philadelphia, he published a translation of the Hebrew Scriptures: *The Twenty-Four Books of the Holy Scriptures: carefully translated*

STYLES OF TRANSLATING

Can we translate a word from another language in every case with the same word in our own language? We may get that impression when we begin to study a foreign language and translate workbook sentences. These artificial sentences are created for student use so the beginner can plug an English word in the place of the foreign word. But as soon as students advance to translating authentic literature in a foreign language, they confront idioms, nuances, and subtleties.

There are essentially two styles of translating, and all modern translations fall somewhere on the spectrum between the two, some closer to one end or the other.

One style of translating is called formal correspondence. Here the translator attempts to follow the form of the original as closely as English will allow. There are degrees in this, from the excessively literal to rather smooth English. Generally, though, the English reader can detect something "foreign" in the style of translation. Most Bible translations, for instance, "sound like the Bible"—that is, the underlying Greek and Hebrew syntax shows through.

The other translation style, called functional equivalence, developed more recently. This approach begins with two questions: 1) When the original readers or hearers encountered this text, how would it have affected them emotionally, intellectually, and behaviorally? 2) What form of English expression would produce an equivalent impact on a modern reader or hearer? The term "crucified," for example, would recall for the people of the New Testament era a horrible, shameful death reserved for criminals and traitors. Today the term has lost much of its earlier horror, partly because it recalls for Christians the work of Christ on their behalf. A functional equivalence translator, therefore, might choose "executed" as a translation. Though not literal, it carries for a modern reader the equivalent impact that "crucified" bore in the Roman world of the first century A.D.

The best way to get a feel for the various styles of translating is to compare the same Bible passage in different versions. Some major formal correspondence versions can be debatably arranged from "rigidly literal" to "loose and expressive" in this way: American Standard Version, Revised Standard Version, New International Version, New Revised Standard Version, and New English Bible. These can be further compared with two functional equivalence translations: Today's English Version and Contemporary English Version.

according to the Masoretic text, on the basis of the English version. This work incorporated his earlier English translation of the Torah, printed in 1845/46, and a revised edition was published in London in 1865.

The outpouring of translations reflected surging currents in biblical scholarship, especially in Germany where advanced critical work was taking place. These trends gradually made their way to England. As early as 1810, Bishop Herbert Marsh sensed the need for a revision that would accommodate these new expansions of knowledge:

Isaac Leeser (1806–1868), Jewish translator of the Hebrew Scriptures. His Twenty-Four Books was first published in 1845–46.

> It is probable that our Authorized Version is as faithful a representation of the original Scriptures as *could* have been formed at *that period*. But when we consider the immense accession that has been made, both to our critical and philological apparatus; when we consider that the most important sources of intelligence for the *interpretation* of the original Scriptures were *likewise* opened after that period, we cannot possibly pretend that our Authorized Version does not require *amendment*. [Italics are his]

Sixty years later, a new and official revision would be undertaken.

The English Revised Version

On February 10, 1870, Bishop Wilberforce of Winchester moved the Upper House of the Convocation of the Province of Canterbury to undertake an official revision of the New Testament. This motion was amended to include the Old Testament, and the Lower House approved the resolution without dissent. By summer, work began on the new revision.

The audience for an English Bible had changed considerably since the days of King James. In their day, the *KJV* translators only dealt with one church body–the established Church of England. Now the Convocation, representing the established church, had to address a nation embracing many denominations. So they invited representatives of other churches to join their work. The British working group of 65 excellent scholars ended up with 41 members from the dominant Church of England, five from the Church of Scotland (Reformed), two from the Episcopal Church of Ireland, one from the Episcopal Church in Scotland, five from the Scottish Free Church, four Baptists, two Methodists, three Congregationalists, and one each from the United Presbyterians and the

Unitarians. They divided into two Companies (committees). C. J. Ellicott, Bishop of Gloucester and Bristol, chaired the New Testament Company, and E. H. Browne, Bishop of Ely, headed the Old Testament Company.

Another challenge the translators faced was the breadth of nationalities who would be using their translation. The *King James Version* translators had a compact audience–the citizens of the United Kingdom. Now more English-speakers lived in the former British colonies than in the United Kingdom itself. Thus, on July 7 the British revisers invited American cooperation. The American Committee, after a slow start, finally organized under the leadership of the distinguished scholar Philip Schaff of Union Theological Seminary. Dr. William Green of Princeton Theological Seminary chaired the American New Testament Committee, while Dr. Theodore Woolsey of Yale University headed the American Old Testament team. The 32 members on the American committee represented nine denominations: Protestant Episcopal, Presbyterian, Congregational, Baptist, Methodist, Reformed, Lutheran, Unitarian, and Friends (Quakers). These scholars met at Bible House in New York City, the headquarters of the American Bible Society. The American scholars began a transatlantic exchange of manuscripts with their U.K. colleagues in 1872.

Like the *King James Version* translators, and the Bishops' Bible team before them, these scholars labored under a set of guidelines. Their first two guidelines are particularly important:

1. To introduce as few alterations as possible into the Text of the Authorized Version, consistently with faithfulness.

2. To limit, as far as possible, the expression of such alterations to the language of the Authorized and earlier English Versions.

Rule 2 created problems for the revisers. When they removed an obvious, now-obscure archaism, or altered some words to reflect more modern texts, they went back to the 16th and 17th centuries for models of expression. Thus, they actually increased the number of such old-fashioned expressions as "howbeit," "holden," "peradventure," aforetimes," "must needs, "behooved," and "would fain."

Their interpretation of "faithfulness," in Rule 1, led them to adopt an extremely literal style of translation. British biblical scholars had been moving toward literalism for some years, so the mood was in the air. Their efforts resulted in English expression that followed more closely the form of Greek and Hebrew than English idiom, creating a translation that was difficult to read.

In their effort to make a careful, word-for-word reproduction of the Greek New Testament, they:

- Used the same English word for each occurrence of a given Greek word whenever possible. (Shades of Julia Smith! By contrast, the *King James Version* had been criticized for using *too many* different English words to translate a given Greek word.)

- Translated every Greek word in the text into a corresponding English word. (The third petition of the Lord's Prayer became, "Thy will be done, as in heaven, so on earth." English does not require all the prepositions used in New Testament Greek.)

- Followed the order of the Greek words and translated the Greek tenses and articles with more precision than English requires. (Compare Mark 1.28, a statement about Jesus. *KJV* reads, "And immediately his fame spread abroad throughout all the region round about Galilee." The *Revised Version* offers, "And the report of him went out straightway everywhere into all the region of Galilee round about." The recent *NRSV* manages to express the statement in idiomatic English: "At once his fame began to spread throughout the surrounding region of Galilee.")

The Work Progresses

The revisers worked diligently, laboriously, carefully—and slowly. The British New Testament Company, for instance, never revised more than 35 verses in a work day.

We might term this a "scholarly" revision. The revisers were anxious to incorporate the recent scholarly findings from manuscript and grammatical studies. Many of these were considered controversial then, though most have survived the test of time. Two of that era's most respected New Testament textual critics—F.J.A. Hort and B.F. Westcott—sat on the British New Testament company. (Their edition of the Greek New Testament text, published later in 1881, became the scholarly standard for some time.)

The revisers' careful attention to the early manuscript sources led them to make some noticeable changes. They separated the traditional ending of Mark's Gospel, Mark 16.9-20, by a break to indicate that it is questionable. The concluding doxology to the Lord's Prayer at Matthew 6.13 was transferred to a footnote. They removed the late trinitarian reference in 1 John 5.7, because it lacked solid Greek manuscript support. The powerful story of the woman taken in adultery, John 7.53—8.11, was placed in brackets with a note explaining how various manuscripts locate this story in different places or omit it altogether.

The Old Testament Company introduced fewer corrections into their underlying Masoretic Hebrew text. For example, at 1 Samuel 14.41 the Masoretic text drops the words that Saul prays. The words appear in all the Septuagint manuscripts and the Vulgate. Scholars generally agree that these sources are correct and that the Masoretic text is in error at this point. Still, the revisers chose to leave them out, as had the King James translators, in the interest of giving precedence to the Masoretic text.

Their decision to render the Psalms and some other poetic passages as poetry, however, marked a major advance. They printed these elements in staggered lines, to make their poetic nature clear to an English reader. This greatly clarifies such passages as Numbers 22–24 or Luke 1–2. Unfortunately, they did not extend this principle uniformly to the writing of the prophets, where poetic passages abound. The Old Testament revisers still viewed these as narrative, prose writings.

THE MASORETIC TEXT

Jews reverentially cared for their sacred scrolls. When one wore out in use, it was destroyed. Since Jewish scribes took great care in reproducing manuscripts, no one felt that older scrolls had any advantage over newer ones.

Still, variant readings crept in and this concerned the rabbis. In the fifth century A.D. the scribal tradition was continued by scholars called Masoretes, a word meaning "transmitters," who sought to perpetuate an accurate text of the Hebrew Scriptures. Two centers of work emerged, one in Babylonia (modern Iraq) and the other in Tiberias (Palestine).

Before the tenth century A.D., the Babylonia center closed and the Tiberian Masoretes carried on the work. Two families competed with each other to produce the best texts, Ben Asher and Ben Naphthali. Scholars have generally preferred the Ben Asher line of manuscripts. The oldest Masoretic text available dates from the ninth century A.D.

Daniel Bomberg of Venice published a Hebrew text with Targums (Aramaic translations of the Hebrew) in 1517. Bomberg's edition became the staple for Bible translators down to the 20th century.

The Revised Bible made a welcome departure from the Geneva-King James tradition by printing the text in sense paragraphs, as had been done for years before the Geneva translation, rather than setting off each verse separately.

The treatment of the Apocrypha reflects the declining fortunes of those books in Protestant circles. The King James revisers worked on the Apocrypha right along with the Old and New Testaments. The Revised Version companies treated the Apocrypha almost as an afterthought. They did not make arrangements for the work until March, 1879, and then decided they would not begin until both Testaments were completed. As a result, the Revised Version Apocrypha did not appear until 1895.

All told, the revisers altered the King James text in some 30,000 places, or at a rate of more than four changes per verse. While their scholarship was commendable, their feel for the English language was less so. They produced an excellent study Bible which was a massive chore to read.

An Eager Public Awaits

The English-speaking world eagerly awaited the revision. The New Testament was completed first and published on May 17, 1881, in England and three days later in America. The new revision generated enough excitement to become a major news item. On May 22, 1881, the Chicago *Daily Tribune* and the Chicago *Times* printed the entire text of the revised New Testament for their eager readers. This massive effort employed 92 typesetters who finished their Herculean task in 12 hours.

Oxford University Press received advance orders for one million copies of the New Testament, and Cambridge University Press, the other publisher, received nearly as many. Some three million copies of the revised New Testament sold in the United Kingdom and the United States during the first year. The Old Testament appeared in 1885, but with much less fanfare.

As people examined the New Testament more carefully, their initial enthusiasm dwindled. The strongest objections came from friends and supporters of the revision. Charles Spurgeon, the best known preacher of the day, call the new version "strong in Greek, weak in English."

Very soon the cry went up for another revision, one that used better than "translation English." The Bishop of Durham by the turn of the century painfully admitted his disappointment. "I feel compelled," he wrote, "after years of use of the Revised Version of the New Testament, to own to the conviction that while it is beyond all praise as an aid to study, it seriously lacks that ENGLISH FELICITY, if I may use the phrase, which should entitle it to take the place of the Authorized Version in our national heart."

In 1904, Samuel Lloyd, a Governor of the British and Foreign Bible Society, published *The Corrected New Testament* which sought to make the scholarly accomplishments of the revisers conform "to the standards of the purest English."

In the face of this criticism of the English style used in the *Revised Version*, the Canterbury Convocation cautiously recommended the revision for church use,

From the front page of the Chicago Daily Tribune for May 22, 1881. This edition carried the entire Revised Version New Testament. The front page of newspapers at the time was devoted to advertisements. To the "pious poor," Sea's Department Store offered free copies of the New Testament as printed in the paper. The store added, "3 cts. charged to those able to pay. Same nicely bound, 12 cts." Three cents was a bargain, since the newspaper cost five cents.

but on a voluntary basis. Two cathedral churches adopted the *Revised Version* for church use. Otherwise, the British churches largely retained the King James for public use and pursued the *Revised Version* for study purposes.

The American Edition

The revisers on this side of the Atlantic were treated a bit like colonial cousins. They were welcome to submit their changes, but the English team didn't feel obligated to adopt their ideas. While some changes were accepted, many more were left out.

A few of the American changes reflected difference in English usage on the two sides of the Atlantic. Americans wanted to use "wheat" instead of "corn" to name the familiar grain. Other suggestions were more profound. The Americans felt more free to change antiquated words than did the British revisers. They wished to clean up some of the more obvious Hebraisms in the Old Testament. They preferred "love" in 1 Corinthians 13 to "charity." Even the American paragraph arrangement differed from the British.

The Americans also wanted to drop "Ghost" (as in "Holy Ghost") in favor of "Spirit." The word comes from the same root as the German "Geist," meaning "spirit." But by the 19th century, "ghost" had taken on spooky associations. The phrase "ghostly counsel" suggested something quite different than "spiritual advice." The Spirit of God when called the "Holy Ghost," suggested someone sent to haunt rather than to comfort. The British revisers, taking a very conservative approach, stayed with "Ghost."

Another difference of opinion centered on the word for God's name. The Americans wished to use "Jehovah" as the divine name, rather than the customary term, "LORD." The British stayed with tradition, as have most translations since.

The Americans also thought it better to leave the Hebrew word "Sheol" untranslated, while the British translated it as "pit," "grave" or "hell" in about one-half of its occurrences. This is a notoriously difficult word to translate because the Hebrew understanding of the afterlife differs considerably from the general Christian view.

The American committee pledged not to publish their own version for 14 years. However, the British university publishers agreed to print in their editions an appendix containing some 300 of the major American alterations. The American preferences, though, ran into the thousands. The appendix only listed the chief ones, as examples.

Unlike their British counterparts, the Americans continued to meet after the new version was published in England. After 1896 the American work was subsidized by the publishing firm of Thomas Nelson & Sons, which would hold rights to any eventual American edition. (Before 1896, private contributions supported the American Committee.)

Three unauthorized "American" editions appeared, incorporating the American preferences from the appendix directly into the text. Two of them were published in 1881 by American firms: Hubbard in Philadelphia, and Fords, Howard & Hulbert in New York City. The third, appearing in 1898, was a venture of the Oxford and Cambridge University presses. They issued an edition, destined for the American market, with the subtitle, "...with the readings and renderings preferred by the American Revision Companies incorporated into the text." It, too, only incorporated those American readings that appeared in the appendix.

The American committee decided to meet these challenges head on. The spurious editions did not incorporate all their preferences and thus misrepresented their work. For instance, they wished to eliminate a large number of archaic words the British chose to keep: to use "cakes" instead of "cracknels," "fined" instead of "amerced," "betray" not "bewray," "lewd" rather than "whorish," and many more.

A copyrighted publication would provide the best protection. They arranged for publication with Thomas Nelson and the *American Standard Version* appeared in 1901, incorporating all of the American preferences. Nelson held the copyright for 28 years. In 1929, it was transferred to an interdenominational group, the International Council of Religious Education. That copyright transfer laid the foundation for developing the *Revised Standard Version* two decades later.

Usefulness of this Version

The *ASV* won far greater acceptance in American churches than did the *RV* in Britain. It was, in fact, a definite improvement. The *ASV* employed fewer obscure, archaic words. It offered better paragraphing and marginal notes. Several of the American textual readings were superior. A number of American denominations adopted the *ASV* for their church school curricula.

The excessive literalness of the *ASV* and the *RV* holds one advantage. Since the translation follows the Hebrew and Greek word order and sentence structure so closely, it offers the serious Bible student who lacks command of the biblical languages the closest approximation of the originals that English can provide. Consistent translation of each original word by the same English word wherever possible makes it easy to use a concordance for Bible study. Because of these specialized advantages, enough interest remained in the *ASV* to induce the

Lockman Foundation, an independent group, to issue the *New American Standard Version*. In 1960, the *NASV* Gospel of John appeared, followed by all the Gospels in 1962, the complete New Testament in 1963, and the entire Bible in 1971. This version updated the language–dropping the "thees" and "thous," replacing outmoded words, being more consistent with the use of "it" as a neuter pronoun, and so forth—but retained the *ASV* literal attention to tenses and word order.

From the standpoint of readability and natural English expression, however, the changes in the American edition can only be considered improvements when compared with the problematic English version. Tyndale, working nearly four centuries earlier, had created a translation that in many instances sounds more modern than either the American or English Revised versions.

The stilted language of the *RV* and the *ASV* awakened interest in translations that would recapture the vigorous English expression characteristic of the great Tyndale. While both the *RV* and the *ASV* acknowledge their debt to Tyndale, the master of English translations, their translators, more concerned with scholarly issues, lacked the sensitivity for vigorous, everyday English which characterized Tyndale.

11 THE BIBLE COMES ALIVE IN MODERN ENGLISH

The English *Revised Version* and *American Standard Version* were barely stocked on booksellers' shelves when new discoveries made them out of date. Even if these versions had been in clear, natural-sounding English, they would have needed replacing. To keep up with the rapid pace of scholarship, the 20th century set off an explosion of creative translation activity unmatched since the days of Tyndale and his successors.

New Light on the New Testament

At the turn of the century, archaeologists B. P. Grenfell and A. S. Hunt dug amid ancient graveyards near the ancient town of Oxyrhynchus (modern Behnesa, Egypt), about 120 miles south of Cairo. They uncovered one of the great rubbish heaps of history, an enormous collection of papyrus documents of all kinds—letters, bills, legal notices, and even portions of Scripture–written in Greek and dating as early as the second century A.D. In this and other excavations, the desert sands yielded our oldest New Testament fragments, dating from about A.D. 150 to 300. By 1998, 65 volumes of these documents were published and available to scholars, presenting the text of more than 4,400 papyrus fragments.

These papyri transformed the understanding of New Testament Greek. Biblical scholars had long known that the Greek of the New Testament differed substantially from the classical Greek of Plato and Aristotle. They thought of it as "Holy Spirit Greek," a special dialect used by the Spirit when God revealed the Scripture to the apostles. Now they discovered letters and correspondence written in the same form of Greek, which was, it turned out, the common Greek dialect spoken around the Mediterranean. Scholars called it *koine*, or "common," Greek.

This new awareness would come to alter the approach many translators would take to translating the New Testament. Translators could now make a letter from Paul sound like a real letter, dashed off in haste and amid the passions of the moment. They didn't have to honor "Holy Spirit Greek" with an artificial elegance when rendering it into English. "Common speech" English translations would actually come closer to the style of the originals than more self-consciously literary renderings.

HOW DOES THE BIBLE REALLY READ?

The New Testament writers used the common Greek idiom, the language of commerce and the streets rather than the academies and lecture halls. This koine Greek was the lingua franca of the vast and diverse Roman Empire. This "common" Greek simplified the grammar and vocabulary of classical Greek, used prepositions more frequently and more loosely, and generally lacked the precision of expression which made classical Greek so suitable for philosophical discussions.

In addition, many New Testament writers used koine as a second language, their native tongue being Aramaic, a language akin to Hebrew. Some parts of the New Testament read like "translation Greek," for they use Semitic word order and phrases borrowed from the writer's native Aramaic. Some New Testament writers, we might say, wrote "Greek with a foreign accent." The Book of Revelation is the worst offender in this regard.

In contrast, Luke, author of the Gospel and Acts of the Apostles, writes the best Greek in the New Testament, coming close to classical standards. He is at home with Greek rhetorical forms, and seems familiar with the methods and style of Hellenistic historians. Luke's skill in Greek is one argument supporting the understanding that he was a Gentile.

Paul falls somewhere between the two extremes. Paul was born in a Jewish community outside of Palestine and was raised among people who spoke koine Greek. However, it is doubtful if he spent much time studying classical Greek poets and authors. The only writings we have of his are all letters, mostly penned in the heat and passion of a crisis and often dictated to a secretary. We can't expect these to display the neatly balanced, formal prose style that marks the best Greek literary writings.

The New Testament uses a relatively limited vocabulary of 5,000 words. Eliminate place names, personal names, and words that occur only once or twice, and the number drops to about 1,000 words. By comparison, a good dictionary of classical Greek includes at least 150,000 words. In general, the New Testament is not a literary work by the best standards of Hellenistic Greek writing. Ordinary, everyday English represents the feeling of these texts very well.

The Old Testament presents another situation. Most of it was written in classical Hebrew when the language was at its peak. A more formal English style suits the Hebrew Scriptures better than the Greek Scriptures.

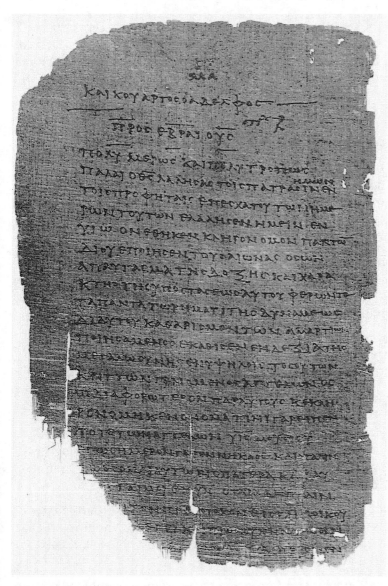

A portion of Papyrus 46. It was recovered in the early 1930s by Mr. A. Chester Beatty and a team from the University of Michigan. The codex dates from the early third century and includes Paul's letters. It is about three-quarters intact. P46 is the earliest substantial portion of the New Testment known to exist.

In the 1920s and 30s a number of other papyri were discovered in Egypt, many of them containing fragments of biblical writing. One, dating from about A.D. 130 and now in the collection of the John Rylands Library in England, contains fragments of John 18. It is the oldest manuscript of the New Testament now known.

Today there are more than 4,500 New Testament manuscripts and fragments to work with. Scholars carefully compare them as they develop critical editions of the New Testament Greek text. The monumental work of Westcott and Hort before the turn of the century has been supplemented by more recent critical editions, including those by von Soden and Nestle, father and son. Nestle's later editions were revised by Kurt Aland, who also contributed to the critical edition prepared for translators by the United Bible Societies, a project in which the American Bible Society played a major role.

New Light on Hebrew Scriptures

As archaeologists dug deep into the ancient Middle East, they unearthed a massive number of monuments and tablets carrying inscriptions and writings in Akkadian, Canaanite, and Aramaic, all languages related to Hebrew. These finds added immeasurably to the understanding of the grammar of biblical Hebrew, especially of Hebrew poetry.

These discoveries also helped translators figure out obscure words. The Hebrew Scriptures include many words used only once or twice, such as names for specific objects. These had always been very difficult to translate. The archaeological finds clarified many difficult terms. For examples:

- The Hebrew *menorah* used to be translated "candle" or "candlestick." Archaeology revealed that the ancients did not use candles but rather oil lamps. Thus, the new translation is "lamp" or "lampstand."

- The *KJV* translates the Hebrew *kaph* as "spoon." Inscriptions reveal this word likely referred to a censer. So the modern *Revised Standard Version* reads "dish for incense." *Chamman* was an obscure word translated as "image" (*KJV*) or "sun-image" (*ASV*). Archaeologists found this word inscribed on a special kind of altar, so the *RSV* translates it as "incense altar" (see Leviticus 26.30).

- Names for animals and jewels have long puzzled translators. Inscriptions unearthed have given many clues. For instance, the stone formerly translated as "sapphire" is not the gem we know by that name but rather lapis lazuli.

This new information, plus ever improving textual sources, combined with an urgent desire to get God's Word out in understandable, contemporary English, led to a vast outpouring of translations from the pens of numerous scholars. (The famous Dead Sea scrolls appeared too late to influence the translations discussed in this chapter.)

Independent Translations Blaze the Trail

Several independent translations appeared in the first half of the twentieth century. Many of these are excellent works that remain in print and in use as the century closes. They influenced the next major official revision in the *King James Version* tradition, the *Revised Standard Version*, by establishing the norms for using contemporary English in a readable form while maintaining the highest standards of scholarship. These translations also experimented with different ways to present God's Word on the printed page.

The Twentieth-Century New Testament

The Twentieth-Century New Testament—the first modern speech version—truly bridged the centuries. A "Tentative Edition" appeared in three parts between 1898 and 1901, with a complete, revised edition following in 1904.

A group of twenty Christians in England, mostly lay people and including some women, determined to produce a contemporary New Testament translation reflecting the latest scholarship. They elected to remain anonymous. English universities of that day concentrated on the classics, so many educated lay people had a good command of Greek and, sometimes, even had the leisure to pursue scholarly studies in the language.

The group met at a country estate in England to produce a version that would make the New Testament come alive in the language and thought forms of their contemporaries. A story has come down suggesting that they were a cluster of eccentrics of the "inspired amateur" type so characteristic of Victorian and Edwardian England. Another story claims that most of the group suffered in various degrees from poor health. Still, they produced a remarkable translation which some scholars place near the front rank of modern versions.

They based their work on the Westcott-Hort text. The group wrote smooth, idiomatic British English and converted weights, measures, coins, and official titles into contemporary British equivalents. To convey the scholarship of their time, they arranged the books according to the chronology scholars assigned them rather than in the traditional order. Thus, the Gospels were arranged as Mark, Matthew, Luke, John. First Thessalonians precedes the rest of Paul's letters. They placed passages with weak manuscript support in square brackets. Major Old Testament references were printed in italics, and minor reference in single quotes. They adopted modern conventions of paragraphing, titles, subheads, and quotation marks, and provided a one-page introduction for each book.

Weymouth's New Testament

Richard F. Weymouth was also a layman, a graduate of University College, London, and a school headmaster. He produced *The New Testament in Modern English* in 1903. It became very popular on both sides of the Atlantic, although an American edition (revised by James Alexander Robertson) was not published until 1943.

Weymouth worked from his own edition of the Greek text (which he called the "Resultant Greek Testament") in which the work of several other scholars was blended.

Weymouth provided brief introductions to the books. He utilized paragraphing, section titles, and quotation marks. He took a rather conservative approach to his English style. Weymouth felt that many older words and phrases were still being used and he did not want to reduce the dignity of the Scriptures by using too many everyday words. He hoped that his work would encourage development of an official contemporary English version that would replace the *KJV* and the *RV*.

Moffatt's Bibles

James Moffatt, who taught in Scotland and later came to Union Theological Seminary in New York, could be considered one the most important individual translators of this century. He produced two influential translations.

The first, *The Historical New Testament*, was published in 1901 while Moffatt was still in Scotland. A leading student of the literary growth of the Bible, Moffatt based this translation on Nestle's edition of the Greek New Testament. He wanted to present the literature of the New Testament in a fresh translation arranged according to its literary growth and the dates of the various documents. Thus, he begins this translation with the letters of Paul, the earliest canonical writings. He added an enormous set of scholarly notes, tables, and articles. He used square brackets to indicate passages he felt were displaced or added later. Moffatt employed different typefaces to distinguish passages he thought were drawn from an earlier source.

Influential translator James Moffatt (1870-1944) prepared one of the first modern language translations done by an individual.

This specialized work prepared the way for his next effort, *A New Translation*, which still enjoys wide use. He published the New Testament in 1913, working this time from Hermann von Soden's Greek text. Moffatt declared he wanted to translate the New Testament exactly as he would any other Greek prose. He used a graceful English style with many beautiful renderings, although in a British idiom. While he retained the traditional order of the books, he transposed some passages within a book to reconstruct what he thought to be the original order.

For instance, he inserted John 3.22-30 between John 2.12 and 2.13. Some scholars consider his translations of Paul's letters to be his finest achievement.

His Old Testament appeared in 1924/25 in two volumes. Here he took more liberties with the traditional text than in the New Testament. Using various typographical means, he indicated where the Hebrew text was broken or missing, marked passages in the Pentateuch (the five books of Moses) which came from various earlier traditions (based on the J, E, D, and P theory of Pentateuchal composition), and indicated sections he thought were later additions. Moffatt frequently changed the Hebrew text for various reasons, but chose not to indicate where nor to explain his reasoning.

This great translator adopted some interesting renderings. For the divine name, Yahweh, he chose "the Eternal," the title often used in French translations. He called Noah's ark a

WHAT ARE J, E, D, AND P?

In the middle of the 18th century, French scholar Jean Astruc began to explore the origins of the five books of Moses. Work continued in the 19th century, especially by Julius Wellhausen, a German scholar. These scholars concluded that Pentateuch was not written by Moses himself but had developed from traditions that circulated orally in Israel which were written down later in different forms, in different places and times. Eventually four strands of tradition were identified. The theory helped to explain how repetitions in these writings occurred and how two tellings of the same incident (like the giving of the Ten Commandments) could display so many differences.

The "J" tradition (named for its use of J[Y]HWH for the Lord's name) was thought to come out of Judah. The "E" tradition (named for the use of Elohim for God's name in its texts) was thought to come from a northern Israelite source. The Deuteronomic source, or "D," is associated with the reforms instituted by King Josiah (see 2 Kings 22–23). The Priestly tradition designated by "P" was linked with the Babylonian exile in the 6th century B.C.

Contemporary scholars feel far less confident than scholars of Moffatt's time when it comes to determining precisely where one tradition in the text ends and another begins.

"barge." He termed Israel's kings or clan leaders "sheiks." He writes that the high priests "made fun of" Jesus on the Cross and begins some sentences with the highly idiomatic, "Well then...."

The complete Bible appeared in 1926 and has gone through numerous editions. His translations adopt a free style, bordering on what some might call paraphrasing to make the point clearly in English. He broke the chains of excessive literalism which had bound the *Revised Version* and opened new possibilities for later translators. His wide use of emendations and his indication of sources—both of which depend on scholarly theories—gives his work some aspects of a commentary.

The Riverside New Testament

William G. Ballantine, teacher at the Oberlin Graduate School of Theology and later President of Oberlin College in Ohio, published *The Riverside New Testament* in 1923. Ballantine was eager to free the New Testament from the museum language of older versions, all of which echoed language from three centuries before, although his style, like Weymouth's, is more traditional than collo-

WHAT TO DO WITH VERSE NUMBERS?

When one sets Scripture in coherent sense-paragraphs rather than separate verse-paragraphs, the verse numbers pose a problem. Placing a full-sized number boldly in the middle of a sentence or paragraph, as the ASV and some modern versions do, is one solution. The disadvantage is that the numbers tend to interrupt the flow of reading. The independent modern English translations typically placed verse numbers in the margin, usually without indicating exactly where in the line the verse break occurs. This preserves the flow of the text, but makes it difficult to locate the beginning of a verse. The Jerusalem Bible uses marginal numbers, but adds dots in the line to indicate where the verse break comes.

Tiny superscript (above the line) numbers placed in the text, the system adopted by the Revised Standard Version, seems to offer the best compromise for achieving both goals of preserving the flow of the text and making it easy to locate verses.

quial. Ballantine also thought that Scripture should look like any other modern book, so he eliminated verse numbers and added an index keyed to pages in the back to locate persons and subjects. That decision may have enhanced readability, but it restricted use of his translation because very many Bible readers depend on verse numbers for reference and citation.

The Centenary Translation of the New Testament

This work appeared in 1924 from the presses of the American Baptist Publication Society to celebrate the hundredth anniversary of that organization, which is now part of the American Baptist Churches in the U.S.A. It was translated by Mrs. Helen Barrett Montgomery, a graduate of Wellesley College who lived in Rochester, New York. Mrs. Montgomery was a leading figure in church life and had travelled extensively around the world in support of mission work. A remarkable person in many ways, she attended seminary and devoted much of her energies to the study of Greek. Her translation aimed at creating a readable, modern translation which would help the Word of God come alive.

The Smith-Goodspeed Bible

This was the first translation to consciously adopt the American idiom. Other translations, even though written in America, leaned toward the British style which still set the standard for many educated Americans. It is significant that the translator, Edgar J. Goodspeed, worked at the University of Chicago in America's heartland, rather than at an eastern university where transatlantic influences prevailed.

Goodspeed published his *The New Testament, An American Translation* in 1923 at The University of Chicago Press, which had initiated the project. He wished to present the meaning of the New Testament "in English of the same kind as the Greek of the original" and added, "For American readers, especially, who have had to depend so long upon versions made in Great Britain, there is room for a New Testament free from expressions which, however familiar in England or Scotland, are strange to American ears."[5]

Goodspeed thus has Jesus tell the paralytic whom he has healed, "Get up, pick up your bed and go home!" (Matthew 9.6).[6] Other modern translations had dropped "thee" and "thou" in ordinary speech but kept it when addressing God. Goodspeed adopted "you" even in prayer. The American flavor of this translation becomes very clear when a reader compares a passage in Moffatt with the same passage in Goodspeed. Goodspeed's "American English" has deeply influenced subsequent translations done in America.

Helen Barett Montgomery (1861-1934) was a leader in missions and a notable church-woman, in addition to translating the New Testament.

Edgar Johnson Goodspeed (1871-1962) was the first Bible translator to consciously adopt the American idiom.

The University of Chicago Press then invited four scholars to translate a companion Old Testament. The Press enlisted T.J. Meek of the University of Toronto, Leroy Waterman of the University of Michigan, A.R. Gordon of McGill University in Montreal, and J.M.P. Smith of the University of Chicago. The first edition was published in 1927 but showed some unevenness, the result of having four scholars working independently on various parts. A later edition in 1931 smoothed out these differences. In 1939, Dr. Goodspeed finished translating the Apocrypha and *The Complete Bible, An American Translation* appeared.

J.B. Phillips

During World War II, J.B. Phillips was ministering in London, conducting Bible studies with the war-weary residents. He soon realized that the available translations, even the so-called "modern" ones, did not speak in a style with which his students could relate comfortably. Being an accomplished Greek scholar, Phillips undertook to translate Scripture on his own, using the speech rhythms and style of language his students could understand.

At the end of the war, he sought a publisher for his work, but with no success until C.S. Lewis—Oxford professor, novelist, and renowned Christian writer—came to his aid. Lewis suggested a title for Phillips' initial translation of Paul's letters: *Letters to Young Churches*. With an introduction written by Lewis, this volume came off the press in 1947 to be received by a huge and enthusiastic audience on both sides of the Atlantic. Other parts of the New Testament followed and the complete *The New Testament in Modern English* appeared in 1958. Phillips later published translations of portions of the Old Testament, notably the major prophets.

Phillips adopts a loose style of translation, though his respect for and understanding of the underlying Greek text prevents him from slipping into what some might consider a paraphrase. Blessed with an elegant and simple English style, he also uses subheads effectively to help readers follow the trend of the narrative or argument of the letter. He makes no apologies for modernizing expressions, titles, and terms. He willingly translates Greek words differently to suit different contexts. In 1958, he wrote, "I feel strongly that a translator, although he must make himself as familiar as possible with Greek New Testament usage, must steadfastly refuse to be driven by the bogey of consistency."[7]

He also wrote that the final test of a translator "is that of being able to produce in the hearts and minds of his readers an effect equivalent to that produced by the author upon his original readers."[8]

Williams' New Testament

In 1937, Charles B. Williams completed *The New Testament: A Translation in the Language of the People*. The copyright was acquired in 1949 by Moody Press which has published it since. A competent scholar, Williams worked from a conservative theological stance and his contemporary translation gained the trust of many Bible readers who doubted the credentials of anyone who tampered with the *KJV* or the *ASV*. Williams paid very close attention to the tense distinctions in Greek, as did the *ASV*.

Simplified Versions

Can the Bible be translated with a limited vocabulary? S.H. Hooke of the University of London, in cooperation with the Orthological Institute of Cambridge, published *The New Testament in Basic English* in 1941, followed by the complete *Basic Bible* in 1950. C.K. Ogden assisted in editing some of the Gospels. Basic English uses a vocabulary of 850 basic words in which any normal thought can be expressed intelligibly. For the Bible, the list was expanded to 1,000 words.

In 1952, Charles Kingsley Williams published *The New Testament in Plain English*, through The Society for the Promotion of Christian Knowledge (SPCK) in London. Eleven years later it was reprinted in the United States by Wm. B. Eerdmans Publishing Company. Williams used a set of 1,500 basic English words, plus another 170 which he explained in a glossary.

The Berkeley Version

Gerrit Verkuyl, for many years associated with the Board of Christian Education of the Presbyterian Church, U.S.A., published in 1945 in Berkeley, California, his *Berkeley Version of the New Testament*. He worked from Tischendorf's Greek text edition, but consulted many other texts. Later, he joined with 20 conservative scholars to produce *The Holy Bible: The Berkeley Version in Modern English*, published in 1959. The version contains annotations which reflect the translators' theological views. A revised edition was issued in 1969.

Other Modern Translations

The Four Gospels, translated by E.V. Rieu, appeared in the paperback Penguin Classics series, of which he was General Editor, in 1952. E.V. Rieu was respected for his translations of Homer and he did a very competent job with the Gospels. His introduction is worth reading for its insights into the problems with which translators must deal. In 1957, *The Acts of the Apostles*, translated by his son, C.H. Rieu, was published in the same series. Though the original intention was to translate the entire Bible, Penguin dropped the project when the *New English Bible* came out.

Another translation was the work of an English scholar, Hugh J. Schonfield, who was perhaps the first Jewish scholar to translate the New Testament. Published in Aberdeen in 1955, he titled it *The Authentic New Testament* and explained, "I have approached these records as if they had recently been recovered from a cave in Palestine or from beneath the sands of Egypt, and had never previously been given to the public."[9] He rearranges the order of the books and leaves out verse numbers to make the writings appear less "Bible-like." His introduction and notes deal extensively with the Jewish background and heritage in Christianity. He uses fresh titles. Second John, for example, becomes "Letter of John (II) to the Elect Lady and Her Children." A paperback version in the United States was issued in 1958 by the New American Library in their Mentor Religious Classics series.

Roman Catholics were also active in creating independent translations. Francis Spencer, a Dominican who had converted from Anglicanism, published in New York in 1898 a modern translation of the Gospels done directly from the Greek. The Gospel translation

WHERE DOES JESUS STOP SPEAKING?

Many Bible editions highlight Jesus' words in red ink, after the fashion of Spencer's italics. Few Bible readers realize, however, that the original Greek does not indicate where quotations begin and end. Translators must exercise textual and editorial judgment to decide where Jesus stops speaking and the Evangelist's narrative begins. Earlier English versions avoided this problem by simply not using any quotation marks.

John 3.10-21 offers an example. The RSV ends the quotation of Jesus at verse 15, leaving the well-known John 3.16 as a comment from the Evangelist. The NIV continues the quotation through verse 21, making John 3.16 a statement by Jesus. Each of these versions notes the other, different interpretation in a footnote.

was reprinted in 1901. He completed the New Testament by 1913. Left unpublished for a number of years, it was finally issued in 1937 by The Macmillan Company in New York. The translation became very popular and went through several reprints. Spencer used paragraphs and subheadings, and introduced something new: he printed the words of Jesus in italics.

Just before World War I, British Jesuits under Cuthbert Lattey began a scholarly *Westminster Version* based on the original languages. Translators for various sections were enlisted in both England and America. The translation appeared in parts, as various translators completed their work. The Old Testament, never completed, appeared in portions between 1934 and 1953. The New Testament, which was completed, appeared in parts from 1913 through 1935. The New Testament, in a revised edition, was issued in a one-volume pocket edition in 1948. Although the translation lacks a sense of uniformity because of so many translators, it reveals careful scholarship and reads well as English.

Bishop Ronald Knox, an Oxford professor and convert to Catholicism, was asked in 1939 by the Roman Catholic hierarchy in England to produce an independent translation from the Vulgate. Knox was known as a literary wit, and he produced a stimulating translation of high literary quality and great readability. The New Testament was published in 1944, with the Old Testament following in 1949, and a complete Bible in 1956. Because of its scholarship and literary style, Knox's translation was welcomed by both Protestants and Catholics.

12 Continuing the King James Tradition

The pioneering work of independent translators before World War II prepared the way for a host of official translations after the war. These official versions were prepared under ecclesiastical supervision and were written with an eye on liturgical, public use as well as for private reading.

The goal of public use cautioned translators against radically innovative phrases which might disturb a worshipper. These versions should sound modern, yet traditional.

The Revised Standard Version

The *Revised Standard Version* was the first of these postwar translations. It stands firmly in the King James family and was the first official modern language version produced in the English-speaking world. The New Testament appeared in 1946, with the Old Testament following in 1952. The Apocrypha did not appear until 1957. The *RSV* became the standard version for most major Protestant churches in America and found a good reception in Great Britain as well. It began as a project to revise the *American Standard Version*.

HOW TRADITIONAL?

In the 1940s, J.B. Phillips could translate "Greet one another with a holy kiss" (Romans 16.6) as "Give each other a hearty handshake all round for my sake." Many people delighted in Phillips' phrasing for private reading or study, but not in church. Scripture read in church, many believe, should have a linguistic style similiar to that of the liturgy or service. In the 1940s and '50s, worship language was generally shaped by the King James tradition. More recently, worship language in many churches has been updated to contemporary standards. In such settings, Scripture that is idiomatic or even a bit colloquial sounds appropriate.

The *American Standard Version*, while superior in some respects to its parent *Revised Version*, left much to be desired in terms of readability. Thomas Nelson & Sons in 1928 transferred the *ASV* copyright to the International Council of Religious Education, a body which represented 40 American and Canadian denominations. The Council established the American Standard Bible

Committee (later the Standard Bible Committee) to serve as trustees and custodians of the copyright and gave the Committee permission to proceed with a revision when they deemed it appropiate. After only a few meetings, the Committee began work on the new revision in 1937. Funding the project posed seemingly insurmountable obstacles in those Depression years. In the end, Thomas Nelson & Sons agreed to finance the work from advance royalties in exchange for ten years of exclusive publication rights to the new Bible.

The Committee began with 15 scholars and later expanded to 22 members. Luther A. Weigle of Yale Divinity School chaired the group, and it included some of the best biblical minds of the time, including James Moffatt and Edgar Goodspeed. An extensive advisory committee was created to supplement the work of the Committee. The Committee itself divided into New Testament and Old Testament sections. Over the years, 32 scholars served on the Committee, all but one, who was Jewish, connected with Protestant denominations.

Between three and five Committee members were chosen for their literary skills or their experience in the public use of the Bible in worship and teaching. This was an attempt to insure readability and usability.

On September 29, 1952, Dr. Luther A. Weigle, right front, presented the first printed copy of the complete RSV to President Harry S. Truman, as part of the National Capitol Bible Observance.

The translators met during academic vacations, most of them being professors, to review the drafts individual Committee members had translated. They usually gathered at Yale Divinity School. Some sessions were held at Union Theological Seminary in New York and others at a hotel in East Northfield, Massachusetts.

When the sections met to discuss the initial drafts they had previously received and evaluated, they went over each word in a laborious fashion, often working 12-hour days. The New Testament section used a variety of Greek texts, but most of their choices appear in the text or margin of Nestle's edition, according to Dr. Frederick C. Grant, one of the leading scholars on the Committee. They made decisions by vote. In case of a tie, the *ASV* rendering prevailed. Often the resulting manuscript bore little resemblence to the initial draft. Once they finished, copies of the revised draft were circulated to the advisory committee and some British scholars for further suggestions. (The outbreak of war in 1939 limited British involvement in the New Testament work; but when the work continued on the Old Testament after the war, they took a more active role.)

In the end, the whole Committee—representing both the Old and New Testament sections—reviewed all suggestions and determined the final form of the text, now requiring a two-thirds majority to decide disputed matters.

The New Testament section met for 145 days total, and the Old Testament section for a somewhat longer time, not counting the days individuals had spent on creating the first drafts. (Later, the Apocrypha section would labor together an additional 101 days.)

The final New Testament manuscript circulated for review in 1943. It was assigned to a small editorial committee to prepare it for publication. Because of the wartime shortages, publication had to await the arrival of peace. The New Testament was officially published on February 11, 1946, amid an impressive ceremony in Columbus, Ohio.

Meanwhile, the Old Testament section continued their work. They completed their final manuscript in June, 1952. A subcomittee of four worked feverishly through the summer to prepare the text for publication and the entire *Revised Standard Version* of the Bible was published on September 30, 1952.

In 1950, the Federal Council of Churches reorganized as a new and larger organization, the National Council of the Churches of Christ in the USA, and the International Council of Religious Education became part of the Division of Christian Education within the new ecumenical body. The new Division assumed the copyright for the *RSV*.

The Style of the New Version

These revisers were given more flexible guidelines than those placed on their 19th-century predecessors. The Council asked the Committee to produce a

> revision of the present American Standard Edition of the Bible in the light of the results of modern scholarship, this revision to be designed for use in public and private worship, and to be in the direction of the simple, classic English style of the *King James Version*.[10]

The Council desired a revision which "preserves those qualities which have given to the *King James Version* a supreme place in English literature,"[11] but their general phrasing of the guideline—"in the direction of"—freed the Committee from a slavish commitment to antiquated and obsolete expressions.

And they took that freedom to heart. While the 19th century revisers had actually increased the number of outmoded expressions and words, the *RSV* translators removed all of the old-fashioned language. Many words in earlier versions had radically changed their meaning, which could lead to serious misunderstandings. "Suffer" was one, as in Jesus' invitation, "Suffer the little children to come unto me and forbid them not." "Suffer" once meant "permit, allow;" now it carried the connotation of agony. The word "prevent" had once meant "come before, preceed," but no longer. And the word "let" in the 17th century could carry the sense of "prevent, stop." All told, there were some 400 words like these that needed changing.

The new version also updated grammar and usage. It dropped the obsolete use of "is" and "are" as auxiliaries of the perfect tense, as in "is come," and adopted the modern "has" or "have." Out went old-fashioned verb forms such as "sware" "drave," and "gat." Prepositions were revised to reflect current usage. In the 17th century, "of" was used in the sense of "by," "from" or "for." So the phrase "of a child" in Mark 9.21 became "from childhood."

Less fortunate, perhaps, was their decision to translate the Greek word for "fornication" as "immorality." Immorality is a broad term which covers much more than fornication, and this word choice obscures the fact that in certain passages the New Testament specifically denounces fornication and not necessarily all "immoralities."

Changes in vocabulary and grammar alone would have made this a much more readable version. But the *Revised Standard Version* went further to smooth out the "Bible language" quality that comes from translating Semitic texts literally. Hebrew uses "and" constantly as a means to bind sentences together. Under the influence of their mother tongue, some New Testament writers (notably Mark) use the same grammatical device in their Greek. The *RSV* drops many of these connectives, or replaces "and" with an English word that better expresses the original sense: "then," "so," "while," "although," and others. Semitic idioms such as "And it came to pass" were replaced by current English equivalents. The use of "saying" to introduce a quote (He spake, saying...) was changed to modern quotation marks (He said, "..."). Some literal renderings, such as "beasts of the field," were expressed in modern terms, such as "wild beasts."

The *RSV* translators chose Lord as the divine name and eliminated "thee" and "thou" except when addressing to God, as in a prayer or Psalm. The translators worked toward a consistent yet flexible policy for translating key Old Testament words. While they did not seek to translate with the same word every time, they did set up guidelines defining which English word should be used in specific contexts. Thus, the Hebrew word *hesed* became "steadfast love" when referring to God's dealings with Israel, and "kindness" or "loyalty" when speaking of interpersonal relationships. The revisers presented poetry in poetic printed form and realized that much of the great writings by the prophets was done as poetry. Paul's "epistles" became "letters," and his name was dropped from the title of the Letter to the Hebrews as it had been long recognized that Paul had not written this letter.

This version also modernized capitalization and the spelling of proper names. It used the same spelling for the same name in both Testaments. At the same time, the *RSV* avoided slang and colloquial expressions because they sought a dignified, elevated style suitable for public worship.

An interesting ancedote illustrates this concern. James Moffatt in challenging the use of certain words to translate a verse, asked the translator where he had gotten the expression. "From your own translation," came the reply. Dr. Moffatt answered, "It was suitable there, but not here." These men were acutely aware of the difference in style possible for an individual translation and for an official version intended for public use.

Still, they prepared a very readable, forceful translation that the average person could read with ease. One example, Philippians 4.14, shows how they clarified the language of earlier versions:

> Notwithstanding ye have well done, that ye did communicate with my affliction (*KJV*)

> Howbeit ye did well that ye had fellowship with my affliction (*ASV*)

> Yet it was kind of you to share my trouble (*RSV*)[12]

Speaking at the publication ceremonies, Dean Weigle expressed the role the translators envisioned for the *Revised Standard Version*:

> We do not imagine that the *King James Version* will cease to be used...We have no thought, moreover, of discontinuing the publica-

tion of the American Standard Version. Each has its use, the first as a great literary and religious classic and the second as a meticulously literal word-for-word translation. It is our hope, however, that the Revised Standard Version may quickly come to be used by ministers and by people generally, for... teaching, preaching, and Christian religious education, and in public and private worship... We sorely need this direct, vital phrasing of the Word of God in language that can readily be understood by the people of our time.[13]

To which sentiments the great Tyndale could only have added, "Amen!"

Received as a New Standard

The 1946 edition of the New Testament came out in a blue-covered, quarto-sized hardback volume with very readable typography. It featured a one-column page and the notes, mostly on textual matters or explaining the meaning of names or places, were clear and legible. Cross references were placed at the bottom of the page in easier-to-read type than some other Bibles used.

Professor Clarence T. Craig, one the translators and later President of Drew Theological Seminary, was granted a leave of absence from teaching to interpret the new version to the supporting denominations. The New Testament Section had prepared a pamphlet, "An Introduction to the Revised Standard Version of the New Testament," which clearly explained the principles behind the translation, in the fashion of the extended Preface to the *King James Version*. Rather quickly, most mainline denominations adopted it as their standard text for edu-

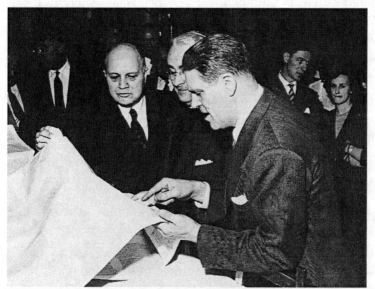

Dr. Roy G. Ross, left, and Dr. Samuel McCrea Cavert examine the first page of the RSV to come off the press in 1952. William R. McCylleyt, right, of Thomas Nelson & Sons, the publishers, points out the type chosen for the Bible.

cational materials. The first printing sold out right away and an eager public purchased over 2 million copies of the New Testament by the time the Old Testament was ready in 1952.

The complete Bible of 1952 came out in two editions. Some 50,000 two-volume, single-column sets were printed initially to match the format of the New Testament volume. But since most people would prefer a single volume Bible, 825,000 two-column, one-volume editions also were printed. It was said to be the largest single order ever placed with a commercial printing house. That first run of nearly 1 million copies required 1,000 tons of paper, 2,000 gallons of ink, 10 tons of type metal, and 140 tons of binder's board. The 23-karat gold leaf used to emboss the title on the cover amounted to 20 million square inches, enough to pave more than one mile of residential street.

The publication of the entire Bible was marked by 3,000 simultaneous interdenominational gatherings around the country, and churches observed that year's Religious Education Week with the theme, "The Word of Life in Living Language," in celebration of the new version.

In 1962, the exclusive rights granted to Thomas Nelson & Sons expired and additional publishers were granted permission to print the version. The American Bible Society was also licensed to print editions for its missionary and evangelistic work. By then, 12 million copies of the whole Bible had been sold, plus 5 million copies of the New Testament and 20,000 large pulpit Bibles. As the new publishers brought out different editions, sales continued to climb.

A second, definitive edition of the New Testament came out in 1971 incorporating some changes and correcting certain oversights that had come to the attention of the Committee through 25 years of widespread use.

Opposition to the Version

The *Revised Standard Version* met some strong opposition. There were those who simply preferred the sonorous language of the *King James Version*. Others felt the King James translators used the best possible manuscripts in preparing their work. For them the *RSV* was a "new" Bible, not quite the true Word of God.

Other objections to the *RSV* were based on a blend of politics and religion. The early decades of the 20th century had been torn by the modernist-fundamentalist controversy. Fundamentalists declared that each word of Scripture, at least in the original writings, was the inerrant Word of God. So-called "modernists" accepted scholarly findings and thought that while the Bible truly spoke God's message, it contained some material that could best be understood in light of its historical context. The slogans for this battle were, on the fundamentalist side, "The Bible *is* the Word of God," and on the other side, "The Bible *contains* the Word of God."

By 1950, the fires that roared in the 1920s had dwindled but the embers still glowed. The members of the Standard Committee were attacked as "liberals." Not being "true believers," it was claimed, they could not translate the Word with integrity.

The version's association with the National Council of the Churches of Christ in the USA, (NCCCUSA) didn't help either. That organization provoked controversy from its start. It united the "mainline" denominations which were considered too liberal by many conservative groups which refused to join the new ecumenical organization. Conservative groups formed their own interdenominational organization, the National Association of Evangelicals. And twenty years later, the conservative tradition in the church would produce its own modern language version, the *New International Version*.

The politics entered in because the United States was torn by a pervasive fear of Communism in the 1950s. In that fearful atmosphere, some groups accused the *RSV* translators of being Communists, "Commie sympathizers," "pinkos," or, more gently, "dupes." In certain circles, people thought of NCCCUSA as a clear and obvious Communist front. Americans now look back on that period with embarassment and even remorse. But it did some damage to the *RSV*.

The New Revised Standard Version

NCCCUSA retained control of the *RSV* copyright and supervised the fortunes of this version through a standing committee, the Policies Committee of the Revised Standard Version. Although no Bible version in America can claim the title "authorized," the *RSV* came as close to this status as any modern Bible because of its broad acceptance. The Policies Committee wanted to keep this version alive to continue the King James tradition of translation.

Scholarly advances and new discoveries soon created a need to rework the *RSV*. A number of important manuscript finds, especially in the Old Testament area, had become available since the late 1940s.

The best-known of these finds are the Dead Sea Scrolls, which came to light in 1947 having been hidden in caves near Qumran, on the Dead Sea, since A.D. 68. The story of their discovery and publication reads like a novel of intrigue and mysterious dealings. But that story cannot obscure the fact that this represents the most significant manuscript find since the unearthing of the *koine* papyri.

The first manuscripts were found in a cave by Bedouin shepherds and some were bought by the Metropolitan of St. Mark's Syrian Orthodox Monastery in Jerusalem for less than $100! It was the next year when Dr. John Trever of the American School for Oriental Research in Jerusalem discovered what a true find was at hand—a scroll of the Book of Isaiah dating from the second century B.C.,

Qumran *Rediscovered?*

The early Christian biblical scholar Origen (c.185–c.254) prepared the Hexapla, a six-column book in which he paralleled the Hebrew Old Testament text with a Greek transliteration and various Greek translations. One of these translations, he writes, was found in a jar near Jericho, along with other Greek and Hebrew books. The Dead Sea Scrolls were kept in jars, and Qumran is near Jericho. Did Origen have some early "Dead Sea Scrolls"? Since Jerome used some of Origen's Greek texts to produce his Vulgate Old Testament, that may explain why the Vulgate shows some parallels to the texts found at Qumran in 1947.

The caves at Qumran, showing Cave 4, where several important manuscripts were found at the end of World War II

making it at least 1,000 years older than any previously known Hebrew Scripture manuscript. A fine scroll of the prophet Habakkuk was also unearthed, along with parts of other biblical books. The writings of the Qumran sect itself also shed important light on the time of Jesus and the formation of the Christian movement.

Many Qumran manuscripts reveal resemblances to the texts Jerome used for his Vulgate, demonstrating again that the Vulgate remains an important text source. Since the end of the war, too, Vatican-sponsored scholars had made considerable progress in developing a definitive Vulgate text.

The Qumran texts had just appeared when the *RSV* Old Testament was coming to completion. Translators used readings from the Qumran Isaiah scroll in 13 passages, but they could not take full advantage of these manuscript discoveries.

The Policies Committee authorized a complete revision of the *RSV* in 1974. They were mandated to "continue in the tradition of the King James Bible, but to introduce such changes as are warranted on the basis of accuracy, clarity, euphony, and current English usage."[14] The translation committee for what would be known as the *New Revised Standard Version* was headed by Bruce M. Metzger of Princeton Theological Seminary. They followed the maxim, "As literal as possible, as free as necessary."[15]

The revisers stated their purpose in the preface, "To the Reader":

> This new version seeks to preserve all that is best in the English
> Bible as it has been known and used through the years. It is
> intended for use in public reading and congregational worship,
> as well as in private study, instruction, and meditation. We have
> resisted the temptation to introduce terms and phrases that
> merely reflect current moods, and have tried to put the message
> of the Scriptures in simple, enduring words and expressions that
> are worthy to stand in the great tradition of the King James Bible
> and its predecessors.[16]

The *New Revised Standard Version*, which was published in 1989, used as its
basis for the Old Testament the *Biblia Hebraica Stuttgartensia* (fourth edition,
1983), an authoritative text in the Masoretic tradition, and also referred to other
ancient versions thought to preserve an earlier form of the text. The New
Testament used the Greek text edition prepared by the United Bible Societies
(3rd edition corrected, 1983). For the Apocryphal/Deuterocanonical works, the
translators used several texts, but relied primarily upon the Septuagint text published by the Wurttemberg Bible Society in Stuttgart, Germany, in 1935.

The Apocrypha to the *RSV* came as an afterthought, undertaken at the request
of the Protestant Episcopal Church and not authorized until the end of 1952
when the Old Testament was already in print. With the *New Revised Standard
Version* the translators worked on the Apocryphal/Deuterocanonical books right
along with both Testaments. This reflected the new ecumenicity of Bible translations and scholarship. So did the composition of the New Revised Standard
Version Committee which, in addition the the usual Protestant scholars, included several Roman Catholics and one each from Eastern Orthodox and Jewish traditions. Once completed, the full *New Revised Standard Version* Bible gained imme-
diate acceptance from Protestants, Roman Catholics, and Orthodox.

Roman Catholic versions, following the traditional sequencing of the
Vulgate, position the Apocryphal/Deuterocanonical books at appropriate places
throughout the Old Testament. A Catholic edition of the *NRSV* following this
arrangement is available from some publishers. Other editions which include
these books follow a compromise arrangement which generally satisfies all parties. The books appear separately between the Testaments under the title
Apocryphal/Deuterocanonical Books (the former being the Protestant label and
the latter, the term prefered by Roman Catholics and Orthodox). These writings
are further grouped into four sections: the books and additions to Esther and
Daniel that are in Roman Catholic, Greek, and Slavonic Bibles; books such as the
Prayer of Manasseh which are in Greek and Slavonic Bibles but not Roman
Catholic versions; writings in the Slavonic Bible and the appendix to the
Vulgate; and writings that appear only in the appendix to the Greek Bible.

PROTESTANTS AND CATHOLICS CONVERGE ON SCRIPTURE

The story of the English Bible, as told so far, runs in two tracks, that of the Protestants and that of the Roman Catholics. Most of the space in this book so far has dealt with Protestant versions because these were far more numerous. For some centuries, the Bible simply did not play the same role in Catholic spirituality as it did for Protestants. That changed in the 1960s and the RSV was at the center of the change.

In 1943, the Vatican allowed translations from the original tongues, without dependence upon the intermediate Latin Vulgate version. That major step led to the Jerusalem Bible and the New American Bible, discussed in the next chapter, both of which have been welcomed and used by Protestants. But Catholic scholars were not yet permitted by the Vatican to work with Protestants, which explains why no Roman Catholic scholars took part in translating the RSV.

The Second Vatican Council (Vatican II), which met from October 1962 to December 1965, radically changed that situation. Pope John XXIII and his successor, Paul VI, set Vatican II on the path of renewing the Roman church and bridging the separation from other Christian groups. From the Council flowed a vital renewal movement, manifested in an outburst of Scripture study by Catholic laity and a new era of Catholic-Protestant cooperation in Scripture study and translation.

Even before Vatican II met, a spiritual renewal was occuring in Roman Catholic circles. This surge of renewal burst forth at the time when use of the RSV was spreading. The Catholic Biblical Association of Great Britain, working with Thomas Nelson, approached the Standard Bible Committee about the

On December 4, 1993, a copy of the Catholic Version of the NRSV was presented at the Vatican to Pope John Paul II by Rev. Dr. Gordon Sommers, left, President of the NCCCUSA. Joan B. Campbell, General Secretary of the NCCCUSA, center, looks on.

possibility of a Catholic edition of the version. No modern English version based on original texts was available to Catholics at that time (1952) and the need was pressing. A Catholic edition of the RSV offered a good, quick solution. The request was well received. In 1965, after 13 years of cooperative work, the Revised Standard Version, Catholic Edition of the New Testament, was published. The Old Testament followed later.

The Roman Catholic scholars explained their purpose this way:

> In the present edition the aim has been to make the minimum number of alterations and to change only what seemed absolutely necessary in the light of Catholic tradition. It has not been the aim to improve the translation as such. There are some places, however, where, the critical evidence being evenly balanced, considerations of Catholic tradition have favoured a particular rendering or the inclusion of a passage omitted by the RSV translators.[17]

This translation marked an historical moment, the first Catholic and Protestant Bible since the Reformation. In 1973, Collins published an edition called The Common Bible which went further down the ecumenical road by incorporating changes desired by Orthodox communions. Collins rightly labeled it "An Ecumenical Edition."

Most subsequent Bible translations have been done with an eye to the needs of Protestant, Catholic, and Orthodox readers. As a result, many Protestants now possess Bibles with the Apocryphal/Deuterocanonical books, and Christians from the three major families of the faith can study the Word together using the same Bible translation.

In keeping with the changes in English usage which have evolved over the past two decades, the NRSV has adopted gender-neutral language. English carries a masculine bias, and the translators aimed to minimize this tendency without doing violence to the biblical texts. Where a masculine noun or pronoun could refer to either gender, a neutral term was chosen, often a plural form even though the source text had a singular. "Men of Israel" becomes "people of Israel"; "sons of God" might be expressed as "people of God."

For instance, Nehemiah 11.2 in the RSV reads, "And the people blessed all of the men who willingly offered to live in Jerusalem." Those addressed were the first group of people returning from the Exile. Since the group included women and children as well, the NRSV can legitimately state, "And the people blessed all those who willingly offered to live in Jerusalem." In a similar spirit, "mankind" is rendered as "humankind." However, the masculine pronoun was retained when referring to God.

The translators respected the difference in literary style between the Old and New Testaments in a number of ways. For instance, they maintained the "will/shall" future tense distinction of formal English in the Old Testament but not in the New. They chose to use the pronoun "you" universally, even in prayer and addresses to God. They left the matter of headings, references, and section heads to the individual publishers.

Compared with the earlier *RSV*, the *NRSV* adopted a slightly freer style of translation. Even with this freedom of style the translators consider this new version a literal translation. It represents a subtle shift in language style from its predecessor, but the cumulative effect is impressive.

The New King James Version

The *RSV* and *NRSV* uphold the basic aims of the King James tradition while taking advantage of advances in scholarship and textual studies. They strive to be contemporary in both language and scholarship. The *New King James Version* takes a very different approach to the tradition. It attempts to keep as much of the original King James Bible as possible.

The version began in 1975 when Thomas Nelson and Sons, a large Bible publishing firm, recognized that, despite the plethora of new translations, numbers of Bible readers still clung to their King James Bibles. The publisher gathered 100 people from various parts of the world to explore ways to create a new version that would update the language yet still look and feel like the original King James Bible.

Overview Committees were established in Britain and the United States. Translators worked on sections of the Bible, following guidelines that kept them very close to the way the 17th century translators worked. While they used the *Biblia Hebraica Stuttgartensia* for the Old Testament, they also relied on Bomberg's 16th-century text, the same one used by the first King James translators. Their New Testament source was F.H.A. Scrivener's 19th-century edition of the Received Text, a text similar to that prepared by Erasmus in the 16th century and which the King James Bible translators used.

After the Overview Committees went over a draft, it was further reviewed by an executive editorial board and a panel of English stylists. They worked on the final stages of the translating process at a location not far from Stirling Castle, one of King James' residences. The New Testament appeared in 1979. Psalms and Proverbs were finished in 1980, and the entire Bible was published in 1982.

The *New King James Bible* retains most of the features of the old King James Bible, including the use of italics for words not in the original languages but necessary for English sense. Some editions even use the verse-paragraph format, though editions with sense-paragraphs are also available. It also capitalizes pronouns when they refer to persons of the Trinity.

13 NEW FAMILIES OF TRANSLATIONS

The surge in translations we observed in the first half of the 20th century did not abate in the second half of the century. During the 37 years between the first publication of the *RSV* and the appearance of the *NRSV*, at least 20 other English translations of the Bible were produced, plus about as many translations of one Testament. This survey can treat only the most significant of these translations.

While the King James Bible tradition, most recently represented by the *NRSV*, remains popular, other important families of translations have emerged. Among them we find excellent Roman Catholic versions translated from the original languages, a reflection of the new ecumenical spirit in biblical work that has prevailed since Vatican II.

ROMAN CATHOLIC VERSIONS

The Confraternity Version

Long before Vatican II, the American Bishops' Committee of the Confraternity of Christian Doctrine felt a pressing need to replace the prevailing Rheims-Challoner English translation of the Vulgate Bible with something more readable. The Biblical Commission at Rome approved the project. Twenty-eight scholars of the Catholic Biblical Association of America, chaired by the Rev. Edward P. Arbez, began work on a new translation in 1936. The work was conceived as a revision of the Rheims-Challoner version, so the translation was based on a critical edition of the Latin Vulgate, though translators made reference to Greek source texts. The New Testament was published in 1941 by St. Anthony Guild Press in Paterson, New Jersey, and became known as *The Confraternity Version*.

Widely used during the war, this Testament became popular with English-speaking Roman Catholics around the world, despite its American idiom and spelling. It uses paragraphs, quotation marks, and modern phrasing (mixed, though, with a few quaint and outdated expressions such as "It came to pass").

The Old Testament appeared in a series of four volumes beginning in 1952 and was published by the Confraternity of Christian Doctrine.

The Jerusalem Bible

As early as 1903, Dominicans at the École Biblique (School of Biblical Studies) in Jerusalem had translated the Bible from original languages and sent copies to priests in France. For several decades after, progressive priests throughout France read and digested these translations, keeping well-worn copies on their book-shelves.

Since the Vatican did not approve Bible translations from the original tongues until 1943, these priests were acting against church policy. But the interest, hard work, and keen scholarship of French Dominicans at home and in Jerusalem created an underground of biblical scholarship. When peace was restored after the war, the Jerusalem-based Dominicans emerged into daylight, highly respected by the international community of biblical scholars.

The fruits of their long study were embodied in a French Bible published in 1954, entitled *La Bible de Jerusalem*. It was widely acclaimed, though not accessible to those who did not read French. Alexander Jones of Christ's College, Liverpool, with the help of 27 colleagues, undertook to translate this Bible into English. They used the French text as a basic control, but regularly consulted the original texts and the Jerusalem scholars to produce the best possible English rendering. The translation appeared in 1966 as *The Jerusalem Bible* and was widely used both by the growing number of Roman Catholic Bible students and many Protestants.

This Bible, then, was developed in a similar manner as Coverdale's, whose Bible in large part was a translation of Luther's German Bible. Some users called the *JB* "the Bible with a French accent," because some Latinisms associated with Romance languages showed through.

The Jerusalem Bible positioned the Deuterocanonical books throughout the Old Testament, as did the Vulgate. It used Yahweh for the divine name. Poetry was printed as such and where the Septuagint has different chapter and verse numbers in the Old Testament (the numbering adopted by the Vulgate), they are indicated in the margin. The translators translated some idioms loosely when it was necessary to clarify meanings.

What sold the Jerusalem Bible, however, was less its English style than its scholarship, especially in its notes which the English version translated directly from the French. It was prepared deliberately as a study Bible, with the original purpose of reinvigorating biblical studies in the Roman Church. Many pages would give more space to notes than to text. The notes dealt with dates, language, history, inconsistencies, history of interpretation, and other important issues. They brought a high level of scholarship from one of the world's centers for biblical study. *The Jerusalem Bible*, in effect, combines the biblical texts with an introductory course in biblical studies.

The full set of notes, chronological tables, extensive introductions to each book, maps, articles, and other helps in the Standard Edition made for a heavy, bulky volume. The publishers brought out a somewhat more compact Reader's Edition, with brief introductions, a minimum of notes, and eliminated most of the other helps. Doubleday & Company, Inc., publishes *The Jerusalem Bible* in the United States.

The New Jerusalem Bible

In 1973, a new edition of *La Bible de Jerusalem* appeared which incorporated new concepts and ideas in biblical studies that had emerged since the first edition and introduced many important changes in the notes. Henry Wansbrough of Ampleforth Abbey, York, supervised the translation of this revised version into English, with Alan Neame doing much of the work on the Old Testament.

Wansbrough recognized that the first Jerusalem Bible had been criticized for sometimes following the French more closely than the original languages. He and his colleagues made a thoroughgoing revision from the original languages. However, when the text allowed more than one interpretation, they opted for the choice in *La Bible de Jerusalem*.

Dom Henry Wansbrough, OSB, General Editor of The New Jerusalem Bible, a revision of the earlier and popular version, The Jerusalem Bible

The New Jerusalem Bible was published in 1985. It strove to maintain this Bible's tradition as a study tool. The translators tried to be as literal as possible. In parallel passages, as in the Gospels, they made efforts to mirror the parallel similarities and differences exactly. For words with important theological meaning, they usually translated each instance with the same English word. They also spent "considerable efforts...to soften or avoid the inbuilt preference of the English language, a preference now found so offensive by some people, for the masculine; the word of the Lord concerns women and men equally."[18] With an eye on its use for public reading in worship, the translators adopted a dignified style free of colloquialisms.

The updated notes in *The New Jerusalem Bible* express the same careful scholarship and informed understanding as those in the original edition, and are just as extensive.

The New American Bible

The 1943 Papal Encyclical *Divino Afflante Spiritu* opened the door for Catholic scholars to translate Scripture directly from the original tongues. Very soon after the encyclical was published, work began on a version of the whole Bible by a committee under the chairmanship of the Rev. Louis F. Hartman, C.SS.R., S.S.L. The editorial committee included four Protestant scholars. The new version first appeared in a series of preliminary editions. The definitive edition, published in 1970, bore the name *The New American Bible*.

The translators wanted to put "the word of God into the vernacular in rigorous fidelity to the meaning of the original, expressed in simple and intelligible language." They consulted the Vulgate for some renderings that Catholic tradition had revered over the centuries. For the most part, though, they produced a fresh and careful translation. Sponsored by the Bishops' Committee of the Confraternity of Christian Doctrine, the *NAB* was a revision of the earlier *Confraternity Version*.

The *NAB* provides copious notes, mostly devoted to clarifying the line of argument expressed in the different books of the Bible, especially in the New Testament. The Old Testament notes clarify terms and names of the characters. In the standard text edition of the *NAB*, however, the notes are not as extensive as those in *The Jerusalem Bible*.

The language chosen is dignified since the version was intended for liturgical use. The New Testament was revised in 1986. The revision addressed the issue of gender inclusive language, but took a somewhat conservative approach. For example, it continued to translate the Greek term *adelphoi* as "brothers," while the *NRSV* usually treated the term in the general sense of "my friends," or "people," or "brothers and sisters."

MODERN JEWISH VERSIONS

The translation of the Hebrew Scriptures done by Isaac Leeser in 1853 had received wide acceptance in both home and synagogue. Leeser essentially worked within the framework of the King James translation "which for simplicity cannot be surpassed," in his words.

Jewish scholars, gathered by the Jewish Publication Society of America, located in Philadelphia, worked on a new, independent translation which would, at the same time, be faithful to both the Masoretic text and the traditional style of the English Bible. The Psalms appeared in 1903 and the whole Hebrew Scriptures were published in 1917 with the title, *The Holy Scriptures according to the Masoretic Text*, and reprinted many times since.

When the need for a modern speech translation became apparent, The Jewish Publication Society developed what they called "A New Translation of The Holy Scriptures according to the traditional Hebrew text." It appeared in three volumes. *Torah* was published in 1962 and revised five years later. This was followed by *The Prophets* (1978) and *The Writings* (1982). One committee of scholars worked on the first two sections, leaving *The Writings* to another committee. It is a readable yet dignified rendering into modern English. The translators honored the Masoretic text, as basic to Jewish translators as the Vulgate had been to Catholic translators. Yet they were open to corrections from other sources and recognized clearly that a faithful translation of Hebrew cannot go slavishly word by word.

PROTESTANT VERSIONS

The New English Bible

In the United Kingdom, the desire to do something about the *Revised Version*, which had not fully replaced the *King James Version* in Great Britain, was growing. The University Presses of Cambridge and Oxford had circulated some proposals for a revision, along the lines of the *RSV*, without success. The successful proposal came from another source in 1946 and represented a more radical turn.

The General Assembly of the Church of Scotland in that year recommended a new, modern translation rather than a revision. They approached other churches with the idea. The Church of England, Methodists, Congregationalists, and Baptists responded initially. Later, these were joined by Presbyterians, the Society of Friends, Churches in Wales, Churches in Ireland, the British and Foreign Bible Society, and the National Bible Society of Scotland. Still later, the hierarchies of the Roman Catholic Church in England and Scotland sent observers.

The planners determined to make a totally new translation which would "employ a contemporary idiom rather than reproduce traditional 'biblical' English."[19] The University Presses joined in the project, directed by a Joint Committee, and agreed to finance it.

The Joint Committee appointed four panels of experts, drawn from the best talents in the United Kingdom and chosen for ability rather than church affiliation. Three panels dealt with the Old Testament, the New Testament, and the Apocrypha. The fourth panel addressed matters of literary style and reviewed the work of the other three panels for literary quality, appropriateness of English expression, and style—both when read privately and when spoken aloud in public worship.

Professor C.H. Dodd, a world-class scholar, headed the New Testament panel and served as director of the enterprise. Among the translators whose work is well-known in the United States are the Rev. Professor C.F.D. Moule, the Right Reverend J.A.T. Robinson, and Professor T.W. Manson.

The translators worked in a similar fashion as the *RSV* translators. Individuals would generate an initial draft of a book and circulate it in typescript to their colleagues on their panel. Then the panel members would meet around a table to discuss the draft verse by verse, sentence by sentence. When they agreed on a final draft, they sent it to the literary panel. That panel would rewrite as necessary to see that the English was appropriate to the original literary form, such as narrative or poetry. The literary revision went back to the originating panel which checked to make sure that no meanings were lost in the pursuit of literary excellence. They sought "timeless English," but were not bound by any older English biblical terminology. Sometimes this process meant passing the manuscript back and forth several times between the translation panel and the literary panel. When everyone agreed on the final version, it was submitted to the Joint Committee.

The work was called *The New English Bible*. The New Testament was published simultaneously in the United Kingdom and the United States on March 14, 1961, the 350th anniversary of the publication of the King James Bible. The entire Bible was published, in editions with and without the Apocrypha, in 1970. In Great Britain alone, the initial press run of one million copies of the *NEB* sold out on the first day. The Bible used marginal verse numbers with no indication of the verse break in the paragraph. Notes are few, mostly dealing with alternative readings and philological matters.

The literary panel was a brilliant innovation. They made the most of a translation done independently of the King James tradition. (This is the first "official" English version to step out of a conscious association with the King James tradition.) Semitic expressions such as "sons of wrath," "children of light" and phrases with loosely attached, adjectival genitives, such as "the hope of your calling" are rendered into idiomatic English. The narratives in the Old Testament, especially, read rather like a modern novel. The vocabulary and style represent the English spoken by educated persons.

The *NEB* is less of a formal correspondence translation than the *RSV*. Some informal renderings were done to make the point of the text more clear to a reader. C.F.D. Moule, one of the *NEB* translators, explained this procedure by using the example of Colossians 3.9, 10. He offered this as his own example of a literal translation of these verses:

> Do not lie to one another, having stripped off the old man with his deeds, and having put on the new which is being renovated into knowledge according to the likeness of the one who created him.[20]

The crucial question, Moule observed, is, What does "into knowledge" refer to or mean? A formal correspondence translation can leave that question to the reader and simply render the Greek as it stands (see, for example, the *RSV, NRSV,* and *NIV.*) The *NEB,* however, in the interest of clarity, adds some words (here put in italics):

> Stop lying to one another, now that you have discarded the old nature with its deeds and have put on the new nature, which is being constantly renewed in the image of its Creator *and brought to know God.*[21]

The added words simply make it easier for the reader to comprehend. Additional words of this kind constitute the difference between a functional equivalence and a formal correspondence translation.

Any member of the translation panels could ask for a marginal note if they insisted on a reading different from that adopted by the majority. *NEB* marginal notes thus reveal many places that other versions do not cite where the Greek of the New Testament is ambiguous and open to multiple renderings.

The *NEB* was also innovative with the format it used. The text appears in one column. Verse numbers run down the outer margins. Only a minimum of sub-heads are included. Instead of section heads to indicate a shift in subject or thought, the *NEB* inserts a space and begins the new section with the initial words set in small capital letters. The result is a very attractive and readable page.

THE CASE OF THE APOCRYPHA

For better than two centuries after the *King James Version,* the Apocrypha was included in Protestant Bibles, treated not as canonical Scripture but as useful and edifying material. The Puritans found this practice objectionable, but the Church of England liked it. Early in the 19th century, the British and Foreign Bible Society formed and became a major supplier of English Bibles. Scottish members of the Society, influenced by the spirit of the Westminster Confession and the Puritan tradition, objected to including the Apocrypha in Bible Society Bibles. After five years of struggle, their views prevailed and the Apocrypha was dropped. This established a precedent soon followed by commercial publishers, thus beginning the tradition of Apocrypha-less Protestant Bibles in English.

The Revised English Bible

As a major new translation gets used, many suggestions for improvement are offered by readers and other scholars. At the same time, scholarship marches on. Renderings that seemed best to a previous generation of scholars may now appear inadequate in the eyes of a newer generation.

Thus, 19 years later, the *New English Bible* was revised and published under a new name: *The Revised English Bible*. The revision was developed under the same Joint Committee structure that guided the original version and was published in 1989.

The revision panels expanded to include Roman Catholics as full participants, joined by the Salvation Army and the Moravian Church. The revisers dealt with gender bias in language, added more subheads to make it easier to follow the argument of various books, replaced marginal verse numbers with superscript numbers in the text, and reverted to the more traditional two-column page layout.

Some users had complained that misunderstandings arose in some passages when the *NEB* was read orally. Certain words and phrases, especially in the Psalms, were not clear when spoken, so the revisers corrected those problems. They also dropped the "thou" form in prayer and Psalms, replacing it with "you."

The New International Version

Despite the proliferation of good modern language translations, many conservative Protestant Christians clung to the King James Bible for reasons more theological than literary. They weren't convinced of the theological soundness of many of the churches which sponsored the *RSV* and *NEB*, and felt that Roman Catholic translations were not sufficiently "Protestant." To meet their needs, the New York Bible Society (now the International Bible Society) sponsored a conservative, contemporary English translation on which work started in 1967.

A group of 100 scholars from America, Great Britain, Canada, Australia, and New Zealand, representing a variety of denominations but led by the Christian Reformed Church, assembled to work on the project. All members of the team were selected for holding "a high view of Scripture as set forth in the Westminster Confession of Faith, and the statement of faith of the National Association of Evangelicals." The translation was to be faithful to the original languages, to "reflect the unity and harmony of the Spirit-inspired writing," to avoid injecting elements of "unwarranted paraphrasing," and to be equally useful for public worship, private study, and devotional reading. The new version was to "communicate God's revelation in the language of the people—to do for our time what the *King James Version* did for its day."

SPECIALTY BIBLE EDITIONS

In addition to versions that represent fresh translations of Scripture, there are a number of specialized editions that add supplementary material to the text of an existing version.

Some "reference Bibles" apply a scheme of interpretation to the Bible and add an apparatus to make it easier to follow their scheme in the Scriptures. The Thompson Chain-Reference Bible assigns nearly every verse to one of several themes. The Scofield Reference Bible applies a pattern of "dispensations" or ways God has dealt with humanity in different eras, a method first developed by the Plymouth Brethren in England. The Rainbow Bible uses colors to show which passages are related to 12 key themes.

On a more scholarly level, we find a number of "study Bibles." These supply footnotes with historical or theological insights to help interpret passages and verses, along with extensive background articles. Study Bibles reflect different theological views. The Oxford Study Bible, Westminster Study Bible and The Harper's Study Bible are in the tradition of middle-of-the-road Protestantism. The latest editions of these are based on the NRSV; earlier editions used the KJV or RSV. The NIV Study Bible, based on that translation, reflects a more conservative tradition. The Jerusalem Bible, with its abundant notes, must be considered among the study Bibles.

More recently, a number of "life-related" study Bibles have appeared. Traditional study Bibles focussed on historical background to help the user understand what the Bible meant to its first readers. They left it to the reader to determine what it means today. Life-related study Bibles, such as The Life Application Bible, focus on what Scripture means in life today. The notes resemble brief commentaries, drawing out the implications of a passage, taken at face value, for morals, behavior, attitude, and piety in today's world. They have become very popular and generally reflect a literal understanding of Scripture with conservative moral and spiritual interpretations. These editions often use the *New King James Version* or the *New International Version*.

All these specialty editions can be very helpful so long as users realize that they are not a "new Bible" but an existing translation supplemented with material to help readers apply the text to their lives.

The Anchor Bible presents a special case. Publication of this multi-volume commentary series on the Bible, including the Apocryphal/Deuterocanonical writings, began in 1964. Each book of the Bible discussed is accompanied by an independent translation done by the commentator. Some of these are considered excellent. But the reader should understand that no effort has been made to harmonize the style of the translations and that the translations are designed for scholarly use rather than continuous reading.

The translators used the Masoretic text in the latest edition of *Biblia Hebraica Stuttgartensia* and a variety of editions of the Greek New Testament. The Gospel of John appeared in 1969 as a preliminary, with the whole New Testament following in 1973. Portions of the Old Testament were published between 1975 and 1977, with the entire Bible in publication in 1978. Zondervan Bible Publishers of Grand Rapids, Michigan, a firm close to the Christian Reformed Church, published the version.

In the translating process, each book was assigned to a team of scholars. The initial drafts were revised by three other groups: first, one of the Intermediate Editorial Committees; second, one of the General Editorial Committees; and finally, by the overall Committee on Bible Translation. During the process, the translations were reviewed by stylistic consultants to insure smooth English. Two consultants reviewed every book twice—once before and once after the final major revision.

The Apocrypha was not included in the translation project because the Westminster Confession, which guides many Reformed churches, specifically states that the Apocrypha is not Scripture.

The result is a readable and clear translation. The English is as international as possible, avoiding obvious Americanisms and Briticisms. (However, a separate British edition was issued to address matters of spelling and varying word choices.) The translators used "you" both in narrative passages and in addresses to God. They achieved an idiomatic style while retaining dignity of expression. They were not interested in the issue of gender-inclusive language. The NIV has gained wide use far beyond the conservative circles which sponsored it.

14 A NEW DYNAMIC IN TRANSLATING

Through the centuries of the English Bible, translations have fallen somewhere along a line marked at one end by literalness and at the other end by clarity. A single translation simply cannot provide 100 per cent of both of these important qualities. Every translator or translation team must decide which end of the scale they will favor. Still, the great Tyndale tradition of translating sought to make Scripture understandable and accessible to the common person as well as the university professor.

Is there a way to do quality translating with a powerful stress on clarity without straying too far from the literal phrasing and word sequence of the original language? The answer came from lands far away from English-speaking countries.

Cross-cultural Communication

Scripture has provided the core tool for missionary endeavors especially since the rise of the worldwide mission movement in the 19th century. Bible societies, which were formed in most Western nations during that century, along with other translating organizations, became involved in translating the Scriptures into regional and tribal languages. Often, missionaries had to create a written language where none previously existed. But a written language and literacy did not fully open the Scriptures to people who lived their lives in a world far different from the one in which Christianity had been shaped.

The problem was one of communication across diverse cultures.

For example, how does one translate the 23rd Psalm for a people who have never seen sheep or a shepherd? How do you communicate the full meaning of "Father" as a reference to God to people in matriarchal societies? What meaning can a Roman or Pharisee have to a tribe in the remote Amazon basin? A host of problems like these challenged translators.

An approach to a solution emerged with the development of functional equivalence translation. Instead of translating the original language literally, this approach expresses the original writer's intention in words and concepts that draw from the contemporary readers' experience and culture. The aim is to make the experience and meaning of Scripture in the new language the *equivalent* of the experience of those who first heard or read it long ago. It interprets faithfulness to the original message of Scripture in terms of contexts and meanings rather than of words and forms.

The task of functional equivalence translation is arduous. It begins with an exegesis (analysis of meaning) of the original text. What did the writer intend to say? What situation was being addressed? In what sort of cultural context was it written? Given the culture of the original writer, what could be left unsaid, assuming the readers would understand?

After this analysis, the translator determines how to express that intention in a new language and culture. What are equivalent situations in the new culture? What must be added to make clear those points which the writer had assumed the original readers would understand? This results in a first draft in the receptor language (the language of the translation).

The proposed new translation is now analyzed. Does it convey the whole message and thread of argument, rather than merely summarizing? Does it go beyond what the writer intended? Has the message been bent to apply to a situation other than that which the original writer intended?

The next step refines the translation by finding the nearest equivalent for the message in the natural patterns of thought and speech in the language of translation. In the process, the translator prefers contextual consistency over verbal consistency, the spoken form of language over the written form. And in the choice of idioms and words, the translator prefers common, everyday usage. Although the goal of a functional equivalence translation is to be as clear as possible to as many people as possible, the translator is not limited to an arbitrary or fixed list of words. Any word in common use can be used if it fits the context.

Dr. Eugene Nida (1914 —-), linguist and translator, pioneered in the theoretical and practical development of functional equivalence translating. He recognized that the problems in translating went beyond finding words in one language to fit those in another. He studied the deeper issues of communicating text from one culture and worldview to those in a very different culture. In addition to writing major theoretical works on linguistics and conducting seminars around the world, he and his colleagues have assisted Bible translators working in more than 500 languages. For many years, Dr. Nida headed the Translations Department of the American Bible Society and now serves as a special consultant. He was deeply involved in developing the Today's English Version. In 1976 he received the Diamond Jubilee medal of the Institute of Linguistics and in 1977 he received the Alexander Gode Medal from the American Translators Association.

The example of Acts 20.32 may help to clarify how functional equivalence addresses a specific passage. In the *RSV*, a translation which attempts to stay close to the sentence structure and forms of the Greek, this New Testament verse reads:

> And now I commend you to God and to the word of his grace, which is able to build you up and to give you the inheritance among all those who are sanctified.[22]

People familiar with Greek grammatical forms and educated in "church language" may have little or no problem understanding this rather literal translation. But for others, several problems arise in making the meaning of this passage clear in English:

1. *Word of his grace.* "Word" here means "message," not a single term. "Of" indicates a relationship between "word" and "grace," but does not make that relation clear. "Grace," always meaning God's merciful dealings with humankind, is an event rather than a word.

2. *Build you up.* This is "Bible English." One doesn't hear the expression in ordinary conversation.

3. *Inheritance.* In everyday use, this term refers to what people leave to designated persons in their wills. The Bible, though, uses it in the special sense of what belongs to God's people.

4. *Those who are sanctified.* Another phrase in "Bible English." The New Testament meaning always refers to God's people.

5. *Which.* In the Greek, this pronoun refers to "word" rather than to "grace," a point easy to overlook as translated by the *RSV*.

Functional equivalence, in contrast to the literal approach to translation, translates across cultures, making the meaning of a message from one culture understandable both verbally and psychologically to another culture. As the previous example shows, the same principles apply as well when translating the New Testament Greek into another modern language, English.

Today's English Version

In 1963 the American Bible Society became aware of a need in the United States for a Scripture version designed for people for whom English was a second language. Most of the existing English translations at that time were too difficult for this group to read easily. Also, there were many English-speaking people who were not brought up in the church and for whom the usual terminology of the English Bible seem strange and foreign. The Society called upon an experienced

AROUND THE WORLD

Common language Bible translations based on the same principles that guided the TEV have appeared around the world. Complete Bibles have been translated into a number of languages, including German, Spanish, Korean, Portuguese, Tagalog, and Chinese.

American Bible Society translation consultant, Dr. Robert G. Bratcher, to undertake a totally new translation on the principles of functional equivalence (then known as "dynamic equivalence").

It may seem that a simpler solution could be found, perhaps by using a very limited, simplified vocabulary. Bratcher realized, however, that the problem of communicating went beyond mere choice of vocabulary; it also involved cultural issues and ways of thinking. These latter issues posed the most difficult challenges, but they could be dealt with in ways that enhanced understanding with the help of functional equivalence principles.

Today's English Version, perhaps better known by its popular title "The Good News Bible," marked a radical departure from the traditional, formal correspondence approach to Bible translating. No one was sure how the new translation would be received. A preliminary Gospel of Mark was issued in 1964 to test the waters.

Encouraged by the positive response, Bratcher continued his work, aided by a consulting committee of five members. Two were connected with national and international mission work; one was a literacy expert; another was an experienced translator with the British and Foreign Bible Society; and the fifth was a noted biblical scholar. They translated the New Testament from the United Bible Societies' Greek New Testament.

The entire New Testament was published in 1966, illustrated with very simple line drawings by the Swiss artist, Annie Vallotton. It bore the title *Good News for Modern Man/The New Testament in Today's English Version*. The widespread acceptance of the new translation astonished the Bible Society. What had begun as a specialized translation found a warm welcome with a broad audience. Within ten years of its publication, some 50 million copies of the New Testament were in print! The New Testament was revised in 1971 and again in 1976, at which point it was checked against the 1975 third edition of the UBS Greek New Testament. All editions received the Imprimatur for Roman Catholic use.

Meanwhile, work was underway on the Old Testament as the New Testament went though its revisions. Preliminary editions of various Old Testament books, translated from Rudolf Kittel's *Biblia Hebraica* in the third edition of 1937, were issued between 1970 and 1975. The entire Bible was published in 1976, combining the newly completed Old Testament with the fourth edition of the New Testament. When the translation of the Deuterocanonicals/Apocrypha was completed in 1979, these books were added to some editions, making it possible for the Roman Catholic church to grant the Imprimatur to "The Good News Bible." A revised edition of the complete *TEV* Bible was issued in 1992.

The printed Bibles incorporated user-friendly features, such as superscript (above the line) verse numbers. Sometimes one verse citation would include a number of verses (such as Numbers 13.17-20) because the brief text following was restructured in the translators' efforts to attain natural English syntax in a way that made the original dividing points between verses unidentifiable. The census reports in Numbers 1–2 were arranged in chart form, as they might appear in a daily newspaper. Genealogies were treated in a similar fashion. Names and unusual words were explained in footnotes. A word list defined terms that have specialized religious meanings or which have no modern, everyday equivalent—such as Pharisee, Passover, and the like. The inclusion of subheads simplified the task of following the argument of a book. When parallel passages existed (as in the Gospels) they were noted beneath the subheads. Maps, a subject index, and a chronological outline added, along with a list of passages where the New Testament quoted Old Testament texts from the Greek Septuagint to help the reader see where these differed from the Masoretic Hebrew text.

In many ways, the *Today's English Version* can be seen as a fulfillment of Tyndale's dream for an English Scripture that almost anyone could read and understand.

The approach taken toward translation by the *TEV* resembles that of the *NEB* in that both translations often restructure a passage in order to make its original meaning as clear as possible. The *NEB*, however, chose the language style of an educated English speaker, while the *TEV* used the common, popular style. A comparison of Romans 1.5 from these two versions with the *RSV*, a traditional formal correspondence translation, shows the difference of approaches:

...through whom we have received grace and apostleship to bring about the obedience of faith for the sake of his name among all nations. (RSV)[23]

Through him I have received the privilege of a commission in his name to lead to faith and obedience men in all nations. (NEB)[24]

Through him God gave me the privilege of being an apostle for the sake of Christ, in order to lead people of all nations to believe and obey. (TEV)

And how did the TEV handle the example of Acts 20.32, examined earlier in the RSV translation?

And now I commend you to the care of God and to the message of his grace, which is able to build you up and give you the blessings God has for all his people. (TEV)

The TEV rendering addresses most of the "meaning challenges" noted on page 193. Note, however, that the translators chose to use the "Bible English" phrase, "build you up" and the word "grace" in its narrow, specifically religious sense.

Besides gaining broad acceptance as a Bible for personal reading, the TEV entered into the lives of churches. The American Bible Society is supported in its ministry of Bible translation, publication, and distribution by more than 80 denominations and the TEV has enjoyed ecclesiastical endorsement or acceptance by many of them. Some denominations have even adopted it officially as their basic Bible for educational purposes. It is used for public reading in churches and TEV lectionaries (books of appointed lessons for each Sunday) have been printed. Because the version uses spoken forms of language, it is well suited to reading aloud in public.

The TEV has also found an audience with youth and young adults. There is a growing recognition that we are seeing the emergence of a "post-literate" generation, a group of people who know

ONE MINOR DRAWBACK

For the gain in clarity, a functional equivalence translation loses the support of a concordance. A concordance is a reference listing every occurrence of a word in a Bible version. Over the years this important tool has helped Bible students do word studies and trace themes by looking up occurrences of words such as "reconciliation" or "justification." But a functional equivalence translation renders these key Scriptural terms by several different English words or even phrases, depending on the context. The TEV addressed this problem by adding a subject index of passages related to key themes and concepts.

how to read but, because of the pervasiveness of television, feel more comfortable with visual and aural forms of communication. Print is not always their first choice and they have less patience with print media than their parents or grand-parents had. When they read they prefer straightforward, simple text.

Contemporary English Version

As noted earlier, the *Today's English Version* began as a translation for people for whom English was a second language. The translators avoided expressions and allusions which, though familiar to all who grew up in an English-speaking environment, might not be immediately understood by those who were less at home with English. But what would happen if functional equivalence principles were applied to a translation addressed specifically for those nurtured in English-speaking culture?

Observing how the *TEV* was used across all age groups, the American Bible Society in 1985 authorized a new translation specifically intended for English-speaking children as well as adults. One translator and one reviewer were assigned to prepare an initial manuscript on the life of Jesus based on selected passages from the four Gospels. Later, a team of translators would be assembled and set to work translating the full Bible.

The first drafts were prepared by the ABS team of translators whose members represented several Christian traditions. These drafts, after review by the ABS Translations Sub-Committee to its Board, went to a large, international circle of reviewers from countries where English is used. The drafts were then revised in light of the critical comments, and reviewed again by the Sub-Committee. The reviewers included Bible scholars, English language experts, poets, linguists, special reading consultants, a wide variety of denominational representatives, and over 40 translation consultants serving the United Bible Societies around the world. The *CEV* translators used the 1983 corrected third edition of the United Bible Societies' Greek New Testament text and the fourth edition, 1967-83, of the *Biblia Hebraica Stuttgartensia* for the Old Testament.

Two additional guidelines directed this translation: aurality and "right-hand extension." Aurality means paying attention to how the English sounds when read aloud. Having in mind a cross-generational translation, it was important to consider users who would read aloud in public or in intimate, family settings. This consideration led the *CEV* translators to go beyond the *TEV* reliance on the syntax of the spoken language to a commitment to choose words and phrases which, when read aloud, could easily be understood by those listening.

THE ROLE OF BIBLE SOCIETIES

The first Bible Society was formed in Halle, Germany, in 1710 as an outgrowth of the missionary-minded Moravian movement. The Halle center produced Scripture for Jews and Muslims, as well as for the poor in Germany.

But the worldwide Bible Society movement began when the British and Foreign Bible Society organized in 1804. Within thirty years, other Bible Societies organized in most European and North American nations. Bible Societies supplied affordable Scripture to their own people, but as the world mission movement expanded in the 19th century, they became increasingly involved in translating Scripture into the languages of places in the world where missionaries from their countries were at work.

With the end of colonialism after World War II, a number of national Societies emerged in newly independent countries. In 1946, the United Bible Societies formed to provide a cooperative framework through which the national Societies could work. The UBS has taken significant leadership in the task of translation. It has developed significant scholarly resources for Bible translating, including excellent editions of the Greek and Hebrew source texts as well as handbooks and monographs which address exegetical, cultural, and linguistic matters important to practicing translators. It was through UBS- sponsored linguistic conferences and translation seminars that the principles of functional equivalence translation were refined and advanced. The UBS also provides a means by which Bible Societies in wealthier countries can support Societies in emerging nations.

The first Bible Society in the United States was the Philadelphia Bible Society established in 1808. It was followed by Societies in Connecticut, Massachusetts, New York, and Maine. These merged in 1816 to form the American Bible Society, though several of these Societies continued to operate under a separate identity for some time.

Through the work of Bible Societies and other Bible translating organizations, at least a portion of Scripture is now available in more than 2,000 languages and dialects. Bible Societies produce nearly 30 million Bibles, New Testaments, and Scripture portions each year. Since they are supported by participating denominations and private gifts, most Bible Societies can distribute Scripture at or below cost.

"Right-hand extension" is a term which simply reflects the fact that when we read English our eyes move from left to right. Complex subordinate clauses, for instance, often force a reader to glance backward to find the appropriate antecedents. This interrupts the natural left-to-right reading flow and is one of the reasons many readers are reluctant to read aloud in public. The *CEV* avoids sentence structures that force this kind of backward eye movement. The result is a pleasant, easy-to-follow text that "flows" smoothly "to the right."

The first edition of the complete New Testament came off the press in 1991. Meanwhile, work continued on the Old Testament. The Psalms and Proverbs were published in combination with the New Testament in 1992, and the full Bible in 1995. Some editions of the *CEV* have appeared under the title, *New Testament with Psalms and Proverbs*.

Like the *TEV*, the *CEV* does not use certain terms familiar to readers accustomed to more traditional translations, such as "reconciliation," "sanctification," "redemption," and so forth. There are two reasons for this. First, the religious meaning of these words is simply not recognizable to those outside the church (and is often difficult for many within the church). The second reason is linguistic. Such nouns as "sanctification" really refer more to *actions* by God than to a static concept or idea which can be named. The biblical meaning is that of a specific action by God in the life experience of God's people. Thus, the *CEV* translates these terms by words and phrases that more clearly express the action involved.

How does the *CEV* translate Acts 20.32, the passage we've been using for comparison?

> I now place you in God's care. Remember the message about his great kindness! This message can help you and give you what belongs to you as God's people.

Even though the words and structure differ from those of a formal correspondence translation such as the *RSV*, the *meaning* of the verse has been expressed in a manner faithful to the sense of the Greek and in a form of English which nearly any English-speaking reader can understand.

This Bible version pays as much attention to an easy-to-read appearance on the page as it does to easy-to-read language. Like the *TEV*, this version uses clarifying subheads and superscript verse numbers. The *CEV* also adopted some interesting typographical innovations:

- Brief quotations within the text appear in quotation marks, but longer quotations, such as a parable told by Jesus, are indented and printed without quotation marks. This is clearer than the traditional, but confusing, string of paragraphs with opening quotation marks and no closing quotation marks. It also makes it easier to identify quotations within quotations by totally dispensing with single quotation marks.

- Poetry is set in verse form, but with great attention paid to its appearance on a page and its oral readability. Translators carefully broke lines at the point where a sense-unit ends and another begins.

The American Bible Society is also working on a *CEV* study Bible. Because the ABS is committed to expressing no doctrinal bias in its Bibles, the notes and helps in the *CEV* study Bible will focus on helping the reader bridge the gap between two cultures: the culture of biblical times and the culture of today. For this purpose, it will utilize notes, illustrations, maps, graphs, and other aids to understanding, including open-ended questions to interact with the reader.

Into the Computer Age

Every translation discussed so far has appeared in the form of a book to be read. Yet electronic communications may be pushing print media into the role of "yesterday's technology." Computers have introduced us to interactive and multimedia programs, where the user engages in a dialogue with the computer. And VCRs have placed an enormous supply of visual resources at our disposal, to use at our convenience.

Can the Bible's important message be communicated through these new electronic forms? The American Bible Society believes it can and in 1989 started its Multimedia Translations Project. The Project applies the principles of functional equivalence translation to a multimedia context which combines visual and aural experiences with participant interaction, all made possible through the power of computers.

The experience of "reading and studying" the Bible in this form gains some important dimensions. A printed book can deliver text and static illustrations, such as

The opening computer screen for "Out of the Tombs," an interactive, multimedia translation of Mark 5.1-20. The user can select from three interactive options: "See & Hear," "Explore," and "Do."

pictures, graphs, and charts. A computer-based program includes all these elements, plus images in motion and sound. One can hear how some present-day scholars believe a New Testament passage sounded when read in the original Greek. An interactive program allows the user to move around at will among all the resources the program offers, as well as providing a means for noting his or her own observations and comments. A program on one small CD-ROM disk can provide 2 1/2 hours or more of fascinating experiences interacting with a Bible passage–encountering its message, exploring its background, and seeing how it has influenced culture.

From Past to Present and Beyond

Our story of the English Bible has carried us through many centuries. We have watched the English language evolve and seen how it grew into an expressive vehicle for God's Word. We have followed the struggles to make God's Word available to all people. We have met some heroes, and we have encountered a few questionable characters. We have seen the impact of politics and social forces on the English Bible.

We began with missionaries crossing the bogs of Britannia, learned of monks copying manuscripts in drafty scriptoria, saw the emergence of the printing press and the mass production of Bibles, and reached the present where the dazzling possibilities of computers seem boundless.

It has been quite a journey, one that reminds us how intimately God's Word connects with daily life. One thread, though, ties the story together. It was best expressed by Tyndale's vision for Bible translating: to bring God's Word to the common person in a form they can understand and use in their lives.

The pursuit of that vision will continue into the future. As our language changes, as our culture diversifies, as new information technologies emerge, fresh approaches to Bible translation will keep pace. Because God's Word endures forever, and new generations will need to hear and receive it, the task of translating the Bible will never end.

TIMELINE OF MODERN ENGLISH BIBLES

At the start of the 20th century, the large majority of Bible readers used the *King James Version*. Some chose the Revised Version. The English language, however, was undergoing great changes on both sides of the Atlantic. Translators now sought to render God's Word in the same idioms that were appearing in English literature. This timeline shows how modern English translations correspond to developments in literature, history, and technology.

Modern Translations	Literature	History	Communications
1900			
American Standard Version (1901)	*The Wonderful World of Oz*, L. Frank Baum (1900)	U.S. President Theodore Roosevelt (1901-09)	First significant silent movie (1903)
The Twentieth-Century New Testament (1898-1901, rev. 1904)	*The Hound of the Baskervilles*, Arthur Conan Doyle (1902)	U.S. President William Taft (1909-13)	First nickelodeon (movie house) opens in Pittsburgh (1905)
Moffatt's *The Historical New Testament* (1901)	*Typhoon*, Joseph Conrad (1902)	Model T Ford (1909)	First speech transmission by radio (1906)
Weymouth's *New Testament* (1903)	*The Souls of Black Folk*, W.E.B. Du Bois (1903)	National Association for the Advancement of Colored People founded (1909)	First color movie (1906)
	The Jungle, Upton Sinclair (1906)	Boy Scouts founded (1910)	First daily newspaper cartoon strip (1907)
		U.S. institutes income tax (1913)	
		Panama Canal opens (1913)	
1910			
Moffatt's *The New Testament* (1913)	*The Love Song of J. Alfred Prufrock*, T.S. Eliot (1915)	U.S. President Woodrow Wilson (1913-21)	First modern crossword puzzle, *N.Y. Times* (1913)
Westminster Version New Testament begins to appear in portions (1913-1935)	*The Mysterious Stranger*, Mark Twain (1916)	Panama Canal opens (1914)	
Jewish Publication Society *The Holy Scriptures according to the Masoretic Text* (1917)	*Renascence and Other Poems*, Edna St. Vincent Millay (1917)	World War I (1914-18)	
	My Antonia, Willa Cather (1918)	U.S. enters World War I (1916-18)	
	The American Language, Henry L. Mencken (published in parts, 1919-48)		

Modern Translations	Literature	History	Communications

1920

Ballantine's *The Riverside New Testament* (1923)	*Babbitt,* Sinclair Lewis (1922)	Prohibition begins (U.S., 1917)	First continuously broadcasting radio station, KDKA, Pittsburgh (1920)
Goodspeed's *The New Testament, An American Translation* (1923)	*Ulysses,* James Joyce (1922)	Women gain right to vote (U.S., 1920; U.K., 1928; Canada, 1917)	*Time* magazine introduced (1923)
Montgomery's *The Centenary Translation of the New Testament* (1924)	*The Great Gatsby,* F. Scott Fitzgerald (1925)	U.S. President Warren G. Harding (1921-23)	First "talkie" movie (1927)
Moffatt's *The Old Testament* (1924); *The Holy Bible: A New Translation* (1926)	*The Sun Also Rises,* Ernest Hemingway (1926)	U.S. President Calvin Coolidge (1923-29)	First Technicolor movie (1935)
Smith's *Old Testament, An American Translation* (1927)	*Winnie-the-Pooh,* A.A. Milne (1926)	Scopes trial challenges teaching of evolution (1925)	
	To the Lighthouse, Virginia Woolf (1927)	Charles Lindbergh makes first non-stop solo flight across the Atlantic (1927)	
		Stock market collapses. Great Depression begins (1929)	

1930

Work begins on *Revised Standard Version* (1937)	*As I Lay Dying,* William Faulkner (1930)	U.S. President Herbert Hoover (1929-33)	First sight-and-sound television broadcast (1931)
Williams' *The New Testament: A Translation in the Language of the People* (1937)	*Little House on the Prairie,* Laura Ingalls Wilder (1935)	The Great Depression (1929-1941)	First mass-market paperback book published (1935)
Spencer's *New Testament* (1937)	*The Grapes of Wrath,* John Steinbeck (1939)	U.S. President Franklin Roosevelt (1933-45)	British Broadcasting Corporation begins television broadcasting (1936)
Smith-Goodspeed's *The Complete Bible, An American Translation* (1939)		New Deal policies enacted (1933)	Columbia Broadcasting System begins TV broadcasts (1939)
		World War II erupts in Europe (1939)	

Modern Translations	Literature	History	Communications
1940			
Hooke's *The New Testament in Basic English* (1941)	*The Screwtape Letters,* C.S. Lewis (1940)	Pearl Harbor bombed, U.S. enters World War II (1941-45)	FM broadcasting begins (1941)
Confraternity Version New Testament (1941)	*Native Son,* Richard Wright (1940)	U.S. President Harry Truman (1945-53)	First electronic vacuum tube computer (1946)
Knox's *New Testament* (1944) and *Old Testament* (1949)	*The Glass Menagerie,* Tennessee Williams (1945)	United Nations Charter signed (1945)	
Verkuyl's *Berkeley Version of the New Testament* (1945)	*The Naked and the Dead,* Norman Mailer (1948)	Dead Sea Scrolls discovered (1947)	
Revised Standard Version New Testament (1946)	*Cry, the Beloved Country,* Alan Paton (1948)		
Phillips' *Letters to Young Churches* (1947)			
1950			
Hooke's *The Basic Bible* (1949)	*The Lion, the Witch, and the Wardrobe,* C.S. Lewis (1950)	Korean War (1950-53)	First cable TV systems begin (1949)
Confraternity Version Old Testament (in parts, 1952 through 1961)	*Invisible Man,* Ralph Ellison (1952)	U.S. President Dwight Eisenhower (1953-61)	First color television broadcast (1953)
Revised Standard Version Old Testament (1952)	*A Good Man Is Hard to Find,* Flannery O'Connor (1955)	A.F. of L. and C.I.O. unions merge (1955)	
Revised Standard Version Apocrypha (1957)	*On the Road,* Jack Kerouac (1957)	First civil rights bill (U.S., 1957)	
Schonfield's *The Authentic New Testament* (1955)	*A Raisin in the Sun,* Lorraine Hansberry (1958)	U.S. launches its first satellite, Explorer I (1958)	
Phillips' *The New Testament in Modern English* (1958)	*Our Man in Havana,* Graham Greene (1958)		
The Holy Bible: The Berkeley Version in Modern English (1959)			

Modern Translations	Literature	History	Communications
1960			
New English Bible New Testament (1961)	*In the Clearing,* Robert Frost (1962)	U.S. President John Kennedy (1961-63)	First transatlantic TV broadcast via satellite (1962)
Jewish Publication Society *Torah* (1962)	*Herzog,* Saul Bellow (1964)	Peace Corp created (U.S. 1961)	First mini-computers for office use (1962)
New American Standard New Testament (1963)	*Ariel,* Sylvia Plath (1965)	Berlin Wall built (1961)	Corporation for Public Broadcasting estab-
The Jerusalem Bible (1966)	*The Mask of Apollo,* Mary Renault (1966)	Civil Rights march on Washington (U.S. 1963)	lished (1967)
Today's English Version New Testament ("Good News for Modern Man," 1966)		U.S. President Lyndon Johnson (1963-69)	Floppy disk invented (1970)
The Living Bible New Testament (paraphrase, 1967)		Vietnam War (1965-73)	
		U.S. astronauts land on the moon (1969)	
1970			
The Living Bible (paraphrase, 1971)	*Birds of America,* Mary McCarthy (1971)	U.S. President Richard Nixon (1969-74)	Video cassette recorder (VCR) invent-ed (1972)
New International Version (New Testament, 1973; Bible, 1978)	*A Whale for the Killing,* Farley Mowat (1972)	U.S. recognizes the People's Republic of China (1972)	Video game systems introduced (1972)
Good News Bible (Today's English Version, 1976; with Deuterocanonicals, 1979)	*Pilgrim at Tinker Creek,* Annie Dillard (1974)	U.S. President Gerald Ford (1974-77)	First "home" or per-sonal computer (1974)
	Sophie's Choice, William Styron (1979)	U.S. President Jimmy Carter (1977-81)	Audio CD, using digi-tal sound, introduced (1979)
Jewish Publication Society *The Prophets* (1978)			
New King James Version New Testament (1979)			

Modern Translations	Literature	History	Communications

1980

New King James Version Bible (1982)	*The Collected Stories of Isaac Bashevis Singer* (1982)	U.S. President Ronald Reagan (1981-89)	First Cable News Network (CNN) broadcast (1980)
Jewish Publication Society *The Writings* (1982)	*Modern Baptists,* James Wilcox (1983)	First woman appointed to the U.S. Supreme Court, Sandra Day O'Connor (1981)	First MTV broadcast (1981)
New Jerusalem Bible (1985)	*Beloved,* Toni Morrison (1987)	Berlin Wall taken down (1989)	First video camcorder (1982)
Revised English Bible with Apocrypha (1989)	*Cat's Eye,* Margaret Atwood (1989)		Internet system established (1982)
New Revised Standard Version (1989)			

1990

Contemporary English Version (New Testament, 1991; Bible, 1995; Bible with Deuterocanonicals, 1999)	*Omeros,* Derek Walcott (1990)	U.S. President George Bush (1989-93)	Cable TV reaches 60% of U.S. homes (1990)
ABS *Multimedia Translations* (computer-based, interactive, 1994)	*Generation X,* Douglas Coupland (1991)	Persian Gulf War (1991)	World Wide Web established (1991)
New Living Translation Bible (1996)	*New and Selected Poems,* Mary Oliver (1992)	U.S. President Bill Clinton (1993-2000)	First multimedia CD-ROM available (1992)
	The Information, Martin Amis (1995)	Nelson Mandela elected President of the Republic of South Africa (1994)	First DVD available (1996)

FOR FURTHER READING

Allen, Ward (translator and editor), *Translating for King James: A True Copy of the Notes of John Bois* (Nashville: Vanderbilt University Press, 1969)
Bois left the only comprehensive notes on the translation of the *King James Version*, so this is an invaluable resource.

Bruce, F.F., *The English Bible: A History of Translations from the earliest English Versions to the New English Bible, Revised Edition* (New York: Oxford University Press, 1970)
A revision of a 1961 work, updated when the full *NEB* appeared, this book offers a comprehensive, readable survey of the English Bible, written by a notable British Bible scholar. Chapter 17 gives details on the process of translating the *NEB* and the controversy it stirred.

The Cambridge History of the Bible (Cambridge at the University Press)
This multi-volume work appears in many libraries and contains a series of authoritative articles on all aspects of the Bible. For the story of the English Bible, consult volume 3, *The West from Reformation to the Present Day* (edited by S.L. Greenslade, 1963). For information on earlier versions, the Masoretic Text, and the Vulgate, consult volume 1, *From the Beginnings to Jerome* (edited by P.R. Ackroyd and C.F. Evans, 1970) and volume 2, *The West from the Fathers to the Reformation* (edited by G.W.H. Lampe, 1969).

Daniell, David, ed., *Tyndale's New Testament Translated by William Tyndale: A Modern-Spelling Edition of the 1534 Translation* (New Haven: Yale University Press, 1989)
Clear, easy-to-read setting of Tyndale's New Testament, including the translator's preface ("W.T. Unto the Reader"), Prologues to the Epistles, and marginal notes. Also includes an introduction by the editor and a brief glossary.

Goodspeed, Edgar J., *Problems of New Testament Translation* (Chicago: University of Chicago Press, 1945)
The translator of *The New Testament: An American Translation* discusses tricky passages of the New Testament and shows how translators since 1826 have dealt with them, in comparison with earlier translators.

Herbert, A.S. (editor), *Historical Catalogue of Printed Editions of the English Bible, 1525-1961* (London and New York: British and Foreign Bible Society and American Bible Society, 1968)
> Available from the American Bible Society, this book lists every printed English version of the Bible from Tyndale to the first edition of the *New English Bible New Testament*.

MacGregor, Geddes, *The Bible in the Making* (Philadelphia and New York: J.B. Lippincott Company, 1959)
> A brief, readable summary, still available in some libraries.

May, Herbert Gordon, *Our English Bible in the Making, Revised Edition* (Philadelphia: For the Cooperative Publication Association by The Westminster Press, 1952)
> Written to celebrate the printing of the *RSV*, it gives much information about the preparation of that important version.

Newman, Barclay M., et al, *Creating and Crafting the Contemporary English Version: A New Approach to Bible Translation* (New York: American Bible Society, 1996)
> This collection of articles by the chief translator of the Contemporary English Version describes the features that make this modern translation one that can be easily understood by all English speakers, even those who are unfamiliar with church language, and those whose primary experience of the Scriptures is through hearing them read aloud. Discussion of changes in the English language and audience needs explains why new, simpler translations are needed.

Nida, Eugene A., *Good News for Everyone: How to Use the Good News Bible (Today's English Version)* (Waco, Texas: Word Books, Publishers, 1977)
> This short book, published eleven years after the ground-breaking Good News for Modern Man New Testament became a national bestseller, describes the history of the Today's English Version and provides interesting insights into the scientific and linguistic bases of modern common-language equivalency translations. Out of print, still available in some libraries.

Reader's Digest, *The Bible through the Ages* (Pleasantville, N.Y. and Montreal: The Reader's Digest Association, Inc., 1996)
> Large, beautifully illustrated volume which covers the whole sweep of biblical history. Parts Four and Five treat early and printed translations.

Reumann, John H.P., *The Romance of Bible Scripts and Scholars* (Englewood Cliffs, N.J.: Prentice-Hall, Inc., 1965)
A good summary with some human interest stories, by a Lutheran New Testament scholar.

Rhodes, Erroll F., and Liana Lupas, *The Translators to the Reader: The Original Preface of the King James Version of 1611 Revisited* (New York: American Bible Society, 1997)
Includes a facsimile of the original preface, plus an extensively annotated transcription of the text and a modern English rendering.

Thompson, Craig R., *The Bible in English, 1525-1611*, in the series "Folger Guides to the Age of Shakespeare" (Washington, D.C.: Folger Shakespeare Library, n.d.)
Covers the vital period from Tyndale to the *AV*, with an emphasis on how those translations contributed to the development of the English language and literature.

Weigle, Luther A. (ed.), *The New Testament Octapla* (New York: Thomas Nelson, 1962)
Eight versions of the New Testament arranged for easy comparison. The versions are: Tyndale 1525 (edition of 1535), Great Bible 1539 (second edition of 1540), Geneva version 1560 (second edition of 1562), Bishops' Bible 1568 (edition of 1602, consulted by KJV translators), Revised Version 1881 (in American Standard Version edition of 1901), and Revised Standard Version 1946 (edition of 1960).

Sources of Quotations

Quotations of copyrighted material are identified by superscript numbers in the text.

1. *The Norton Anthology of English Literature*, Volume 1, Revised Edition. M.H. Abrams, General Editor. Copyright 1968 by W.W. Norton & Company, Inc. Reprinted by permission of the publisher.

2. *A Cambridge History of the Bible: The West from the Reformation to the Present Day*, S.L. Greenslade, editor. Copyright 1963, Cambridge University Press.

3. Laura H. Wild, *The Romance of the English Bible*, New York: HarperCollins Publishers, 1929.

4. *The Bible in the Making* by Geddes MacGregor. Copyright © 1959 by Geddes MacGregor. Copyright renewed. Reprinted by permission of HarperCollins Publishers, Inc.

5. From "Preface" in *The New Testament: An American Translation*. © 1923, 1948 by the University of Chicago.

6. *The New Testament: An American Translation*. © 1923, 1948 by the University of Chicago.

7. Reprinted with permission of Simon & Schuster, Inc. and HarperCollins Publishers Limited, from *New Testament in Modern English*, revised Edition translated by J.B Phillips. Copyright 1858, 1960, 1972 by J.B. Phillips.

8. Reprinted with permission of Simon & Schuster, Inc. and HarperCollins Publishers Limited, from *New Testament in Modern English*, revised Edition translated by J.B Phillips. Copyright 1858, 1960, 1972 by J.B. Phillips.

9. Hugh J. Schonfield, *The Authentic New Testament*. Published 1958 by the New American Library. By Arrangement with Dobson Books Ltd.

10. Frederick C. Grant, *An Introduction to the Revised Standard Version*. (International Council of Religious Education, 1946.)

11. Frederick C. Grant, *An Introduction to the Revised Standard Version*. (International Council of Religious Education, 1946.)

12. *The Revised Standard Version of the Bible*, copyright 1946, 1952, 1971 by the Division of Christian Education of the National Council of Churches of Christ in the USA. Used by permission.

13. Herbert Gordon May, *Our English Bible in the Making*. Used by permission of Vanderbilt University.

14. From "To the Reader" in the *New Revised Version of the Bible*, copyright 1989 by Division of Christian Education of the National Council of Churches in the USA. Used by permission. All rights reserved.

15. From "To the Reader" in the *New Revised Version of the Bible*, copyright 1989 by Division of Christian Education of the National Council of Churches in the USA. Used by permission. All rights reserved.

16. From "To the Reader" in the *New Revised Version of the Bible*, copyright 1989 by Division of Christian Education of the National Council of Churches in the USA. Used by permission. All rights reserved.

17. *Revised Standard Version of the Bible, Catholic Edition,* copyright 1965 by the National Council of the Churches of Christ in the USA.

18. From *The New Jerusalem Bible,* copyright by Doubleday, a division of Bantam Doubleday Dell Publishing Group, Inc. and Darton, Longman, & Todd, Ltd. Used by permission of Doubleday, a division of Bantam Doubleday Dell Publishing Group, Inc.

19. *New English Bible,* copyright Oxford University Press and Cambridge University Press, 1961, 1970.

20. *A Cambridge History of the Bible: The West from the Reformation to the Present Day,* S.L. Greenslade, editor. Copyright 1963, Cambridge University Press.

21. *New English Bible,* copyright Oxford University Press and Cambridge University Press, 1961, 1970.

22. *The Revised Standard Version of the Bible,* copyright 1946, 1952, 1971 by the Division of Christian Education of the National Council of Churches of Christ in the USA. Used by permission.

23. *The Revised Standard Version of the Bible,* copyright 1946, 1952, 1971 by the Division of Christian Education of the National Council of Churches of Christ in the USA. Used by permission.

24. *New English Bible,* copyright Oxford University Press and Cambridge University Press, 1961, 1970.

Sources of Illustrations

Illustrations are identified by page number and, where necessary, location on the page.

Cover picture of William Tyndale is from a portrait of Tyndale in the Hall of Hertford College, Oxford, and is used by permission of the Principal and Fellows of Hertford College, Oxford.

6. The Bettmann Archive.

7. The Bettmann Archive.

11. The Bettmann Archive.

12. British Library, Department of Prehistoric and Romano-British Antiquities; used with permission.

17. From *The Book of Kells*: Reproductions from the Manuscript in Trinity College, Dublin, With a Study of the Manuscript by Franáoise Henry. New York: Alfred A. Knopf, 1974. Used with permission of the publisher.

21. From MS 200, folio 62, in the collection of Lambeth Palace Library, London; used with permission.

24. Snark/Art Resource, New York.

26. American Bible Society.

31. The Bettmann Archive.

33. The Bettmann Archive.

37. American Bible Society.

40. The Bettmann Archive.

47. The Bettmann Archive

49. Used with permission of the Principal and Fellows of Hertford College, Oxford.

50. Used with permission of the Principal and Fellows of Hertford College, Oxford.

54. Artist unknown; public domain.

58. Reproduced from The New Testament 1526 William Tyndale translation, with an afterword by F.F. Bruce. London: David Paradine Developments, 1976. Used with permission of the publisher.

61. Public domain.

63. British Tourist Authority.

65. The Bettmann Archive.

67. Top left. Collection of National Portrait Gallery Archive and Library, London; used with permission.

67. Top right. American Bible Society.

70. From Henry Holland Herwodlogia anglica (1620); used with permission of Lambeth Palace Library, London.

72. National Portrait Gallery, London; used with permission.

75. American Bible Society.

77. American Bible Society.

83. National Portrait Gallery, London; used with permission.

86. Artist unknown; public domain.

88. American Bible Society.

95. British Tourist Authority.

96. Art Resource.

97. National Portrait Gallery, London; used with permission.

101. The Bettmann Archive.

102. The Bettmann Archive.

106. Catholic University Press, Washington, D.C. Used with permission.

110. Artist unknown; public domain.

112. British Tourist Authority.

116. American Bible Society.

122. American Bible Society.

127. American Bible Society.

128. Script supplied by American Bible Society.

138. American Bible Society.

140. *Top.* Free Library of Philadelphia, Picture and Print Collection. *Bottom.* General Commission on Archives and History, United Methodist Church.

143. Philadelphia Jewish Archives Center.

148. Harold Washington Library Center, Chicago.

155. University of Michigan.

158. From "Bible collectors' World: Official Organ of The International Society of Bible Collectors," October-December 1992 issue; used with permission.

161. *Top.* American Baptist Historical Society. *Bottom.* From "Bible Collectors' World: Official Organ of The International Society of Bible Collectors," April-June 1992 issue; used with permission.

168. National Council of the Churches of Christ in the USA

172. National Council of the Churches of Christ in the USA

175. United Bible Societies/Maurice Harvey.

177. L'Osservatore Romano/NCCCUSA

183. Longman & Todd Ltd., Publishers.

192. American Bible Society.

194. American Bible Society.

200. American Bible Society.

INDEX

Page numbers set in roman *type indicate that a reference can be found in the running text on the page indicated; numbers set in* **bold** *indicate that the reference is to be found in the shaded box on the page indicated; an italicized number indicates an illustration.*

SHARING GOD'S WORD WITH THE WORLD

This Bible represents a legacy of translating God's Word into the language of the people — into languages that will bring the Scriptures to life in the hearts of readers and hearers. The American Bible Society works with scholars from many countries to faithfully translate the Scriptures into languages and formats that speak clearly to both mind and heart. We encourage people everywhere to engage with the inspired Word of God — to embody its message and to experience a relationship with God through its reading.

To this end the American Bible Society, a not-for-profit Christian organization, offers programs to churches, other Bible-centered organizations, and individuals that connect people with God's living Word, and support the work of more than 100 other Bible Societies worldwide. Since our founding in 1816, people have generously supported the American Bible Society in its global mission to translate, publish, and provide Scriptures that are easily understood and affordable.

In many areas of the world, and even within the United States, the cost of a Bible often represents a hardship for many who thirst for God's Word. Thanks to the faithful support of many individuals, churches, and ministry partners, the American Bible Society continues to respond to the Scripture needs of the underserved and under engaged through effective programs and ministry partnerships.

We invite you to participate with us as we share God's Word with the world. To find how, please contact us at:

American Bible Society
1865 Broadway
New York, New York 10023-7505
1-888-227-8262
www.americanbible.org

Also of interest ...

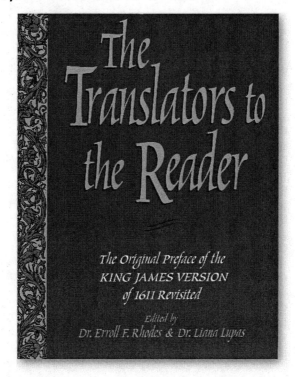

Although no longer included by most modern publishers of the *King James Version*, this fascinating

preface by the translators of this durable and respected translation reveals much about how ancient sacred texts can be rendered in ways that will communicate to new generations of readers.

This edition presents three versions of the Preface: (1) a facsimile from a copy of the original 1611 Bible, (2) a thoughtfully annotated transcription, and (3) an easy-to-read modernized version. And an introductory essay by the editors provides helpful context and background information.

Paperback, 8 1/2 x 10 1/2 inches, 96 pages
ISBN 1-58516-425-9   Item number 106022   *Price: $12.99

*Price subject to change without notice.